Endo … *FRIENDS*

In *No Enemi…* forensic analysis of the "pathologies" of Australia's strategic mindset. Unlike so many of his contemporaries, Behm's detailed and historically grounded explanation of that mindset engages in an important critique of the stale, self-reinforcing orthodoxy of Australia's national security policy club.

Behm skewers the false promise of deterrence, offers a blistering critique of Australia's relationship with the United States and the recently announced AUKUS alliance, and makes a compelling argument for a complete overhaul of Australia's engagement with our region.

And unlike so many of his fellow club-members, Behm refuses to draw artificial boundaries between Australia's domestic and international politics and history. *No Enemies No Friends* faces the truth of Australia's racist history and present head on, showing how central that is to this country's security mindset – and, critically, the reactionary and shameful role Australia plays in the world today. As Behm so clearly demonstrates, there's no remedying Australia's foreign policy morass without first coming to terms, collectively, with our past. It is only then that we might begin the radical reconceptualisation of Australian foreign and security policy that we so urgently need.

No Enemies No Friends calls for a collective reckoning, and a collective renewal of leadership, ambition and imagination. The book outlines practical ways to begin such a transformation, without ever pretending that it would be easy or that one analyst alone could possibly have all the answers. In his embrace of that complexity, Behm offers real hope for a radically different future for this country and its place in the world.

DR EMMA SHORTIS,
RMIT University

This is a necessary and valuable work, bursting with the wisdom of scholarship and to put it plainly, the accumulated confidence of age. Destined to become and remain important long after comparable works have been forgotten.

PROFESSOR MARK KENNY,
Australian Studies Institute, Australian National University

If you have an intuition that Australia could improve its foreign and security policy, you'll enjoy reading this book. If you're comfortable with current policy, you NEED to read this book: not to agree with all its points, but to grapple with the questions it poses. Good foreign policy needs a few stirrers and Allan Behm ably plays this role.

MELISSA CONLEY TYLER,
Program Lead, Australia Pacific Development,
Diplomacy and Defence Dialogue (AP4D)

A provocative book that turns the mirror on ourselves, our delusions, and our assumptions. In arguing for a recalibration of our strategic future it offers insights into the possibilities, more suited to our Realpolitik.

ADMIRAL CHRIS BARRIE AC, RAN (Ret'd)
Honorary Professor, Strategic and Defence Studies Centre,
Australian National University

Deeply informed, finely written and passionate, Allan Behm's *No Enemies No Friends* shows how much of Australia›s ability to successfully navigate an increasingly dangerous world demands that we look with the same sharp clarity at ourselves as at the world outside.

ALLAN GYNGELL,
National President of the Australian Institute of International Affairs

NO ENEMIES
NO FRIENDS

Allan Behm

Allan Behm specialises in political and security risk evaluation, policy analysis and development, and negotiating the policy/politics interface.

Following a career spanning nearly thirty years in the Australian Public Service, he was Chief of Staff to Minister for Climate Change and Industry Greg Combet (2009 to 2013) and senior advisor to the Shadow Minister for Foreign Affairs, Senator Penny Wong (2017–19).

No, Minister – an insider's account of what actually goes on in Parliament House – was published by MUP in 2015. Allan Behm is Director, International & Security Affairs Program at The Australia Institute in Canberra.

Allan Behm

NO ENEMIES NO FRIENDS

Restoring Australia's Global Relevance

UPSWELL

First published in Australia in 2022
by Upswell Publishing
Perth, Western Australia
upswellpublishing.com

ISBN: 978-0-6452480-2-9

NATIONAL LIBRARY OF AUSTRALIA

A catalogue record for this book is available from the National Library of Australia

Cover design by Chil3, Fremantle
Typeset in Foundry Origin by Lasertype
Printed by McPherson's Printing Group

For Paul Barratt AO

1944–2021

Public servant, public intellectual, public commentator

Contents

Prologue

In a deeply troubled world, Australia is in deep trouble. Once admired for its egalitarian, energetic and liberal approach to engagement in world affairs, it is now widely seen, by peers and critics alike, as heartless, hypercritical and mean-spirited. At the beginning of the twentieth century, we were at the forefront of universal suffrage, establishing the dignity of work by mandating fair rates of pay, instituting social safety nets that protected those facing hard times and providing a lifestyle that was the envy of many. Now we are seen as backsliders on critical, indeed existential, issues such as global warming and nuclear disarmament, blind to the deep consequences of the coronavirus pandemic among our nearest neighbours, especially Indonesia, and high-handed in our dealings with the poor and struggling countries of the Pacific. Countries whose respect we once enjoyed regard us as contemptible in our attitude to refugees seeking asylum here, and despicable in our lack of generosity to the millions of people displaced because of wars that we have supported.

What has happened to Australia Felix? What has happened to us?

Surprisingly, nothing and everything. We have relied on our luck and on the amazing natural endowment of this continent, exploiting it and its First Peoples to become the thirteenth-richest nation in the world, with a population that places us at fifty-fifth. Without wanting to belong to our continent, without caring for it and being cared for by it, we declared it *terra nullius* and claimed ownership of it. And we have exploited it – or, rather, we have encouraged multinationals to exploit it while we retain a few of the benefits that are not expatriated. We stand by, doing as little as possible, while our continent makes us wealthy. We have developed a way of thinking about ourselves and the world in which we live that is at once introspective and blind to the remarkable opportunities that surround us.

At the same time, we allow ourselves to be carried along by forces that we neither understand nor control. We signed up for various colonial wars, two world wars and a procession of other conflicts without much in the way of deep reflection on where our interests actually lay. We have successfully transformed ourselves from being an ally of the United States to being its vassal, engaging in conflicts in the Middle East and Afghanistan which were none of our business, terrorism notwithstanding. Indeed, as the 'deputy sheriff' epigone, we risk surrendering what is left of our own agency to American strategic overreach as it seeks to restore its 'pre-eminence' in the face of the confected 'threat' from China.

In one of the safest and more remote parts of the world, far from the theatres of war, we imagine ourselves to be subject to a growing threat of armed attack. The more we fixate on China, the more fearful we become. And the more fearful we become, the more defensive is our approach to our future and our opportunities. The more defensive our mindset, the more we shackle ourselves to the United States. We have persuaded ourselves that the more we invest in the instruments of war, the safer we will be from having the instruments of war used against us. Instead of recognising the value of disarmament, we have become advocates for rearmament. We seem blithely unaware of the paradox that is an enormous continent and its small population. Yet we seem to imagine that we can 'rip an arm off' a potential adversary which, in the words of its founding leader, is able to dedicate a hundred million dead in any war that it might wage.[1]

Why have we gone from the self-confident bumptiousness of Billy Hughes at Versailles in 1919 and the constructive and engaged participation in global affairs of Evatt and Spender in the early aftermath of World War II to the bumbling spectator hovering on the edges of other nations' conversations?

This book seeks to address that question. It argues that our deep lack of confidence has driven us to a position of irrelevance in regional and global affairs that is, quite simply, tragic. It is tragic for us as a wonderfully endowed nation to have stultified our agency. And it is tragic for the regional and global communities that our true talents as a nation are not put at the service of a world that needs ideas and energy if it is to remedy the troubles it currently faces. It also advances the rather simple proposition that to the extent that we recognise the factors that constrain and limit our agency as a nation, the more likely it is that we can reimagine our modus operandi as a constructive international player.

This book is somewhat unusual in that it focuses more on what makes us tick as an actor on the international stage than on the roles that other actors play. Of course, it is not blind to the fact that we live in a complicated, chaotic and often disrupted world. But it attempts self-reflection on why it is that we behave as we do, what colours our apprehension and comprehension of the world in which we live, and how we might conceive of our role in more confident and constructive terms.

Australian bookshelves carry an impressive array of volumes dealing with Australia's military history. Indeed, Australia boasts excellent military historians. There is also a reasonable body of work on international relations and defence policy. But when one combs the shelves for Australian books on the cultural dynamics of Australian security, there is not much to be found. For instance, the Australian Army Reading List – an eclectic potpourri of books 'designed to prepare an officer or soldier for service in the profession of arms' – makes no reference to the foundational works of Hedley Bull, Coral Bell, Robert O'Neill or Des Ball, or to the more recent studies by Paul Dibb, Ross Babbage, Hugh White or Brendan Taylor. But it does include important commentaries by American and British authors.[2]

The last couple of years have witnessed the arrival of two important studies – Hugh White's *How to Defend Australia*[3] and Rory Medcalf's *Contest for the Indo-Pacific*.[4] While entirely different in their take on Australia's strategic position, both volumes present their conclusions within the standard Australian strategic policy framework – the idea that the nation's security depends on a strong military force (demanding high levels of spending). And while White argues that Australia's alliance with the United States is of declining relevance, Medcalf advocates an extension of Australia's strategic dependence beyond the Australia New Zealand United States Treaty (ANZUS), to include the kinds of regional military cooperation envisaged by the 'Quad' – the Quadrilateral Security Dialogue between Australia, India, Japan and the United States. These are important books.

One searches in vain, however, for any extended consideration of how Australia might recalibrate its national security policy to address two quite novel features of the contemporary strategic environment: first, the human security issues resulting from accelerating climate change, particularly in the Pacific and the archipelagic nations to Australia's north and west; and second, the irreversible change in Australia's regional defence superiority resulting from both the accelerating decline in Australia's erstwhile 'capability edge' due to the increased availability of military technology in the region, and, of course, China's increasing strategic dominance.

So, in its own small way, this book attempts to tackle that question too.

The more proximate inspiration for this book lay in an apparently innocuous question posed by a student of the 2019 Master of National Security Policy program at the Australian National University's National Security College. The question was: 'Can you explain the surprising continuity in Australia's national security policy settings since World War II, notwithstanding the changes in the nature and balance of power that have occurred in that period?'

'Nice question,' I replied, mentally dusting off the standard three-part answer that is evidence of long membership of the national security policy community, and so following the general practice of rehearsing and amplifying 'received wisdom': the spatial and temporal constraints of Australia's strategic geography; the enduring nature of the nation's strategic interests; and the strength of Australia's alliance with the United States. Anyone aspiring to become a member of the national security policy club should at least know the pat answers that signal acceptance of the policy mindset. As for the Roman curia, so for the security policy community: the test of fidelity is orthodoxy.

Yet orthodoxy is the last thing that someone who wishes to tread the cloisters of the national security community really needs. To be relevant in a disrupted world in which many issues are unconventional, conventional thinking ill-equips a policy adviser for the innate 'wickedness' of most contemporary strategic problems. 'Wicked' problems usually generate 'messy' solutions, because the multi-dimensional and chaotic nature of the interactions between those dimensions never lend themselves to neat linear analysis or resolution through a dialectical method that depends on confected binaries. In the world of security policy, as indeed in most domains of public policy, neither branch of the term 'received wisdom' holds true: it is 'received' by those who lack imagination, and it is 'wisdom' by default. Wisdom, of course, is experience that has been reflected upon rather than compounded by repetition. Orthodoxy is rewarded. The soundness of one's judgement is validated by the doyens of the security community, and one's career blossoms as one progresses to positions of increasing eminence and seniority, again as in the Roman curia or freemasonry. But orthodoxy confirms the status quo, which is what a disrupted world is all *not* about.

So, instead of trotting out the usual planning determinants at the tactical and operational levels of defence and security policy development, I decided to offer the class a more challenging and provocative commentary on what one might call 'Australia's strategic policy mindset'. If orthodoxy is rewarded by approbation, heterodoxy brings only the quiet comfort which is its own reward. And, as with many solitary pursuits, it has a long gestation. So this book has had a somewhat longer gestation than most. Like several other former practitioners in the field of national security policy, I had been reflecting on structural and theoretical problems in Australia's national security policy, international and domestic, for some years. But unlike these colleagues, I had not formulated my reflections as arguments.

Hence my response to the question was, at best, a partial challenge to orthodoxy. A few quick *obiter dicta* thrown in at the end of a lecture hardly substantiate a serious reappraisal of a couple of centuries of coming to grips with the emergent cultural factors that might have shaped Australia's security thinking. And given the plethora of experiences that contribute to something as intangible as a national strategic mindset, how does one go about sorting them into categories and weighing their impact?

How should the security experiences of the First Peoples of Australia – which of course include dispossession, land seizure, enforced migration, violence, disease, forcible relocation to unfamiliar country, separation of children from their parents, slavery masquerading as indenture, denial of opportunity, denial of rights, degradation of landscapes, destruction of culture, alienation within a continent occupied for 60,000 years before the Western tradition began – play into any consideration of why modern-day Australia thinks and acts as it does on the global stage? How did the fears, isolation and hardship of the first waves of immigrants to Australia, most of them British and Irish convicts, set the early security behaviours of the new settlers and those who exercised control over them? What impact did the arrival of free settlers have? What security prejudices did the non-English-speaking free settlers bring with them as they fled the localised religious, ethnic and political tensions of continental Europe? How did racial sensitivities acquire such prominence following the arrival of Chinese fortune-hunters in the 1850s? How did 'blokiness' come to be such a constraining determinant of the national security discourse when Australia was a world leader in voting rights and universal suffrage?

Each of these questions, of course, merits much more substantial analysis than a relatively short-compass book can record, and more insight than I am able to offer. So this book does not pretend to be a treatise on why it is that Australia has become so good at getting things so bad. What has inspired me to look at what it means for Australia to lack both enemies (who concentrate the mind) and friends (who reassure the mind) is the strong view that we have all the capabilities and skills to be so much better than we are. We can be both diverse and inclusive. We can work in a system that values both contestability and collaboration. We can honour 'having a go', trite though the phrase has become, as much as we can applaud success. We can take as much pleasure from the larrikinism of a tennis icon like Nick Kyrgios as we do from the dignity and grace of a tennis star like Ashleigh Barty. We can be as accepting of people's right to believe what they wish as we can be uninterested in what their beliefs might be. To paraphrase a remark attributed to Voltaire (but in fact written by biographer Beatrice Hall), we can disagree with people's views as strongly as we wish while defending to the death their right to express them.

So this book is much less a lamentation for what might have been than a meditation on why it is that we are so cack-handed, so adept at frustrating the realisation of our own best interests. It is also a contemplation on the steps we might take to become more sure-footed – less a matter of light at the end of the tunnel than of hope springing eternal, perhaps. But just as Finland and its Scandinavian partners, together with the Baltic states, have long had to come to terms with two strategic giants – Russia to the east and Germany to the south – to maintain their prosperity and security, so Australia must learn how to live in a new and, from our perspective, less predictable world. Like the Scandinavians, we need to maintain a credible defence force. But, again like the Scandinavians, we need to examine our hedging options that lessen our dependence on military force and defence alliances for the maintenance of our long-term security.

The considerations and conclusions proposed in this book have become even more poignant and more urgent with the joint announcement by Australia, the United Kingdom and the United States (AUKUS) to collaborate on Australia's acquisition of eight nuclear-powered submarines. This is a truly momentous decision, promoting Australia into the ranks of countries operating nuclear-propelled warships – the first non-nuclear weapons state to do so. While there may be some sound technical arguments supporting nuclear propulsion, the speed and secrecy surrounding the decision and the manner of its announcement were simply extraordinary. According to British reports, as few as ten people in the United Kingdom were aware of this proposal prior to its announcement, and it appears that very few people in Australia outside the Prime Minister's Office were aware either.

Australia has become a country with a formidable reputation for kicking 'own goals', eliciting sympathy and derision in equal measure. With the creation of AUKUS, our diplomatic ineptitude has sunk to a new low. In case anyone was not yet convinced that Australia's promotion of an independent international inquiry into the coronavirus outbreak in early 2020 – provocative to China and subservient to the United States – was crass, the Morrison government has compounded its clumsiness. To deliver a sharp poke in the eye to China, the government decided to poke France in the eye, to poke Indonesia, Malaysia and New Zealand in the eye by blindsiding them, and then its irrelevance was put on public display when the US president forgot the prime minister's name. In response, France withdrew its ambassadors from Canberra and Washington, and Indonesia cancelled a planned visit by the Australian prime minister.

Our closest friend and ally, New Zealand, made it immediately clear that our nuclear-powered submarines would not be permitted into New Zealand waters, immediately distancing itself from what could only be interpreted as a concerted attempt by three Anglophone nations to contain China. New Zealanders excel at gallows humour. *The Civilian*, a satirical electronic media outlet, captured the mordancy of the moment: 'Experts warn that exclusion from AUSUK pact could see New Zealand miss out on future catastrophic wars'. Not to be outdone, Australia's *Betoota Advocate*, another satirical journal, produced the headline 'China panics after learning that they've only got 25 years until Australia gets 8 new submarines'.

Marty Natalegawa, Indonesia's former foreign minister and a person with a genuine affection for Australia, signalled the kind of nuanced response that one might expect of Indonesia.

> The decision on AUKUS strengthens the impression of a region increasingly dissected by geopolitical push and pull. The possibility of a chain reaction by other countries, not simply China, in the Indo-Pacific – noting in particular the qualitative escalation represented in the nuclear-powered submarine capability – cannot be discounted.[5]

And Malaysia's prime minister, Ismail Sabri Yaakob, told Prime Minister Morrison in a telephone conversation that AUKUS could provoke other powers to act more aggressively in the region, especially in the South China Sea.

Some analysts have commented that, by deciding to acquire a nuclear-powered hunter-killer submarine, Australia has crossed the Rubicon. Perhaps the sad truth is that we have crossed the Styx. For the past two decades, imperceptibly, Australia has become increasingly attracted to long-range weapons systems – missiles, drones, advanced submarines – and the need to be able to defend against (and conduct) cyber-warfare. The AUKUS agreement effectively demolishes four decades of national strategic policy focused on the direct defence of Australia by returning to an operational preference for forward defence. The earlier concentration on the 'sea-air gap' that separates Australia from the nations of South-East Asia has given way to a preference for operating in China's adjacent waters. This is a radical policy change. It is also fraught.

Democratic governments wonder why trust between the governors and the governed is in decline, and why support for democracy as a form of government is waning. To spring such a momentous decision on an unprepared public is both cynical and high-handed. Blithely to commit Australia to an exotic technology that we cannot build, maintain or dispose of is simultaneously to cede our sovereignty and to consign us to the status of vassal-state in perpetuity – a 'forever partnership', in Prime Minister Morrison's words. Carelessly to ignore the regional community, particularly Indonesia, is arrogant, condescending and dismissive. And recklessly to announce the acquisition of a submarine that was specifically designed as a hunter-killer to destroy a potential enemy's submarine-based second-strike nuclear deterrence capability is a provocation.

Australia has reached a critical point in its history. Do we remain a fully engaged member of an imperialist white man's world, celebrating past glories and past wars, shackled to a nation whose place in the world is certainly changing, even if it is not declining, or do we begin the taxing task of redefining ourselves and our national interests? Do we take stock of the forces, the pathologies, that have led us to where we now find ourselves, or do we remain unconfident and afraid of abandonment? Do we begin the patient and careful work of coalition-building, planning for peace, prosperity and stability with our neighbours, or do we retreat under the protective umbrella of US military power in the Pacific? Do we become a confident and constructive partner in regional and global affairs, or remain apologetic and irrelevant?

This book sets out to provide some answers to those questions.

1
An Insecure Mindset: Our Strategic Paradigm

Humankind cannot bear very much reality.

T.S. Eliot, *Murder in the Cathedral*

There is a profound insecurity at the heart of the Australian character. As the twenty-first century unfolds, this insecurity shackles our progress and prosperity. More than that, it puts us at risk: of domestic division and of international marginalisation. The complexities of a disrupted world and our deep-seated fear of change have persuaded us to reconfirm historical ways of thinking and acting. Our default position is to return constantly to conventional approaches to unconventional problems. And that serves to exacerbate our general state of befuddled insecurity.

On a continent that has been home to the world's oldest continuous civilisation for at least 60,000 years, the immigrant majority cannot conclude formal recognition of the rights and privileges of Australia's First Peoples. This is a nation whose prosperity has depended on sustained immigration, but equality and inclusion both remain beyond our reach. In a region that is already the engine of the global economy, we remain aloof, detached and disengaged, limiting ourselves to the Anglosphere, which remains separate, superior, increasingly irrelevant and distinctly 'white'. Like the Cyclops, each of the 'Five Eyes' partners is one-eyed. In a world where anthropogenic climate warming is changing the face of continents and putting global populations at risk, we look to increased coal production and a 'gas-led recovery' to sustain our economy.

In a world with serious problems, we are not a serious nation.

We are a nation of flunkeys. With a bit more self-possession and self-confidence, we might have aspired to be a nation of courtiers, currying favour with the powerful nations of the world in the way that has proven reasonably successful for the smaller European and Asian nations. But that takes planning, perseverance and considerable self-knowledge. Courtiers build influence. Flunkeys display fear and weakness. Just look at the sycophants who attended upon President Donald Trump, scurrying around like mindless myrmidons. Following the leader – 'tugging the forelock', as former prime minister Paul Keating was wont to say – is much easier than taking the risk of independent action.

Like most flunkeys, we are eager to display our subservience. A visit to Australia by any member of the British royalty brings on adulation and fawning deference. We baulk at asserting ourselves as a republic. A telephone conversation with US secretary of state Mike Pompeo, an official more given to bluster and bullying than to diplomacy and reason, transforms our foreign minister into an obedient servant, while our prime minister happily becomes a mouthpiece for US hardball assertiveness in pressing for an independent international inquiry into the origins of the coronavirus pandemic. We prefer to be amenable acolytes rather than persuasive partners.

Subservience is a form of sycophancy. In the dying months of what was perhaps the most malign presidency in US history, our foreign and defence ministers, along with their most senior officials, embarked on their pilgrimage to Washington to pay homage at the shrine of fading US strategic power. At least it served as a farewell call on US secretary for defense Mark Esper, who was dismissed by President Trump just two months later. At a time, in late 2020, when the coronavirus had infected millions of Americans and was killing thousands each day, and with the Trump administration in evident freefall, Australia clung on like a flea to a dingo. Instead of creating strategic space – as the NATO partners did, for instance – Australia signalled its fealty.

Even our national honours system does not escape employment as a tool of toadyism. While we continue to find it difficult to recognise and reward women who deserve acknowledgement for their contribution and success, we regularly give honorary awards to US military and civilian defence leaders, all male of course. If the national interest is better served by conferring the Order of Australia on white Americans skilled at maintaining Australia's alignment with US interests than it is by conferring such distinctions on Australian citizens who dedicate themselves, without fanfare or high-level access, to building an inclusive society, then our prostration is complete. And, as Prime Minister Scott Morrison's receipt of the Legion of Merit from outgoing President Trump suggests, prostration is itself rewarded.

Subservience, we might think, relieves us of risk. But risk, the calculated dimension of fear, is exactly what worries us most. And what better way to avoid risk than to shift it elsewhere, decreasing uncertainty by increasing the vulnerability that results from transferring responsibility for our own decisions? Vulnerability, of course, is the necessary precursor to destruction.

History seldom records when the destruction of civilisations and the cultures that define them begins. Was it the arrival in Cuba of Christopher Columbus on 12 October 1492 that initiated the destruction of the Aztec, Inca and Mayan civilisations of Central and South America? Or did Columbus, who repatriated a few slaves as proof of his voyage, merely open the door for Hernán Cortés and his conquistadors twelve years later? They, after all, exploited internal divisions, suppressed indigenous resistance, slaughtered the armed defenders, introduced epidemics and repatriated both slaves and treasure.

Can John Cabot, who allegedly landed in Newfoundland on 24 June 1497 but met no indigenous people, be blamed for the eventual destruction of the indigenous cultures of North America? Or is that claim reserved for Christopher Newport and his colonists, who settled Jamestown, Virginia, on 10 April 1607?

It took the Gwaegal and Dharawal people of Botany Bay almost two decades to grasp the significance of their encounter with Captain

James Cook on Sunday, 29 April 1770. Cook's own journal records the event:

> [I] Saw, as we came in, on both points of the bay, several of the Natives and a few hutts; Men, Women, and Children on the South Shore abreast of the Ship, to which place I went in the Boats in hopes of speaking with them ... As we approached the Shore they all made off, except 2 Men, who seem'd resolved to oppose our landing. As soon as I saw this I order'd the boats to lay upon their Oars, in order to speak to them ... We then threw them some nails, beads, etc., a shore, which they took up, and seem'd not ill pleased with, in so much that I thought that they beckon'd to us to come ashore; but in this we were mistaken, for as soon as we put the boat in they again came to oppose us, upon which I fir'd a musquet between the 2, which had no other Effect than to make them retire back, where bundles of their darts lay, and one of them took up a stone and threw at us, which caused my firing a Second Musquet, load with small Shott; and altho' some of the shott struck the man, yet it had no other effect than making him lay hold on a Target. Immediately after this we landed, which we had no sooner done than they throw'd 2 darts at us; this obliged me to fire a third shott, soon after which they both made off ...[1]

The inhabitants of Botany Bay might have considered themselves lucky. The Māori peoples living along the Tāranganui river saw several of their leaders shot and killed by Cook's crew, a testament as much to misunderstanding as to apprehension, on both sides.[2] But the prosaic quality of Cook's record of his first encounter with Australia's Indigenous people, and his matter-of-fact description of opening fire against naked people armed only with rocks and wooden spears, reveal how accustomed his crew had become to firing on 'natives', how normalised the use of armed violence towards them already was. When in doubt, shoot.

And so Australia's modern security culture began with the discharge of a musket. For anyone with some exposure to national security policy, the expression 'security culture' may seem oxymoronic. There can be little doubt, however, that Australian approaches to national security policy and planning reflect fundamental preoccupations that not only establish a recognisable security mindset but also render the Australian approach to national security unique.

There are seven different but interrelated dimensions that together comprise Australia's strategic mindset:

- An ingrained sense of 'the other' – a genteel sobriquet for racism – that excludes and often dehumanises those who are deemed not to 'belong' to the dominant ethnic and social elite(s), or who are regarded as threatening the dominant ethnic and social elite(s), thereby preventing cultural and ethnic diversity in the national security policy domain;[3]

- An unmistakeable 'gender bias', the misogyny that preserves national security policy as a predominantly male domain, 'boys' business', effectively excluding women from national security decision-making;

- 'The tyranny of distance' that, for the first century and a half at least, forged a sense of homogeneity, which in turn generated a sense of entitlement, a liking for 'big government', a delight in whingeing and a collectivism that is as evident in the national love for sport as it was in the fading trade union movement;

- A profound sense of isolation, a direct corollary of the tyranny of distance, and the insecurities that go with it;

- In consequence, a deep sense of dependence, a compulsive need for a protector and a security guarantor, a 'great and powerful friend' (to use Prime Minister Robert Menzies' term of 1962[4])

- The reflex of dependence, a chronic 'fear of abandonment', to use Allan Gyngell's term;[5] and

- 'The cultural cringe' – the critic and schoolmaster A.A. Phillips' term for the sense of inferiority that pushed Australians to validate themselves using British, and subsequently American, aesthetic and intellectual paradigms, causing generations of artists and intellectuals to descend upon London or New York to establish their identity and find their voice. Consequently, foreign solutions are better than home grown ones, and their foreign solutions to their security concerns are preferred to home-grown solutions to our independent security issues.

Racism, the dominant security pathology

From the day of Cook's arrival, the 'race' binary – white supremacy versus black (and other non-European) subordination – was set. The violence of the initial encounters was the product of a deep-seated sense of 'the other' – of human beings whose customs and language were not understood, in a landscape that was itself as strange as its flora and fauna, all of them alien. For Cook and his crew, these were primitive people whose fear could be assuaged, and whose acquiescence bought, by a few beads, nails and trinkets. Or else they could be coerced with superior firepower. For the Gwaegal and Dharawal people, Cook and his crew were from another world, ghosts perhaps brought to land by a giant bird.[6]

Incomprehension was the shared perception. But whereas the first reaction of the black inhabitants was to wish the white arrivals gone, the first reaction of the white arrivals was to open fire. The power of ball and black powder was to kill and suppress, cementing the tension of race and the supremacy of the white arrivals from the very first encounter between the Indigenous peoples and what would become, less than two decades later, the white claimants to and occupants of this vast continent. As Manning Clark, with uncharacteristic understatement, put it, 'In this way The European began his tragic association with the aborigines on the east coast.'[7] The Indigenous tribes of Botany Bay were nurtured by the land to which they belonged and had no concept that the land might have belonged to them. They could not have imagined the spiritual death – 'a destruction of their past, their future and their opportunities of transcendence'[8] – that was about to be visited upon them.

The arrival of the First Fleet in 1788 immediately reversed the relationship between the land and the inhabitant. It introduced the English concept of property title. More than that, it imposed race as the determinant of social order. It also informed the emerging strategic culture that would come to distinguish Australia's deep-seated anxiety, its sense of remoteness and dependence and its constant geopolitical discomfort.

Australia's strategic paradigm is a function of both its European antecedents and its history as a colony that created the fiction of *terra nullius* – a land belonging to no one – while simultaneously driving the Indigenous inhabitants off their traditional lands, destroying their cultures and rendering them aliens and dispossessed exiles on their own continent. And where dispossession failed to work, the exotic diseases and unsanctioned shootings that are the default precursor to modern genocides rendered the white colonisers 'secure' against the Indigenous savages.

'Race' is a particularly European preoccupation, dependent on preconceptions of 'otherness'. 'Race' and 'ethnicity', as linguistic tools for categorising and classifying people, have a relatively short provenance. They are among the cultural and political artefacts of European exploration and colonisation dating from the fifteenth century, given currency by the explorer and traveller François Bernier in the second half of the seventeenth century.[9] It is important to recognise that Bernier had a significant influence on John Locke, who in turn gave legitimacy to ideas of racism, white supremacy and slavery in the English-speaking world, particularly in the Americas.[10] The superficial phenomena that are generally used to describe 'race' – skin colour, eye shape, hair types, facial features, physical taxonomy and 'phenotypes' – have no genetic or biological validity.[11] Rather than describing and identifying people, 'race' is a term that divides and stratifies. And that was how colonising powers employed racial classification: culturally, politically, socially and economically.

The entrenched dominance of racism and the imbued rejection of 'the other' in the Western colonial consciousness was well expressed by Edward Said:

> Race theory, ideas about primitive origins and primitive classifications, modern decadence, the progress of civilization, the destiny of the white (or Aryan) races, the need for colonial territories – all these were elements in the peculiar amalgam of science, politics, and culture whose drift, almost without exception, was always to raise Europe or a European race to dominion over non-European portions of mankind.[12]

In his mannered but relentless reflection on Australia's early economic, social and political development, *The Fatal Shore*, Robert Hughes draws out the factors that transformed the incomprehension that underpins a sense of 'the other' into the apprehension that underpins racism: the absence of any sense of legal rights or status, the lack of economic value, disponibility (a prerequisite to dispossession), pariahdom and untouchability.

> The aborigine was seen as a mere native pest, like a dingo or a kangaroo. He was a *myall*, a *murky*, a *boong* or (in a phrase that precisely expressed the whites' belief in his inevitable passing) a *darkcloud*. He could be killed without hesitation – and, given the remoteness of the outer settlements and the thinness and inherent racism of the police force, without much chance of detection and punishment.[13]

Indigenous peoples, however, were not the only 'others'. The discovery of gold in Australia brought an influx of American prospectors from the goldfields of California, and Chinese fortune seekers from the southern provinces of China. Many of the Chinese who came to work in the goldfields arrived as indentured labourers: they prospected for gold on behalf of mining entrepreneurs, worked incredibly hard, then returned home. What was more interesting was their practice of working in teams, often reprocessing the tailings dumps of mines that had already been worked, or working mines that had been abandoned. Some of these teams were very successful, which generated envy among the less organised – and often less hardworking – miners from other nations.

It was not long before the colonial governments moved to deter Chinese immigration by imposing poll taxes. The Victorian government, for instance, imposed a £10 poll tax on arrivals from China, which led the shipping companies to land their Chinese workers at Robe, in South Australia. Some 20,000 Chinese miners walked the 400 kilometres to the Victorian goldfields, risking violence and death as they did so. The slaughter of Chinese workers at Lambing Flat (now known as Young, New South Wales) over ten months between 1860 and 1861 was only the tip of a racist iceberg that ultimately found expression in the White Australia policy.[14]

If the gold rushes provided the impetus for a rapid expansion in the fledgling nation's wealth and prosperity, Chinese immigration provided a lightning rod for racism, exclusion and intolerance. The Victorian parliament passed the *Chinese Immigration Act* in 1855, which was followed in 1857 by similar legislation in South Australia, and six years later by the *Chinese Immigration Restriction Act* in New South Wales. Indeed, fear of Chinese immigration was one of the factors that pushed Australia's colonial leaders towards Federation: one of the earliest acts of the federal parliament was the *Immigration Restriction Act* of 1901. Drafted by Alfred Deakin, this statute became the cornerstone of the White Australia policy. And, of course, section 127 of the Constitution excluded Indigenous Australians from being counted among 'the people of Australia' for certain constitutional purposes. While clearly discriminatory, this provision did not exclude them from citizenship or from the protection of the law,[15] or from enlisting and dying in World War I.

Thus, 'White Australia' was the core element of national security policy in the early years of Federation. As early as 1903, Prime

Minister Deakin spoke at length on the need for a racial basis for Australian identity and security:

> You probably believe that a white Australia is secure. I hope it is, but it won't be secure unless a vigilant watch is kept upon proposals to tamper with it. None of a serious character have been put forward by anybody in a responsible position, but there are indications that we may have to defend the principle yet. So far as this Government is concerned it will be ready for the emergency. *(Cheers)* A white Australia does not by any means mean only the preservation of the complexion of the people of this country. It means the multiplying of their homes, so that we may be able to occupy, use and defend every part of our continent; it means the maintenance of conditions of life fit for white men and white women; it means equal laws and opportunities for all; it means protection against the underpaid labor of other lands; it means social justice so far as we can establish it, including just trading and the payment of fair wages. *(Cheers)*
>
> A white Australia means a civilisation whose foundations are built upon healthy lives, lived in honest toil, under circumstances which imply no degradation. Fiscally a white Australia means protection. We protect ourselves against armed aggression, why not against aggression by commercial means. We protect ourselves against undesirable colored aliens, why not against the products of the undesirable alien labor? *(Cheers)* A white Australia is not a surface, but it is a reasoned policy which goes down to the roots of national life, and by which the whole of our social, industrial, and political organisations is governed.[16]

While the White Australia policy, as an instrument of population management and control, has been binned for the discriminatory and divisive policy it was, it lingers in the national security subconscious. Hugh White, one of Australia's pre-eminent strategic commentators, identifies China, India, Japan and Indonesia as 'Asian powers' without any further qualification, as though Portugal and Poland could simply be lumped together as 'European powers'.[17] He also reflects our longstanding ambivalence towards Indonesia, whose people 'are different in more dimensions of their national lives than any other pair of neighbouring countries in the world'.[18] White was comparing Indonesia and Australia, though he might have brought Papua New Guinea into consideration for an even sharper contrast. The point is, of course, that Indonesia is very clearly 'other'.

Preoccupation with race is at the heart of Australia's inability to resolve the unfinished business of reconciliation between the immigrant communities and the First Peoples of Australia and their acceptance of each other as a single nation. The alienation and dispossession of the First Peoples is matched by the inability of the immigrant communities to accept responsibility for what happened. The same consideration applies to the more recent immigration to Australia by people from Asia, Africa and the Middle East. The (Korean) American poet Cathy Park Hong could just as well have been writing about Australia when she considered the issue of 'whiteness' in the United States:

> I have to address whiteness because Asian Americans have yet to truly reckon with where we stand in the capitalist white supremacist hierarchy of this country. We are so far from reckoning with it that some Asians think that race has no bearing on their lives, that it doesn't 'come up', which is as misguided as white people saying the same thing about themselves, not only because of discrimination we have faced but because of the entitlements we've been granted due to our racial identity.[19]

Australia's fear of 'the other' has found its most recent expression in the AUKUS partnership, where the Anglophone and anachronistically white trio – Australia and is former protector (Great Britain) and its current protector (the United States) – have banded together to assist Australia to acquire nuclear-powered submarines. Against which countries might Australia wish to deploy such vessels? Asian ones, of course – countries that remain in our consciousness as determinedly 'other'.

Gender and misogyny

The arrival of the first group of transported women on Australia's shores was marked by rum-fuelled rape and debauchery. Two weeks after the arrival of the First Fleet at Port Jackson, sufficient huts and tents had been erected to land the women prisoners. While many of them had been in sexual relationships during the long voyage from Portsmouth, the crews of several of the ships accompanying the First Fleet saw the women's appearance en masse as an opportunity for unrestrained sexual licence. With wry mordancy, Robert Hughes captures the moment: '[A]s the couples rutted between the rocks, guts burning from the harsh Brazilian *aquardiente*, their clothes slimy with red clay, the sexual history of colonial Australia may fairly be said to have begun.'[20] He might more accurately have said that the discrimination that marked the lot of women in Europe was given even greater salience at the very beginning of Australia's colonisation. As Anne Summers put it: 'Women were transported solely to serve as sexual commodities and the British Government acted as imperial whoremaster.'[21] The 'March4Justice' protests of early 2021 vented the deep-seated anger that continues to energise Australian women because of sustained discrimination and misogyny.

The events of 6 February 1788 were emblematic of Australia's enduring inability to deal with its 'woman problem'. Up to and including the gold rushes of the 1850s, men outnumbered women by as much as three to one. Women generally lived hard lives, the few exceptions being the wives and daughters of the colonial administrators and the propertied class that began slowly to emerge. Even those women had no political rights, and few economic rights. Little wonder that so many poor Catholic girls rushed off to populate the nunneries rather than submit to domestic drudgery and perpetual procreation. But quite apart from their confinement to the kitchen and their lack of rights and opportunity, women were denied any place in the governance of the colonies.

Implicit gender bias lingers in the Australian argot. We continue to avoid enunciating what we stand for – our values – but we have no difficulty agreeing on one aspect of the Australian character: mateship. Prime Minister John Howard enshrined 'mateship' as the cornerstone of his conservative agenda, at once capturing the sentimentalism of the word and giving it a new romantic resonance that appealed to the 'battlers', the 'aspirationals' and the newly emerging, non-unionised, self-employed, blue-collar members of the middle class.[22] His particular sleight of hand was to rebrand a concept that was central to the establishment of trade unionism in Australia – 'the collectivist idea that men should be loyal to the men with whom they lived and worked', as Geoffrey Blainey puts it[23] – while preserving its essential masculinity. It is interesting to note that the word *mate* excludes both women and Indigenous people from its ambit: rarely does one hear an Indigenous person say 'mate'; many prefer instead the US rapper (and Kiwi) term 'bro'.

Security, as it relates to national security, defence and military strategy, has long been the preserve of men. But, as Julie Arostegui has written, times are changing:

> [There] has also come a paradigm shift in the concept of security from one of state security to human security. Whereas traditionally security involved the protection of borders and state sovereignty, the modern concept of security addresses the security of individuals and communities. It broadens both the nature of security threats such as poverty, discrimination, gender-based violence, lack of democracy and marginalization, and the actors involved, including non-state actors and civil society ... Integrating a gender perspective into the security sector is essential: 1) to abide by universally accepted human rights principles; 2) because when both men and women are involved in decision-making processes, there are better outcomes; and 3) using gender perspectives and mainstreaming increases operational effectiveness.[24]

The call for change is implicitly a criticism of established practice. Just as the national parliament continues to be a largely male preserve, particularly on the conservative side, so too very few women attain leadership positions in the cloistered world of the national security community. The first woman to have been appointed National Security Adviser, by the Gillard government, was transferred to the Health department under the Abbott government. A woman served as Deputy Secretary (National Security) in the Department of the Prime Minister and Cabinet prior to her appointment as Ambassador to the Organisation for Economic co-operation and Development (OECD), while five or six women occupy senior positions in related portfolios. But these are the exceptions rather than the rule. The Australian Defence Force, of course, has been notoriously slow to appoint women to senior operational and command roles, positioning them generally in support and management roles.

The tyranny of distance

The title of Geoffrey Blainey's landmark study, first published in 1966, is much more frequently quoted than his book is read. Australia's preoccupation with its long-term economic prosperity began with the arrival of the First Fleet. Blainey deals more with the impact of distance on immigration and trade than with the impact of distance (and its corollaries, remoteness and isolation) on the national character and how we think about ourselves in the world. The title does, however, capture one of the forces that have shaped our national mindset and fed the insecurities that have worried us since famine nearly destroyed the first settlement in 1790.

Of course, the white settlers did not think to learn from Port Jackson's Indigenous people about how they might feed themselves, any more than Burke and Wills might have wondered how the Indigenous people along Cooper Creek maintained nutritional standards while the explorers were dying of beriberi in 1861. Superiority might bring its own rewards, but ignorance (or is it arrogance?) certainly brings its own punishments.

As Blainey wrote, 'Australia continues to be viewed by the outside world as a billabong standing some distance from the global mainstream.'[25] At the same time, '[d]istance still reigns over various facets of Australia's contacts with the outside world. The social, cultural and political effects of historic distance – of that long separation of Australia from Europe – are alive. Moreover, distance within Australia is tenacious.'[26]

Most of us think of distance in terms of physical proximity: the further apart two points are, the more distant they are. The truth is that distance is less a function of proximity than a measure of how far one must actually travel to get from one place to another. Physical obstacles, such as rivers, mountains and ravines, can force us to undertake very long journeys to travel between places that are not so far apart 'as the crow flies'. Anyone who has tried to cross the Burdekin or Clarence rivers in flood knows what this means. So, for the early settlers, distance was measured in the nautical miles travelled from Portsmouth to Sydney via Tenerife, the Cape of Good Hope and the Southern Ocean.

Remoteness and isolation are both consequences of distance. Remoteness describes vast physical separation. Isolation is more complex: it also connotes the cultural, social and psychological separation that may be a function of physical distance, a consequence of other emotional factors, such as feelings of abandonment, disconnection, vulnerability or withdrawal, or a combination of all of these.

Just as distance preoccupied Governor Phillip's administration of the colony in its earliest years, so it has preoccupied Australia's strategic planners. If the strategic culture of the United States is in large measure defined by its rugged exceptionalism, and that of the United Kingdom by its dogged determination to preserve its identity, Australia's is perhaps most defined by the anxiety that comes from being remote and living precariously in an alien land. Australia's strategic policy is typically threat-based, reflecting that deep anxiety: Chinese workers in the nineteenth century, Russia at the end of the nineteenth century, Japan in the interwar years, Russia and China (communism) in the 1950s, Indonesia in the 1960s (and on and off since then), and now China (again).

Since 1788, immigrants to this continent have found it difficult to come to terms with its landscape, flora and fauna. Anxiety breeds nostalgia, among other things, so the early settlers needed the comfort of 'home' (wherever in the British Isles that might have been) and the familiar artefacts that defined 'normal' – the domestic animals, the verdant landscapes with their deciduous trees, the shrubs of the hedgerows (like blackberry and hawthorn) and their fauna (like rabbits and foxes), and the birds (including blackbirds, doves and pigeons, sparrows and starlings) that lent a European character to the new conurbations being moulded onto the remotest outpost of 'civilisation'.

And as the early settlers began to form a distinctive shared strategic narrative, it was built around the idea of a British empire on which the sun never set and its principal military expression, the Royal Navy. The first four governors of this transported colony were naval officers, and the ships of the Australian Squadron comforted the anxiety induced by remoteness, even if their presence was largely symbolic.

Distance also shaped the basic ideas on which we transformed ourselves from a collection of separate colonial administrations into a single nation. Professors Cheryl Saunders and Adrienne Stone, with Joshua Quinn-Watson, for example, charted the influence of distance on Australia's constitutional development. 'While many constitutions are informed by the influences of history, politics and culture; here in Australia, it's also the influence of geography, and in particular, of distance, that has helped to shape the Australian Constitution as it has evolved.'[27]

Among the many factors that encouraged federation, distance – both from London and between the seven major administrative centres (New Zealand participated in the early Australasian Federation Conferences) – was perhaps the most powerful. 'Strength in unity' was as much a driver of Australia's creation as a unitary state as the need for managed economic relations and for common defence.

Remoteness

Botanically, ethnically, geographically and geomorphologically, Australia is the world's remotest populated continent and nation. Remoteness has been one of the key contributors to the formation of the Australian character, the ethnic homogeneity of the immigrant settlers being another. It helped establish the early communalism that united the transportees and their gaolers in the face of shared adversity. It encouraged the racial segregation between the immigrant and Indigenous communities. It fostered the community spirit and mutual assistance that continues to distinguish Australian responses to floods, bushfires, droughts and, most recently, the COVID-19 pandemic (though different responses to the coronavirus by various of the states was seen as a test of the 'we're all in this together' idea rather than a validation). It created the other icons of Australia's self-image, such as 'mateship', the 'fair go', 'tall poppy syndrome' and an aversion to humbug and pretentiousness.

Our remoteness has also been a major contributor to our defiant monolingualism: we draw comfort from sharing a common language with our British cultural antecedents and our American protectors, while maintaining a separate identity as a white society at the bottom of a non-white world. The permeable borders of Europe encourage bilingualism, and in the case of the Nordic countries it is not unusual for people to converse easily in the languages of their neighbours. Switzerland has four national languages, Canada two. In New Zealand, Māori is increasingly spoken among *pākehā*.

In Australia, Indigenous languages are on the critically endangered list: of the 250 or more languages spoken at the time of colonisation, over 100 are extinct; of the 145 still spoken in 2005, 110 were under serious threat.[28] Language is a key ingredient of identity, and as both Indigenous Australians and Australians from non-English-speaking backgrounds attest, the loss of language leads to a loss of identity. But for the dominant language group, imbued with a deep sense of 'the other', the imposition of a single language both buttresses racial dominance and 'assimilates' other ethnicities and races. So the

Commonwealth Department of Home Affairs, in its *Australian Values Statement*, requires temporary and provisional visa applicants to understand that 'Australian society values ... the English language as the national language, and as an important unifying element of Australian society'.[29] Remoteness precipitates defensive homogeneity.

Isolation

The other consequence of remoteness is isolation – the feeling that the small outposts and their inhabitants at the far end of the world are on their own. Those who have lived in isolated communities understand that there are two different but related consequences of sustained isolation. First, isolated communities tend to look inwards, building strong bonds to counter the insecurity and vulnerability that isolation generates. Second, isolated communities become progressively less connected with the outside world, and increasingly reliant on narrowly based mutual help.

At one level, isolation has advantages. Without external interference, civilisations and cultures develop their own identities over very long periods of time, as the Indigenous peoples of Australia did for over 60,000 years. They developed their technologies, their art, their spirituality, their relationship with the land based on their unique experience of a unique continent. And just as there was no single language that united the Indigenous peoples, so too there was no singular culture.

But isolation also brings with it many dangers. The lack of connection with the many other human groups that populate the globe means that advances in technologies, in social organisation and in human thinking remain unshared. And, importantly, long periods of isolation render populations vulnerable to the ravages of disease where there is no herd immunity. So isolation was a significant contributing factor to the decimation of the Indigenous population after 1788 due to smallpox, typhus and the other diseases the immigrants brought with them.

It is noteworthy that, at the very end of *The Tyranny of Distance*, Blainey turns to the question of isolation and its impacts. His words are telling:

> Aboriginal Australia was ... shaped by distance; and the effects of that isolation are still at work. Long after the first Aboriginals reached Australia, the global climate became warmer, and the seas began to rise, largely isolating Australia from the outside world. During a period of isolation extending over 10,000 years, the way of life of the Aboriginals and the outside world increasingly diverged. Even today, many Aboriginal aspirations, values and attitudes reflect a traditional way of life developed in isolation. Traditional Aboriginal attitudes to land, to private property, to the accumulation of wealth, to work and leisure, to travel and to settling down, to kindship and to religion reflect that long isolation. The main reason why, today, the European and Aboriginal attitudes are often far apart stems from that remarkably long period of isolation.[30]

Ultimately, it would seem, the consequences of 'the tyranny of distance' – insecurity and vulnerability – can only be met by the assurance that there is a protector who will provide help, come what may. For many in remote Australia, it is 'the government' that meets their needs through educational and health institutions, or the periodic resupply truck. Notwithstanding the communications revolution that has brought the world together, Australians continue to feel that they are the last stop on the line. Instead of seeing distance and isolation as strategic assets, Australian security planners regard isolation as dangerous.

It might be comforting to think that our fear of isolation is the result of a deeper consideration of the circumstances that confronted Australia's Indigenous peoples before 1770. But the arrival of Europeans, especially after 1788, with their diseases and muskets, inflicted untold damage and misery on peoples whose identification with the land protected both them and it. While adversity often breeds resilience, isolation, it appears, breeds vulnerability and dependence.

Dependence

From the beginning of immigrant settlement, the colony was totally dependent on Britain: victuals from the government stores, resupply, the guards. And of course, until 1840, the colony depended on the British courts for the constant supply of prisoners that grew the population while providing cheap labour. The cost of passage to Australia was prohibitive, which led free immigrants to favour America (from which they could also return, if they succeeded financially). Nonetheless, by 1830 Australia's immigrant population had reached 70,000,[31] which more than doubled to 162,000 by 1840.[32] Emancipated ex-convicts could not compete with serving convicts in the labour market, creating social malaise; for this and other reasons, the British government decided in 1840 to end transportation. Nonetheless, immigrant numbers continued to increase, with convicts arriving at Tasmania and Norfolk Island until 1852, and some 10,000 landing at Fremantle before 1868.

Small populations stretched from Fremantle to Moreton Bay (where the first penal settlement began in 1824), with higher concentrations in Hobart and surrounding areas, in Sydney, and eventually in Melbourne (established in 1835) and Adelaide (established in 1836 for free settlers). Settlement and the beginnings of a trade economy raised concerns about defence and security, prompting the early colonial administrations to establish small defence contingents – mainly militias and inshore naval vessels comprising gunboats, torpedo boats and armed sloops.

Initially, the defence of Australia rested with the Royal Navy's East Indies Station based in Ceylon (Sri Lanka) until the establishment in 1859 of the Australia Station, based in Sydney. This comprised a motley collection of overaged and under-gunned vessels superfluous to British strategic needs in the Northern Hemisphere. Still, they were something – a token, perhaps, but a reminder both of the colonies' dependence and of the comforting power of the Royal Navy.

In the early years of Federation, Britain was commonly referred to as 'the mother country'. In his pre-election speech given in Ballarat in 1903, for instance, Alfred Deakin used the term repeatedly.[33] By 1910, he had secured the services of Field Marshal Viscount Kitchener to advise on Australia's defences. Kitchener's report exploited the nation's insecurities:

> 1. It is an axiom held by the British Government that the empire's existence depends primarily upon the maintenance of adequate and efficient naval forces. As long as this condition is fulfilled, and as long as British superiority at sea is assured, then it is an accepted principle that no British dominion can be successfully and permanently conquered by an organized invasion from overseas.
>
> 2. But in applying this principle to Australasia, considerations of time and space cannot be disregarded. The conduct of a great war depends upon the calculated and proper combination of naval, military and diplomatic forces; and it is quite conceivable that in the future, as in the past, national considerations may require the concentration of British naval forces in one or other theatre of operations. It follows that, in seas remote from such a concentration, the British Naval Forces may find themselves for the moment inferior in force to an actual, or potential, enemy. In such a situation, although our ultimate superiority at sea might not be a matter of doubt, some time might elapse before our command of the sea was definitely assured in all waters. It, therefore, becomes the duty of all self-governing Dominions to provide a military force adequate, not only to deal promptly with any attempt at invasion, but also to insure local safety and public confidence until our superiority at sea has been decisively and comprehensively asserted.[34]

Cleverly, Kitchener played on Australia's growing fears of invasion, specifically by Japan, as grounds for beefing up its military capabilities (both land and sea forces), while also encouraging Australia to develop land forces that could quickly be put at the disposal of imperial force planners. Thus, even before the passage of the *Defence Act 1909*, which introduced universal military service for all eligible males, Australia was caught in the double bind that dependence brought with it: the need for a home-grown force for self-defence, and the need to allocate that force to the protecting power to meet broader strategic purposes. This need for an insurance premium against future need for direct defence was as much evident in the Howard government's decision to allocate Australian forces to the war in Iraq in 2003 as it was in the Cook government's decision to send the first Australian Imperial Force to assist Britain in 1914. And the Curtin government was caught in the middle of the double bind in 1941, when it decided to recall the second AIF from Europe and the Middle East.

The enduring nature of this sense of dependence on Britain was nowhere clearer than in Prime Minister Menzies's announcement of his government's declaration of war on Germany in September 1939.

> Fellow Australians, it is my melancholy duty to inform you officially that in consequence of a persistence by Germany in her invasion of Poland, Great Britain has declared war upon her and that, *as a result* [emphasis added], Australia is also at war ... Our staying power, and particularly the staying power of *the mother country* [emphasis added], will be best assisted by ... maintaining ... our strength.[35]

Dependence also inspired Prime Minister Curtin's dramatic response to Japan's attack on Pearl Harbor and its impact on the war in the Pacific. In his famous essay published in the Melbourne *Herald* on 27 December 1941, Curtin wrote:

> Without any inhibitions of any kind, I make it quite clear that Australia looks to America, free of any pangs as to our traditional links or kinship with the United Kingdom. We know the problems that the United Kingdom faces. We know the constant threat of invasion. We know the dangers of dispersal of strength, but we know too, that Australia can go [that is, withdraw Australian forces from Europe, the Middle East and Greece/Crete] and Britain can still hold on.[36]

The fall of Britain's 'impregnable' fortress in Singapore just a few weeks later brought Curtin to a heightened sense of threat and dependence. He was persuaded to take his case directly to the American people in a radio broadcast:

> It was, therefore, but natural that, within twenty days after Japan's first treacherous blow, I said on behalf of the Australian Government that we looked to America as the paramount factor on the democracies' side of the Pacific. There is no belittling of the Old Country in this outlook. Britain has fought and won in the air the tremendous battle of Britain ... She cannot, at the same time, go all out in the Pacific. We Australians, with New Zealand, represent Great Britain here in the Pacific – we are her sons – and on us the responsibility falls. I pledge to you my word we will not fail. You, as I have said, must be our leader. We will pull knee to knee with you for every ounce of our weight ... But I give you this warning: Australia is the last bastion between the West Coast of America and the Japanese. If Australia goes, the Americas are wide open. It is said that the Japanese will by-pass Australia and that they can be met and routed in India. I say to you that the saving of Australia is the saving of America's west coast. If you believe anything to the contrary then you delude yourselves.[37]

In important respects, however, Australia's dependence on the United States in wartime became even more entrenched by the arrival of a post–World War II dispensation that saw Australia give perpetual expression to its insecurity and dependence in the ANZUS Treaty. But, as the Vietnam war ramped up, dependence descended into a pathetic grovel, with Prime Minister Harold Holt declaring that Australia would 'go all the way with LBJ [US president Lyndon B. Johnson]'[38] – a catspaw in support of American adventurism in Indochina.

Fast-forward to 2001, when we see Prime Minister Howard visiting Washington on 9/11 as the Twin Towers collapse in New York and a passenger aircraft crashes into the Pentagon. The global response to these attacks was overwhelming. But it was the Australian prime minister and his cabinet who went the extra mile to invoke the

ANZUS Treaty. The US did not request Australian assistance under the treaty, since the terrorist attacks were not acts of war, and the United States was not subject to an existential threat. But that did not deter the Australian government from making the biggest peacetime call it could, and then backing up that call with a series of decisions to support US adventurism in Iraq and Afghanistan. Howard gave cloying expression to Australia's fealty:

> In every way, the attack on New York and Washington and the circumstances surrounding it did constitute an attack upon the metropolitan territory of the United States of America within the provisions of articles IV and V of the ANZUS Treaty. If that treaty means anything, if our debt as a nation to the people of the United States in the darkest days of World War II means anything, if the comradeship, the friendship and the common bonds of democracy and a belief in liberty, fraternity and justice mean anything, it means that the ANZUS Treaty applies and that the ANZUS Treaty is properly invoked.[39]

As former prime minister Malcolm Fraser wrote in 2014, 'the need for dependence on a major power lies deep in Australia's psyche – it is in our DNA'.[40] As if to give Fraser's observation contemporary resonance by proving that too much dependence is never enough, the Australian Strategic Policy Institute proposed an extension to the ANZUS Treaty by recommending its invocation in response to the COVID-19 pandemic.[41]

Fear of abandonment

Abandonment is the dependant's nightmare.

'The fear of abandonment lies deep in the history of European settlement in Australia.' So Allan Gyngell begins his insightful account of Australia's foreign policy after the fall of Singapore in 1942.

> For a century and a half after Tench [Watkin Tench, a young naval officer who arrived in Port Jackson with the First Fleet in 1788] scanned the horizon, only one response was conceivable for most of the people who lived here. They thought of themselves as just as much part of the great British Empire as residents of London or Manchester. They were, in the image they used so often, children of the mother country – scattered perhaps, but bound as family. Australia's security and Britain's were, they knew, inseparable.[42]

But their constant fear, reinforced by the two and a half years they waited for the Second Fleet, was that their mother would abandon them, cast them off and leave them to their own devices, as had been the childhood fate of so many of the convicts themselves.

The abandonment nightmare has never left us. The four years of the Trump presidency served only to reinforce that fear. Hugh White, for instance, has warned that, our wish for an ally notwithstanding, we can no longer assume that the United States will be there for us when we think we need it.[43] The fact is that President Trump inflicted massive reputational damage on the United States, eroding its credibility as a global leader and accelerating the decline in confidence of its traditional allies and friends. Abandonment has transcended nightmares and entered the world of possibility.

The cultural cringe

In contemporary usage, the 'cultural cringe' refers to a pervasive lack of confidence in our own ideas and the broad intellectual culture that nurtures them. Back in 1950, A.A. Phillips' original aim was to expose the fundamental diffidence that underlay Australia's literary culture: the need for international (generally British) affirmation to substantiate an authentically Australian voice.[44] Our national broadcaster no longer speaks to us in rounded vowels, resorting to Daniel Jones's *English Pronouncing Dictionary* to bring us news from London. But, as Hilary McPhee has written in her withering and witty commentary on the continuing relevance of Phillips' work:

> A.A. Phillips identified a species he called 'the denaturalized intellectual' as the Cringe's unhappiest victim – and cursed him down to 'his indifferent eyebrows'. The eyebrows may not be indifferent, but ten years of a Howard Government followed by Rudd and Gillard, so far at least, has ensured that the old Cringe, which A.A. Phillips saw as a form of estrangement of the intellectual, has morphed into a kind of stylish but timid conformity. The timid intellectual holds politicians in contempt and feels free to lecture them occasionally, but fails to hold them to account – and imagine new mechanisms that might start them listening again.[45]

The cultural cringe has become a culture of conformity.

It is often the case that jingoism and overenthusiastic nationalism mask more fundamental insecurities and uncertainties. Rodomontade and bravado, two of Australia's less attractive traits, are usually symptoms of deep-seated self-doubt. So too is looking to other authorities to provide answers and solutions to the issues that worry us, and to validate our chosen courses of action.

Australians constantly look elsewhere – to Europe, to North America, to the Nordic countries and sometimes to New Zealand – to find solutions for what are often unique problems and models for organisation and behaviour to improve efficiency and efficacy. Australian security planners, like planners in other public policy domains, are constantly searching for American or European (particularly British) planning models to support solutions to uniquely Australian problems. The current preoccupation with 'decoupling',[46] 'political warfare'[47] and 'comprehensive coercion',[48] for instance, translates a distinctly American take on its strategic relationship with Russia, Iran, ISIL and China and applies it to Australia's relationship with China.

So into Australia's security policy lexicon enter new terms of art such as 'economic bifurcation' and 'decoupling' as economic counterforce strategies that employ tariffs, quotas and prohibitions on cross-border activities to counter the strength of China's economy – as though such measures would be either available or attractive to Australia. Were such decoupling to lead to a repudiation of the open market–based rules established by Bretton Woods, enshrined in the World Trade Organization rules and reflected more broadly in the post–World War II 'rules-based order', the economic and broader national security consequences for Australia would be profound.

Where the cultural cringe takes Australia into the domain of mindless dependency on great and powerful friends for our security policy settings, the inevitable result is national disempowerment.

Is there an exit strategy?

This chapter has explored the intersecting pathologies that condition Australia's strategic mindset, shaping both our understanding of the world around us and the responses we have to it. These implicit biases that distinguish our strategic mindset might suggest that we are in a straitjacket from which there is no escape, predetermining our options by committing us to a future that is only a function of our past.

The gates of Dante's hell carried the warning 'Abandon all hope, you who enter here'. But *The Divine Comedy* is about redemption and hope, the prospect of a reconciled world and a harmony that encompasses the 'other stars' that give Dante's unified universe a dynamic diversity. While we are long way from Dante's *Paradiso*, we do control all the intellectual and physical resources we need to help build a better world. Though we may not recognise it, we still have agency.

The following chapters explore the principal international and security policy themes that have dominated our international and security policymaking since World War II and that continue to steer our thinking in our current disrupted world. In international and security policymaking, as in all other areas of public policy, Australia has choice and freedom of action. To make those choices and to exercise our freedom of action, we need to understand ourselves and the implicit assumptions that drive us. We need to understand the pathologies that constrain us and, having understood them, address them. We need to grasp the opportunity that self-knowledge affords us to change both our analytical paradigms and the parameters within which we frame our policies. We need transformation if we are to realise the opportunities that a disrupted world affords us. This, ultimately, is what it means for us to exercise agency.

As Barack Obama wrote before he was elected to the US presidency, hope is one of the central motive forces of sound public policy. Optimism and vision are two of the key features of political leadership. It is certainly the thesis of this book that we hold our own future in our hands, and that we have the innate abilities to shape an independent, prosperous and secure Australian future.

2
What Is 'Security' Anyway?

Heav'n, the seat of bliss,
Brooks not the works of violence and war.

John Milton, *Paradise Lost*

A nation cannot be secure when its citizens are not. Dictators thrive on the misery, poverty and subjugation of the people, which together destroy the trust that is fundamental to human and national security. Moreover, they also destroy the trust that is the critical starting point of a secure international order. Trust is conspicuously absent in our present disrupted world, which bristles with weapons, as though security is a consequence of preventing violence and war rather than of nurturing peace and wellbeing.

Within fifty years of the arrival of the First Fleet, the security enjoyed by Indigenous peoples for over 60,000 years, measured in terms of their wellbeing, had been smashed. Dispossessed, diseased and reduced to the position of aliens in their own land, they saw their cultures wither and, in many cases, collapse. Their security fell victim to the power of a foreign state to impose its interests over theirs. The advantages of being a citizen, such as they were, were not extended to Australia's Indigenous peoples.

As a term of policy art, 'security' has been misappropriated by those who glorify war and seek to assert the primacy of the state over the citizen. Together with its derivative 'securitisation' (of which more below), 'security' legitimises the expansion of state power at the expense of the basic rights of the citizen. Not only does it prioritise state security over human security, but it does so in a way that has the net effect of reducing the freedoms and social amenity of those whom the state claims to be protecting. It works by fomenting and then reinforcing division and fear within the community, playing on suspicion and instituting controls that centralise power in the defence, intelligence, law-enforcement and corrections arms of government.

That was certainly not what Cicero had in mind when he coined the word, bringing together the Latin terms *sine* (without) and *cura* (worry) to give us 'security' and its cognate 'sinecure' – the absence of worry. For Cicero, security, in the sense of calmness, contentment and tranquillity, was the necessary precondition for the constancy and dignity that were the hallmarks of what we might now call 'a fit and proper person'.[1]

For most countries, security and prosperity exist in entirely different parts of the political lexicon. Treasurers, along with industry and infrastructure ministers, have been responsible for delivering prosperity, while defence ministers, home affairs ministers, attorneys-general and occasionally foreign ministers have been responsible for delivering security. And ne'er the twain have met, except to the extent that security made prosperity possible, and prosperity made security affordable. Yet there is a growing realisation that security and prosperity are inextricably linked, since neither is achievable without the other. More than that, there is a growing recognition that prosperity is better measured in terms of individual wellbeing, contentment and resilience than in gross transactional terms – reduced deficits, balanced budgets or budget surpluses.

For the most part, international security policies reflect a concentration on the principles advocated by the so-called 'realist' school of international relations, articulated principally by Hans Morgenthau in his monumental 1948 book *Politics Among Nations: The Struggle for Power and Peace*. Morgenthau did not devote time or space to a systematic consideration of security – he was much more preoccupied with power. It is clear, however, that the basic premise on which his analysis depends (apart, of course, from the assumption that there is always a rational basis on which international power relationships are struck) is the enduring importance of the 1648 Peace of

Westphalia, which defined the relationships between states following the catastrophic Thirty Years' War. States employ and deploy power in their own interests (as distinct from the interests of their citizens), and it is the use of that power that determines the security of the state.

Morgenthau appears to accept that security means 'the defence of the frontiers as ... established by peace treaties'.[2] This essentially defines security as the absence of threat against the territory or the sovereignty of the state. In other words, security is the ability of the state to maintain its power by addressing threats. This has been the critical premise in most international statements concerning national security.

It is becoming increasingly clear, however, that security comprehends something far more fundamental and compelling than the ability of the state to protect its sovereignty from threats by other states – important though that may be to the safety of the citizens. Citizens are increasingly resistant to the state wasting their lives in its own protection. The 'campaign fatigue' currently affecting many Americans bears witness to that.[3] It is for the state both to maintain the legal consensus that underpins the protection of its citizens' rights, and to provide the economic and social infrastructure that enables the community to generate human, physical and social capital.

As communities everywhere are discovering, security has as much to do with clean air, clean and available water, reliable food supplies, opportunities for children, ethnic and racial harmony, the ability to live a fulfilling life and a dignified old age, along with personal and economic contentment in the face of the consequences of climate change, such as hurricanes and bushfires. In other words, security is about individual and community wellbeing. While, at one level, this emerging concept of security may be understood as freedom from threat, it has more to do with the creation of opportunity, prosperity, resilience and harmony – 'life, liberty and the pursuit of happiness', as the US Declaration of Independence puts it. A key corollary of this changed sense of security is that most citizens in twenty-first century democracies want freedom *from* military service rather than freedom *through* military service.

The UK-based Ammerdown Group has observed:

> The proper goal of security should be grounded in the well-being of people in their social and ecological context, rather than the interests of a nation state as determined by its elite. This first requires a collective effort to build the conditions of security over the long-term. A commitment to the common good should guide the approach, recognising that security is a shared responsibility and its practice should be negotiated democratically; when security is the preserve of a few, it will not serve the many and is likely to fail everyone.[4]

To the extent that security legislation and conventional military spending work to protect and advance community wellbeing, they are worthwhile. But where military spending becomes a substitute for investment in the muscles and sinews that make for a strong nation, it undermines security.

The defeat of fascism and militarism was a defining moment of the twentieth century, even if that defeat unleashed a global nuclear threat. Even more defining, perhaps, was the unimaginable carnage and suffering that attended that defeat. Mankind had looked over the precipice and recoiled, and looked for global mechanisms to prevent a recurrence. So the 'victorious powers' – principally the Western democracies, led by the United States – established the United Nations, which, in important ways, gave political expression to the Bretton Woods agreement, which had stabilised the global economic system.

Central to the Charter of the United Nations was the basic unifying principle of Western humanism, the value and dignity of the human person, which provides the ethical basis for the equality between people that finds expression in the term 'rule of law'. Preambular paragraph 2 of the charter captures the idea: '[We] reaffirm faith in fundamental human rights, in the dignity and worth of the human person, in the equal rights of men and women and of nations large and small ...'

Article 1 of the charter, with its emphasis on equality, human rights and fundamental freedoms, implicitly places the individual at the centre of the 'state'. The state, which consists of individuals who enjoy basic rights, is charged with protecting those individuals and their rights. In that sense, the state is the creature of its members, not the other way around. Yet, over the past few decades, that relationship between the individual and the state has been under stress, as the state increasingly attempts to assert itself over its citizens, limiting their rights while entrenching its 'security'.

As Francis Fukuyama has written, 'A liberal democratic regime based on individual rights enshrines the notion of equal dignity in law by recognizing citizens as moral agents capable of sharing in their own self-government.'[5] This principle, it would appear, is increasingly under challenge in a disrupted world as governments seek to apply old solutions to new problems. Some of our current problems are in fact new manifestations of old problems. But they remain problems because they were never solved: the prescriptions of a procession of governments simply did not work. The issues demanding renewed global attention include climate change, internal societal collapse, pandemics, drugs and transnational crime, weapons of mass destruction, and terrorism.

Climate change

On a national television program in December 2019, former Australian prime minister Malcolm Turnbull declared that climate change was a national security concern.[6] The panel did not demur. But Turnbull could have been speaking for the president of the United States, the prime ministers of Greece, Spain and Sweden, and even the president of Russia, all of whom faced catastrophic forest fires in 2019. In August 2020, giant old-growth sequoias were again under threat in northern California.[7] The catastrophic fire season in south-eastern Australia during December 2019 and January 2020 impacted on the physical and mental health, and the personal and financial security, of hundreds of thousands of citizens. But —this was not a singular event. It was part of an enduring pattern of climate change–induced events. That is why climate change and its effects – among them drought, rising sea levels, soil salinity, oceanic acidification, rising sea and land temperatures – constitute a threat to the long-term security of nations. They demand a global response.

Internal societal collapse

The long arc of history suggests that the greatest threat to the survival of the state is not aggression by neighbours, serious though that is. Rather, it is the internal collapse that comes from civil war and the destruction of social cohesion. The English Civil War, the French Revolution, the collapse of the Mughal Empire, the American Civil War, the Russian Revolution and the Chinese Communist Revolution, not to mention the many revolutions and civil wars in Africa and South America, illustrate the point. And such internal assaults on the cohesion of the state are often the consequence of structural inequality. As the events that attended upon the denouement of the Trump administration attest, inequality saps the internal cohesion of a nation. It is a cancer within, weakening not only the body politic but, just as importantly, rendering the nation vulnerable to external forces.

The disturbing resurgence of nationalism in parts of Europe, Asia and the Americas, particularly the ethno-nationalism demonising minorities and 'outsiders' that has taken root among the more extreme right-wing groups in continental Europe, serves as a reminder of how ancient scourges can metastasise in the body politic generations after they were deemed to have disappeared.

Pandemics

The outbreak of COVID-19 in China and the speed of its spread globally offer another reminder of the vulnerability of the human species to sudden trans-species viral mutations such as occurred in the 1918–19 influenza epidemic,[8] or the severe acute respiratory syndrome (SARS) coronavirus that appeared in 2002–03.

Pandemics constitute an existential threat to individuals and communities. While they may not (yet) lead to the destruction of nations, the spread and lethality of COVID-19 has caused massive economic and social dislocation, driven the global economy into recession, collapsed key industries such as aviation and tourism, caused significant unemployment and consequent economic insecurity, and left governments around the world scrambling to provide medical facilities, social safety nets and vaccines.

It is sobering to consider, for instance, that by the end of 2020 more Australians had succumbed to the COVID-19 than Australian troops were killed in the Vietnam War. In the United States, the figures are even starker. By the end of 2020, the number of US citizens killed by the coronavirus was over five times the number of US service personnel killed during the entire Vietnam War. By the end of 2021, the number of US deaths from the coronavirus was greater than the total number of US service personnel killed in conflict during the entire twentieth century. In terms of morbidity and mortality, at least, national security far transcends the ability of citizens simply to survive war. It extends to the ability of citizens to live without the fear of premature death from a pandemic.

With entire cities and states in lockdown, citizens everywhere are wondering just why their governments were so slow to recognise the risk and undertake preventive measures. When first-world nations such as Italy, Spain, the United Kingdom and the United States are unable to protect their populations, and when governments around the world embark on stop-gap measures that lack consistency and coherence, when nations pursue dog-eat-dog policies to secure vaccines, blind to global need, it is little wonder that citizens feel insecure and fearful. And it is little wonder that their trust in government erodes substantially.

The coronavirus does not have nationality and knows no boundaries. It is indiscriminate, affecting the healthy and the vulnerable wherever they are. As a global phenomenon, it demands global cooperation if it is to be contained, treated and eradicated.

Drugs and transnational crime

According to the most recent *World Drug Report*, drugs killed 585,000 people in 2017.[9] The number continues to rise. The number of drug users was estimated to be 271 million, or 5.5 per cent of the global population aged between fifteen and sixty-four. Cannabis remains the most used drug, though opioids are by far the greatest cause of death.

The global cost of transnational organised crime is estimated to be between US$1.6 trillion and US$2.2 trillion,[10] illicit drugs accounting for about half the total and significant funds also deriving from trafficking in people, firearms, natural resources, wildlife and counterfeit goods, and cybercrime. The ongoing but unresolved debate in many international jurisdictions about pill testing at music festivals underscores both the availability of so-called recreational drugs and their lethality. Yet in many countries – the Benelux (Belgium, the Netherlands and Luxembourg) and Portugal being notable exceptions – law enforcement continues to focus on apprehending those in possession of drugs, with drug syndicates continuing to be successful at evading detection and arrest. A focus on the health and wellbeing of citizens would suggest that the decriminalisation of drug possession and the legalisation and regulation of drug supply offer more constructive avenues for the control of drug use and supply.[11] They would also enhance the personal security and safety of drug users.

Weapons of mass destruction

WMD, especially nuclear weapons, remain an existential threat to humanity. While the global community has lived with them for three-quarters of a century, proliferation has continued while non-proliferation efforts under the Treaty on the Non-Proliferation of Nuclear Weapons (NPT) have stalled. The reduction in the nuclear use threshold by the United States, as contemplated in the 2018 Nuclear Posture Review, where the boundary between nuclear and conventional warfare has become blurred, is a particularly worrying development.[12]

Groups such as the International Campaign to Abolish Nuclear Weapons (ICAN) have galvanised the international community to accelerate its efforts to eliminate nuclear weapons. But the fact remains that the states possessing nuclear weapons – France, Great Britain, India, Israel, North Korea, Russia, Pakistan, the United States and potentially Iran – have completely disregarded the UN Treaty on the Prohibition of Nuclear Weapons, while the allies of the United States – except the Netherlands – refused to participate in the treaty's negotiations.

The NPT had a solid early record in delivering nuclear arms control and disarmament, though it too is under threat as the nuclear weapons states party to the treaty continue to disregard their obligations under Article VI. 'Negotiations in good faith' on general and complete disarmament have given way to cynical improvements in the destructive capacity of nuclear weapons and the accuracy of their delivery systems. The fact remains that nuclear weapons constitute an existential threat to humanity, and their eradication is essential if people are to live in a more secure world.

Terrorism

Since the attacks on the World Trade Center and the Pentagon on 11 September 2001, terrorism has become *le problème du jour* for many nations. Some countries embarked on a frenzy of legislation at once, responding to and fomenting public concern about acts of Islamist politically motivated violence. As of 30 September 2019, Australia, for instance, has enacted eighty-two anti-terror laws, with another six in the pipeline – far exceeding the legislative responses of the United Kingdom, Canada and even the United States.[13] Fifty-four pieces of legislation were enacted in the decade following 9/11,[14] legislative hyper-activity that exacerbated both popular anxiety and the tendency towards social exclusion by singling out the Muslim community for special attention.

Around the world, calls for an increased emphasis on social policy tools – interventions aimed at building stronger, more inclusive and more tolerant communities – have gone largely unheard, the default position being ever greater reliance on expanded surveillance and law-enforcement powers. The question is whether a community can be more secure when it is more fearful and less free.

The so-called war against terrorism offers a salutary lesson in this regard. The military capabilities and doctrines developed to ensure victory in any possible war against an aggressor state have already proved largely irrelevant in the fight against groups that resort to a form of asymmetric warfare (terrorism) to promote their cause. They do this either to penalise those states that pursue policies against the interests of such groups (for instance, the United States and its coalition partners prosecuting the war in Iraq and Afghanistan), or to force actions (such as legislated restrictions on individual and group freedoms) that would have the net effect of undermining liberal democracy itself. Random acts of violence and terror simply cannot be prevented by air strike, tanks and prolonged military occupation. Indeed, all that those actions seem to do is sap the strength and resolve of the nation that deploys such forces, and provide the rich, sludgy soup of anarchy that is the perfect incubator for terrorism. As General David Petraeus tried to demonstrate in Iraq and, subsequently, Afghanistan, 'search and destroy' must be matched against 'hearts and minds': negotiation with the enemy is just as important as the annihilation of the enemy's hard core. The modern history of Iraq is a testament to the failure of annihilation of the enemy's hard core as a strategy.

The basic problem is that, like security, the very concept of terrorism is misconceived. It is seen as an attack on the state when it transparently is not: it is an attack on the values that unite the community in common purpose and joint endeavour. It is hardly surprising, then, that a misconception of the nature of terrorism invokes an entirely inappropriate form of response – military force, in the case of Iraq, or an overreliance on statutory instruments, in the case of Australia, Canada, the United Kingdom and the United States. This is, after all, the old security paradigm: where armed violence is employed against the state, the state retaliates with armed force, because it is the only entity that is constitutionally empowered to do so. If all you have is a hammer, everything looks like a nail. But the response exacerbates the problem, because the aim of the terrorist is to generate fear in the community, thereby eroding whatever support the community might have for legitimate military force.

As Philip Bobbitt has noted, since the emergence of modern states during the Renaissance, the world has been divided into states of consent and states of terror. States of consent derived their legitimacy from the consent of the community, given freely and renewed frequently – consent that can be withdrawn. States of terror govern through oppression of the people, and their regimes do not cede power freely.[15] Terrorism is the weapon of choice when the aim is to prevent states from operating through popular consent. Consequently, as Bobbitt notes:

> The threats we will soon face are such that we cannot afford to lose, yet to win we must reconceive victory; now that war must aim at victory newly conceived, we must change our ideas of what counts as war: the new warfare attacks innocent civilians because it challenges rights and opportunities, not nationhood or wealth or territory; finally, war is changing because states go to war on behalf of their legitimacy and the basis for legitimacy is changing.[16]

Securitisation: Turning problems into threats

'Securitisation' is a relatively new tool by which states exercise control over their citizens. It is the practice that accords significant public danger, menace and threat to politically and socially important issues, and accordingly seeks to deal with such issues by employing personal and social controls, enhanced intelligence gathering powers, law-enforcement protocols and national military capabilities. 'Securitisation' simultaneously creates, exploits and assuages fear.

To deliver its intended effects, securitisation relies on two messaging techniques that magnify the significance of the issue that a government may want to exploit.

First, security is given exceptional status among the various domains of public policy, and an importance out of all proportion when measured against other characteristics of a well-functioning society – health, employment, education, public and social amenity and so on.

Second, securitisation invokes the rhetorical manipulation of issues. Refugees and asylum seekers, for instance, are described as 'boat people', 'queue jumpers' and 'illegal immigrants', which has the effect of both dramatising the issue and demonising the victims. Suburbs in which unemployed or underemployed youths congregate are 'war zones', and the youths in question are 'criminal gangs' and 'young thugs'. There is scarcely an aspect of Indigenous policy and ethnic minority youth law enforcement, for example, that is not subject to both messaging techniques.

Securitisation also encourages a significant, though sometimes subtle, change in the role of those who advise on intelligence and operational matters. Oftentimes analysts move from their role as objective assessors of evidence to a more ambiguous role in which they and their agencies focus instead on the dynamics of threat management, proffering advice based on 'professional judgement' as distinct from a hard assessment of the facts. In other words, securitisation both relies on and promotes the amplification of views and advice based on professional judgement – a kind of group-authorised subjectivity – rather than an objective evaluation of evidence and data.

US president Franklin D. Roosevelt began his first inaugural address, delivered on 4 March 1933, in terms that capture the incapacity of many contemporary governments: paralysis in the face of problems that they can neither comprehend nor resolve. Roosevelt's words reverberate today: 'Let me assert my firm belief that the only thing we have to fear is fear itself – nameless, unreasoning, unjustified terror which paralyzes needed efforts to convert retreat into advance.'

Roosevelt understood implicitly that fear is pernicious, sapping the nation's energy while it breeds mistrust and kills the hope that inspires vision. As he said, 'when there is no vision, people perish'.[17] President Roosevelt's response was to offer a leadership of 'frankness and vigor', as he put it, to restore the confidence that 'thrives only on honesty, on honor, on the sacredness of obligations, on faithful protection, on unselfish performance'.

So Roosevelt embarked on the 'New Deal', a suite of public policy reforms, public works projects and relief programs that not only set the United States on the road to recovery, but also positioned it to defeat the global security challenge that Pearl Harbor would catastrophically deliver in 1941. Roosevelt did not announce a 'war on poverty', a 'war on unemployment', a 'war on inequality', a 'war on greed' or any of the other rhetorical but otherwise empty expressions that work to securitise wider policy domains. Roosevelt offered systematic solutions to address systemic problems.

By way of contrast, the first response of many contemporary government leaders is to securitise national problems. Issues that may be either causes or consequences of anxieties within the community are portrayed as existential threats demanding military or quasi-military responses. The language employed to inflate risk is always replete with hyperbole and rhetoric, and the solutions offered are usually couched in the confected language of urgency and overreach. In Australia's case, 'Operation Sovereign Borders', for instance, remains Orwellian both for its confected language and for its ability to dramatise the policy response while dehumanising and demonising the targets of the policy.

In the lead-up to the 2001 election, the Howard government securitised the MV *Tampa* incident, deploying armed special forces troops to control unarmed refugees rescued from a sinking vessel.[18] Little more than a month after the *Tampa* incident, HMAS *Adelaide* intercepted a disabled Indonesian fishing vessel (SIEV 4) carrying over 200 asylum seekers, initiating what became known as the 'Children Overboard Affair', as well as 'a certain maritime incident'. This was also securitised, with the government falsely claiming that refugees had thrown their children overboard to force the Australian authorities to accept them into the country.[19] It is important to note that while the government was securitising the activities to manage refugee flows, it was also securitising the very language used to describe the refugees and the vessels in which they sought refuge: 'suspected illegal entry vessel' became 'suspected irregular entry vessel' (SIEV), attaching criminal and security labels to what were, after all, clapped-out fishing boats.

These incidents prompted legislation to exclude asylum seekers from landing in Australia (principally by excising points of entry from the Australian migration zone), principally on the grounds that people seeking asylum were a national security threat to Australia's sovereignty, and that some of the asylum seekers might have been terrorists.[20] The defence minister of the time, Peter Reith, leveraged his earlier remark that boat people could provide a pipeline for terrorists to say that 'it is irrefutable that part of your security posture is your ability to control your borders'.[21]

The securitisation of the refugee issue led to a build-up of defence resources in northern Australia, and enhanced aerial surveillance of Australia's northern waters by the RAAF and private contractors. Immigration and customs border controls that had worked well for decades were suddenly found to be defective, and in need of a more overtly paramilitary character. Even the Department of Customs officers' white uniform shirts were subsequently replaced with black shirts (they call it 'barathea blue') to make them look more intimidating.

The fear of fear itself resulted in the appearance of black-uniformed border security personnel not only at our airports and ports, but on our inner-city streets, as part of an expanded law-enforcement character assigned to our national immigration and border control functions. 'Operation Fortitude', for instance, the misconceived joint Victoria Police–Border Force operation planned for August 2015, was widely seen as a law-enforcement/paramilitary targeting of ethnic communities.[22] It was.

More recently, the footage of camouflaged police officers with automatic laser-sighted weapons confronting Indigenous children at the Don Dale Youth Detention Centre in the Northern Territory should be of concern to all Australians, not just First Australians.[23] Domestic law-enforcement agencies have progressively become more militarised as they have become more Americanised: police constables routinely carry sidearms, tasers, truncheons and handcuffs, all on clear display, to inject that 'little bit of fear' of police, as advocated by the New South Wales police commissioner Mick Fuller.[24]

The operations of Australian police services have become more intimidating, whether in detaining a mentally ill disabled pensioner,[25] responding to peaceful demonstrations and protests, such as occurred outside the prime minister's residence in Kirribilli in 2019,[26] or maintaining law and order at music festivals, where strip searches, including of juveniles, have become ever more common.[27] Indeed, terms of art such as 'proactive policing' may mask the implicit securitisation of law enforcement. And where 'proactive policing' is managed by the imposition of quotas – the number of 'proactive policing' interventions whereby members of the public are stopped, questioned, searched and/or detained – quite fundamental questions of legitimacy and legality arise.[28] When specific communities and ethnicities are singled out for special attention, as so often happens with Indigenous, Asian, Muslim and African communities, securitisation begins to morph into racial discrimination. This form of securitisation is a direct assault on human rights.

Perhaps the most extraordinary example of the securitisation of social issues was the 2007 Northern Territory Emergency Response initiated by the Howard government, and subsequently continued by the Rudd government. At the instigation of the then minister for Indigenous affairs, Mal Brough, a former army officer, the government appointed a serving major-general to head a task force to deal with the recommendations of a Northern Territory inquiry into child sexual abuse in Aboriginal communities. Enabling legislation, *The Northern Territory National Emergency Response Act* 2007, was rushed through the national parliament, and subsequently amended four times by the Rudd and Gillard governments. Securitisation is not the preserve of Coalition governments alone.

Ten years later, the ABC's Indigenous affairs editor, Stan Grant, described the intervention as a 'dark time' for Indigenous people.[29] The controls it imposed were seen by many, including the UN High Commissioner for Human Rights, as a violation of human rights.[30]

While the emergency intervention may have been well-intentioned, it was a tactical response to a long-term strategic issue for Indigenous Australia: the restoration of dignity and recognition to people who had been alienated and dispossessed. It is far from clear that the intervention delivered the results it promised. Indeed, many Indigenous people in the Northern Territory claim that it failed.[31] And to judge by the most recent *Closing the Gap* report, Indigenous disadvantage remains entrenched.[32] The securitisation of disadvantage does not help. Rather, it exacerbates the problem.

Maybe it is fear itself that continues to persuade Coalition governments to generate panic and urgency in legislating additional powers for the police and security agencies, powers that further constrain the civil liberties of the community as each bill is railroaded through the parliament.

'Hyper-legislation', so described by University of Toronto professor Kent Roach, is a key feature of Australia's approach to securitisation.[33] As at 30 September 2019, Australia had enacted eighty-two anti-terror laws, extending from the retention of metadata by telecommunications companies to the revocation of citizenship from dual nationals convicted of terrorism offences.[34] This is compounded by the demonisation of ethnic minorities, especially from Africa and the Middle East, and the extraordinary claims made by Department of Home Affairs minister Peter Dutton that Melburnians were scared to go out to dinner because of gang violence.[35] All these contribute to making people fearful and insecure – they create anxiety for political effect.

Securitisation is also reflected in the 'law and order' campaigns that argue for increased militarisation of police services. Commenting on this issue, Michael Pembroke, a judge of the New South Wales Supreme Court, offered a timely reminder when he said that 'the mission of the police is not to wage war but to protect and safeguard'.[36] Judge Pembroke's comment goes to the essence of what security is all about: the ability of the community to live in peace and harmony, going about their business in the confidence that they can live rewarding, fulfilled and happy lives.

Even the landscape has been securitised, at least in Canberra. Like Abuja, Brasília, Islamabad, Naypyidaw, Ottawa and Washington DC, Canberra is a purpose-built city. Its business is government. But unlike most of the other purpose-built national capitals, Canberra's parliamentary landscape is surprisingly securitised. The federal parliament has been transformed from an open parliament – the electors could literally walk across the top of Parliament House – into a fortress, protected by armed police officers with automatic weapons, armed patrols, the display of sidearms within the secure spaces inside the parliamentary building, and an array of physical security barriers and CCTV monitors.

Prime real estate close to the federal parliament is dominated by the Department of Defence (occupying Russell Hill), the Australian Security Intelligence Organisation (overlooking Lake Burley Griffin), the Australian Federal Police (in a building that once accommodated six federal departments and agencies), the Office of National Intelligence, the Attorney-General's Department, the Department of the Prime Minister and Cabinet, the senior executive component of the

Department of Home Affairs, and the Department of Foreign Affairs. The Treasury and the Department of Finance are also close by.

The applied economics departments, along with the social policy departments, are distributed across the rest of Canberra. This landscape implicitly reinforces the power of the national security establishment in the national subconscious. Moreover, it reinforces government's preoccupation with the security of the state vis-à-vis the security of the citizen. The departments and agencies that help build the deep infrastructure on which an inclusive and strong community rests (education, health, community services, industry and infrastructure) are dispersed and out of sight – and this in one of the world's first federated constitutional democracies.

Securitisation is pernicious, for two reasons: it diminishes the autonomy and dignity of the individual citizen, and it normalises the practice whereby the state succeeds in confecting emergency or panic to address the symptoms of problems rather than their causes. In a subtle sense, securitisation is anti-democratic, since it uses the instruments of state control over its citizens and other individuals to manage non-defence and non-military problems without engaging the citizens to act in their own interests. In particular, securitisation usually involves the use of military, paramilitary, law-enforcement and intelligence-gathering capabilities to resolve matters that are fundamentally economic, political and social.

An expanding global approach to security

The past decade or so has seen the beginnings of a paradigm shift in the global approach to security. National security has begun to include more basic concepts of values and rights – concepts that have not thrown over the need for states to be able to protect themselves against aggression but rather have expanded the basic connotation of security to accommodate human security concerns. Security as a function of the power of the state to protect itself has progressively expanded to incorporate the basic need for personal and community wellbeing in a world where threats from states are diminishing while threats from other sources are increasing.

An expanded concept of security is not new. This evolution was captured nicely by Francisco Aravena, writing in 2002, when he noted that:

> a conceptual transition is taking place from a Cold War perspective that visualized an enemy expressed in strongly military actions carried out by a state, to a post-Cold War perspective in which threats are diffused, the weight of military factors has diminished and many of the threats appear not to be linked to state actors, and even not to be linked to any particular territory.[37]

Aravena went on:

> Four substantial elements need to be emphasized in today's security landscape:
>
> - International security extends beyond its military components;
> - International security is transnational, global and interdependent;
> - International security is produced by a plurality of actors, the state is no longer the exclusive actor; and
> - International security in the twenty-first century has enlarged its agenda and demands that actors work together.[38]

Although armed conflict and its antecedents are ultimately arational and chaotic, it would be wrong to suggest that the global community now needs to replace its traditional concept of security with one that focuses exclusively on values and rights. Rather, the challenge is to expand its understanding of security to include the management of climate change, pandemics, nuclear weapons, international criminality, pollution and environmental degradation, the creation of human and social capital, the expansion of institutional and other arrangements that enhance social equity, and the recognition that resilience and social inclusion are of greater significance in maintaining and enhancing national security than are defence and law-enforcement systems of themselves. Breakdown in internal social cohesion and the resultant civil wars are a greater threat to the survival of the state than is war against other nation-states. In this context, it is important to recognise that social inclusion erodes, and community cohesion dissipates, when the rule of law is in any way compromised. It is paradoxical that a scrupulous adherence to due process offers a better defence of social inclusion and community cohesion than does the creation of arbitrary exceptions in the name of 'national security'. In other words, adaptability, flexibility, resilience and legality are the new hallmarks of security, as they are of economic prosperity.

As a disrupted twenty-first century unfolds, declining relative prosperity (as measured by the widening gap between the world's rich and poor) and increasing insecurity go hand in hand. That inversion largely defines the disruption the global community currently confronts. This is what security policy needs to address, and it demands a realignment of prosperity with security. Security will not be guaranteed by a clinical preoccupation with military threat (and/or its absence) and freedom from crime, while more devastating possibilities – with potentially greater costs in terms of human lives and national treasure – progressively dominate the national and international consciousness.

For governments, this creates a new set of challenges. Whereas, during the twentieth century, governments of all persuasions looked to 'hard power' (that is, military capabilities) to assert their authority, to protect the nation against attack and to promote their strategic interests, the demand of the twenty-first century will be to develop appropriate forms of 'soft power' that at once realise the security aspirations of the community while constraining those circumstances in which 'hard power' might be required.

So, where to?

This chapter has identified some of factors that constrain the way national security policies are designed and framed. It has also identified several symptoms of misalignment between the security needs of communities and the policies that are intended to meet those needs. But we are yet to discover a systematic treatment for the symptoms of misalignment.

There are four intersecting binaries that need to be addressed if 'national security' is to be reframed in ways that address the disrupted global environment in which nations now find themselves and the disruptive forces that are reconfiguring the 'global rules-based system' that has underpinned global economic, political, social and strategic security since World War II:

- The fundamental relationship between the individual (citizen) and the state.

- The reactive planning dynamic that focuses on threats and risks to security, as distinct from the proactive dynamic that might focus on the constructive and positive elements of national harmony that is characterised by harmony, inclusion, resilience, tranquillity and wellbeing.

- The 'control mentality' that seeks to isolate (and marginalise) problems and manage the people who have those problems, as distinct from the 'empowerment mentality' that seeks to enable individuals and communities to take charge of their own lives and prospects.

- The 'intervention model' of public policy design that deals with matters after they arise, as distinct from the 'prevention model' of public policy design that deals with matters proactively.

Think tanks across the globe have attempted to resolve these seemingly intractable tensions. Yet in the past couple of decades the pendulum has swung noticeably in favour of the state when it comes to the rights of the individual. Whether it is the passage of bills that afford greater powers to police and security agencies, the collection of telecommunications metadata, the surreptitious introduction of facial-recognition technologies, the profiling of individual preferences in order to develop manipulative choice algorithms or the use of artificial intelligence to generate individual and social controls, the privacy and rights of individual citizens are increasingly restricted, all in the name of 'security'. Yet the question remains: how can the state be secure if its citizens are not? This is a fundamental problem that governments have failed to address.

The new security issues that affect nations in ways that traditional security solutions are unable to resolve perhaps demand a new suite of conceptual and policy frameworks if the citizen and the state are to enjoy the wellbeing that is the goal of all sound policy. The reactive, control and interventionist models will simply not cut the mustard if the global community is to develop systematic solutions to systemic problems.

3
Dependence and Faith-Based Policy: ANZUS

We only speak of faith when we wish to substitute emotion for evidence.

Bertrand Russell, *Human Society in Ethics and Politics*[1]

Governments of all persuasions trumpet their adherence to evidence-based policy, except when it comes to national security. Here, deep-seated anxieties and uncertainties colour the assumptions on which security policy is based, giving it a quality that is at once doctrinaire and, like religious faith, unassailable. It is an orthodoxy, the broad acceptability of which is demonstrated in its 'bipartisanship' – that killer of conversation, whereby trawling through the collective ignorance produces a lowest common denominator on which everyone can agree. Contestability is limited to the margins. The fundamental tenets are unchallengeable, and unchallenged. Governments and oppositions share the one faith.

As an exercise in government policymaking, this practice is dangerous because it is fundamentally anti-democratic. There is little accountability attaching to the premises on which national security policy is based, since the system that produces it is shrouded in secrecy and those who inhabit the cloisters of security policymaking are distinguished by their conformity and convergence. And their silence. They are as monochrome as they are generally mono-gendered. They form the entitled elite that is self-important enough to think that it answers an ancient question: 'Who guards the guardians?'

While, at one level, secrecy (which, in soft tones, its proponents usually call 'confidentiality') may appear to allow frank and fearless debate about problems and their solutions, as one might hope takes place in the national cabinet room, it far too often creates the preconditions for alignment and uniformity. Policy, as a result, becomes arcane and the policy process becomes self-referential. Consequently, historical precedent and prior experience establish the default frameworks within which security decisions are taken, regardless of the specific dynamics of the problem at hand or the unique circumstances that might provide its context.

This means that it is difficult to escape the stultifying constraints of the strategic mindset identified in Chapter 1. We are hardwired to deal with fundamental issues of national security on the basis of entrenched fears that reflect our preoccupation with race, distance, isolation and dependence. Our default position is to see every security issue through the lens of what we assume to be US interests, and how any option pursued by Australia might strengthen or otherwise impact on our relationship with the United States. Our approach to national and international security is totally conditioned by the ANZUS Treaty, itself an artefact of our strategic dependency.

But sentimental attachment to the ANZUS Treaty does not amount to a security policy. For the best part of sixty years, the treaty has been both the touchstone and the anchor of Australia's national security. It is an enduring reminder of Australia's strategic dependency on the United States, and a concession by the Americans that both recognises and mitigates that dependency. In a radically changed world, however, the global strategic dominance of the United States, and the authority and credibility that went with it, have declined. This decline was accelerated by the mercurial actions of President Trump. For all his reliance on mantras and slogans to substantiate his presidency (witness his 'Make America Great Again' catchcry), the inescapable fact is that slogans do not make for good policy, and America is less great for his presidency.

ANZUS so dominates government discourse on Australia's relations with the United States that the security relationship has come largely to define the entire relationship. Yet our relationship with the United States is significantly deeper and more diverse than the defence relationship can ever be. Governments find it convenient, however, to overlook the deep constitutional links between Australia and the United States – constitutional links that ground the operation of the rule of law that defines both of our democracies – preferring instead to be distracted by the glitter of gold braid and the spectacle of sailpasts, flypasts and military parades.

So it came as no surprise that Prime Minister Morrison, in his October 2019 speech to the Lowy Institute, proclaimed that 'our alliance with the United States is our past, our present and our future – it is the bedrock of our security'.[2] The term used was 'alliance', not 'relationship', 'association' or 'connection'. In the context of the prime minister's speech, 'alliance' is about defence, defence being the raison d'être of the ANZUS Treaty.

The political import of a reference to the Book of Revelation and a term like 'bedrock' is clear: ANZUS has become both a central tenet of our national security faith and the sine qua non of our national interest, consolidating both our identity and our power. While hyperbole is increasingly the currency of political discourse, it is incumbent on policy thinkers to consider the impact of such overheated political claims on the authority, credibility and legitimacy of public policy. And they must consider whether the political and strategic dimensions of policy statements are convergent. After all, public policy is what establishes the foundations of government action and the reasons for government decisions.

So we must ask ourselves: is the political power of the ANZUS Treaty as a panacea providing national psychological comfort in the face of anxiety and a deep sense of dependence matched by its strategic effect? Does the treaty afford the security 'guarantee' and the ensuing confidence that has long been the holy grail of the nation's political leaders and defence planners?

A little history

Mythmaking has long surrounded Australia's strategic relationship with the United States. While a former Australian ambassador the United States, Joe Hockey, trumpeted his '100 Years of Mateship' campaign[3] to construct an image of a strategic relationship greater than the sum of its parts, no one bothered to recollect the more self-serving purpose of the Great White Fleet's visit to Sydney, Melbourne and Fremantle in 1908.[4]

This was a 'bread and circuses' display of US naval power, the grandest spectacle seen by the newly formed federation, and the greatest concentration of naval power in Australia since the arrival of the First Fleet 120 years earlier. For Prime Minister Alfred Deakin, who enjoyed issuing an invitation to the US president, Theodore Roosevelt, without the agreement of Whitehall, it was an opportunity for a spot of defence policy freelancing. As he wrote (anonymously) before the fleet's arrival, 'The entrance of a fleet under the Stars and Stripes into the Pacific is an incident of the utmost significance.'[5] And, just a few days later: 'Its chief inspiration has been racial and political.'[6]

But rather than initiating an act of enduring friendship, President Roosevelt's intention was to gather intelligence on the port capabilities and defences of Sydney and Melbourne to support US military contingency planning, should it become necessary to control Australian ports in the event of a war with Japan and a split from the British empire.[7]

Both the Prime Minister's and the President's objectives were met. But the very fact of such contingency planning reveals a constant feature of US relationship management – America First. As a former Premier of NSW Jack Lang once said, "In the race of life, always back self-interest – at least you know it's trying". From Washington to Trump, the US has always put its self-interest first.

It was Australian self-interest that gave birth to the ANZUS Treaty, a self-interest driven by anxiety and insecurity, as distinct from the independence and self-affirmation that distinguished early American self-interest as it fought for independence from Britain. At the end of World War II, Australia's longstanding strategic dilemma – how to defend a large continent with a small population – had reappeared starkly. The experience of two world wars in quick succession, and an overwhelming sense of the cost of war, in both blood and treasure, powerfully reinforced our sense of isolation and dependency. The war with Japan, an ally (of sorts) in World War I, reinforced a deep antipathy towards 'the Asian hordes', reinforced by the powerful anti-Chinese sentiment generated during and after the gold rushes.[8] By the end of World War II, 'White Australia' reigned as the unifying national policy.

It was not long after Prime Minister John Curtin's famous 'realignment' from Great Britain to the United States[9] that Australian concerns about the nature the strategic relationship with the Americans began to take root. The attorney-general and minister for foreign affairs, Dr Bert Evatt, held firm opinions about the need for equality and mutuality between the United States and Australia, and a clear recognition of Australia's interests in both Asia and the Pacific – interests to which the United States was inclined to give scant consideration and then dismiss, or simply ignore altogether. It should be noted that Australia's claims were perhaps not greatly assisted by Evatt's forthright and often abrupt demeanour in advancing his arguments, both to his cabinet colleagues and to his American interlocutors.

The more serious contention between the two sides arose in the immediate aftermath of Japan's surrender in 1945. Like Prime Minister Billy Hughes, who had supported a punitive treaty with Germany in 1919, so Evatt was committed to a hard treaty with Japan that would restrict its ability to rearm, which in turn meant tight constraints on its ability to reindustrialise. This was anathema to General Douglas MacArthur and the Truman administration, which was already looking to a strong Japan as a cornerstone of US strategic power in the North Pacific and as a key element in the containment of China as the inevitability of its Communist Party control loomed.

As we shall see, this latter element of US strategic policy – the rise of China – in no way informed the negotiation of the ANZUS Treaty.

So when, in 1949, the newly elected Liberal–Country Party coalition government, led by Prime Minister Robert Menzies, was contemplating the implications of a soft treaty with Japan, Mao Zedong's expulsion of General Chiang Kai-shek's forces from mainland China and accelerating tensions on the Korean Peninsula provided an as yet unrecognised backdrop to Australia's traditional strategic anxiety. In a conversation with the US special representative John Foster Dulles in September 1950, Menzies' external affairs minister, Percy Spender, made it clear that Australia's primary concern was security against future Japanese aggression. He indicated that a formal commitment by the United States guaranteeing Australia's security against Japanese aggression might go some way towards allaying Australia's fears.[10]

Australia's fear of a rearmed Japan was also an artefact of the racial anxiety that found expression in the White Australia policy and the deep sense of grievance held across the Australian community at the atrocities committed by the armed forces of Japan during the Pacific War, sentiments that lingered long after the war's end.[11]

Spender was no Evatt in having a visionary approach to a post-war world, or the intellectual qualities needed to deliver it. But he had the sound diplomatic skills that Evatt so lacked, and the realist's capacity to pounce on opportunity. By means of some careful political manipulation, Spender succeeded in convincing the acting prime minister, Sir Arthur Fadden, to announce Australia's early commitment of air and ground forces to the Korean War – without Menzies' knowledge. (Menzies was in the middle of the Atlantic Ocean, aboard the *Queen Mary*, where Spender unsuccessfully – whether by design or by accident – attempted to contact him by telephone.)[12] The Australian decision was well received by the US administration.

So it was that Spender was able to exploit the confluence of regional strategic events to secure a security treaty with the United States as the price for lenient treatment of Japan. While it took another year of diplomatic wrangling for Spender to persuade Dulles and Secretary of State Dean Acheson, and to dissuade Menzies from indulging his Anglophilia by bringing the United Kingdom into the Pacific pact, the ANZUS Treaty was signed in San Francisco on 1 September 1951. Basically, America's need for a reliable ally and Australia's need for a 'great and powerful friend' converged, although neither side got exactly what it wanted.[13]

The arrival of a revolutionary Marxist-Leninist government in China and the outbreak of armed conflict on the Korean Peninsula – developments, one might have thought, of greater strategic moment than a 'soft' peace treaty with Japan – did not influence Australia's quest for a security treaty with the United States in any substantial way. ANZUS was all about Japan. In a conversation with Dulles on 22 September 1950, Spender 'made it quite clear ... that Australia's primary concern was security against future Japanese aggression and said that Australia would not subscribe to any treaty with Japan unless there were adequate assurances that Australia would be protected against Japanese aggression'.[14]

So far as the United States was concerned, the treaty was the price that it was prepared to pay to have Australia's compliance. From the US perspective, the treaty did not address a potential China threat, or a threat from anywhere else. In other words, at its origin, the treaty was of limited strategic application. It is important to bear this in mind as we look at ANZUS in contemporary circumstances.

At the end of World War II, the United Kingdom retained significant colonial and political interests in India, Burma, Malaya and Borneo, Hong Kong, the South Pacific and, of course, Australia. It had a devoted acolyte in Menzies, who continued to look to it rather than to the United States as the ultimate guarantor of Australia's economy and security. As late as 3 August 1950, Menzies told Fadden that 'we do not need a pact with America – they are already overwhelmingly friendly to us'.[15] Assistant Secretary of State Dean Rusk certainly shared Menzies' view, though for altogether different reasons:

he saw the participation of 'Asiatics' as essential in US regional treaty-making.[16]

In early 1951, the British government was giving serious consideration to its interest in joining the ANZUS Treaty and contemplating the consequences of its exclusion. The British were concerned that the United States was attempting 'to supplant and undo us in the Pacific' – a somewhat odd position, given the disproportionate cost of US victory in both the European and Pacific wars – and communicated that view to Menzies.[17] But the fact of the matter was that the balance of power in the Pacific had changed forever, and it was the United States that finally thwarted Britain's expectations, rather than New Zealand or Australia. Menzies raised Prime Minister Anthony Eden's interest in gaining ANZUS Treaty observer status for the United Kingdom with Acheson, though one suspects that Menzies' efforts were half-hearted. Indeed, by late 1951 it had dawned on Menzies that if he continued to press for British association with ANZUS, the result may well be the scuttling of the treaty in toto, given US reluctance. Eventually, Britain was thrown a bone with the establishment of the 1954 Manila Pact, which provided for the collective defence of South-East Asia under the Southeast Asia Treaty Organization (SEATO) and, following the withdrawal of UK forces from east of Suez in 1968, the Five Power Defence Arrangements (FPDA), providing for the integrated air defence of Malaysia and Singapore. FPDA continues to operate in a vestigial way but is of decreasing contemporary strategic relevance.

So, at its inception, ANZUS was indeed a treaty of both political and strategic moment.

- It confirmed the place of the United States as the pre-eminent power in the Pacific.

- It provided for the security of Australia and New Zealand as the price paid for a lenient treaty with Japan.

- As an artefact of the Japan Peace Treaty, it consolidated Japan's position as a critical element in the US strategic dominance of the North Pacific and the US force disposition, particularly the home porting of the United States Seventh Fleet at Yokosuka, the US Air Force's 18th Wing (initially the Seventh Air Force) at Kadena, and the III Marine Expeditionary Force in Okinawa (arrangements that remain largely in place more than seven decades later).

- It provided Australia with the 'security blanket' it had always wanted – an external solution to the 'big continent/small population' dilemma.
- It aligned Australia with US policy that sought to re-create imperial Japan as a constitutional democracy that would provide a critical strategic stabilising factor in North Asia.
- It established a model for a set of US treaties in Asia: the Mutual Defense Treaty with the Philippines in 1951; the Security Treaty Between the United States and Japan in 1951; the Mutual Defense Treaty with the Republic of Korea in 1953; the Treaty of Mutual Cooperation and Security between the United States and Japan in 1960; and, notwithstanding its dissolution in 1977, the Manila Pact that still operates in Thailand – the linkages with 'the Asiatics' that Rusk sought.
- And, unintentionally, it sealed the fate of Britain as a strategically significant power in the Pacific.

But ANZUS was, nonetheless, a treaty forged in the context of its times: a period of uncertainty and anxiety for Australia as it tried to come to terms with the decolonisation of Asia, the victory of a revolutionary communist movement in China, the rise of communist movements throughout Asia, a cold war between the United States and the Soviet Union that had clear consequences for the Pacific, and, perhaps most importantly, a United States that was determined to back its immediate post–World War II power with the authority and legitimacy that came from its establishment of a remodelled United Nations.

While Prime Minister Howard was the first head of government to invoke the ANZUS Treaty, it was Menzies who first tested the waters. Australia's commitment of forces to the defence of Malaysia against Indonesian 'Confrontation' in 1963 was made under the assumption that, were Australian forces to come under direct attack by Indonesian forces, the United States would commit forces to support Australia. Discussions between US Under-Secretary of State for Political Affairs Averell Harriman and the Australian government in June 1963 skirted around US policy in South-East Asia, with Harriman apparently adopting a more committed interpretation of the ANZUS Treaty than President John F. Kennedy subsequently adopted in his conversations with Prime Minister Menzies and Treasurer Harold Holt, and the Australians seemingly hearing what they wanted to hear.

So when Prime Minister Menzies met President Kennedy in July 1963, the key topic of conversation was the applicability of the ANZUS Treaty to an Australian force under attack in Malaysia. Menzies assumed that ANZUS was operable in such a situation. Kennedy was equivocal.[18] In a subsequent conversation with Treasurer Holt, Kennedy was more forthright: the United States was not going to be the backstop behind UK and Australian power in Malaysia. Kennedy is recorded as saying: 'We have not said "if you [Indonesia] do so and so [attack British or Australian forces] the result will be war with the United States".'[19]

The record of this meeting ends with: 'As the party took their leave the President repeated that he did not want the Australians to think that the United States was not with them, but he did want some idea of the direction we were going and what specific commitments the Australians understood we had made.'[20] And the footnote to the record drives home the basic difference between Australian and US interpretations of the automaticity of Articles 4 and 5 of the ANZUS Treaty.

In a memorandum for the president on 8 August 1963, Acting Secretary Ball suggested that, under ANZUS, the United States was only committed to consult and to act in the event of an attack on a treaty member's forces in the Pacific. The term 'act' covered a broad range of measures, from diplomatic support to the use of troops. The Department of State did not want to give Australia a 'blank check' for support of their troops anywhere in the Pacific.

In October 1963, Harriman evidently began correcting the record. In a draft memorandum for the Australian ambassador, he summarised previous conversations against the backdrop of President Kennedy's remarks.[21] Harriman's draft was not conveyed to the Australian ambassador. What was finally provided to the Australian Ambassador by Kennedy's national security advisor, McGeorge Bundy, was a carefully drafted paper, with all the necessary disclaimers, that appears to have been based on Harriman's earlier draft. It represents a tighter interpretation of the ANZUS Treaty, useful but not nearly as generous a promise of US military support in any or all circumstances as Australian security needs might dictate. Indeed, it cautions Australia. The paper advises Australian policymakers, then and now, as follows:

> In view of the extensive commitments of the United States throughout the world ... further consultations would be necessary before any United States armed forces were committed. In case it was decided that such forces were necessary ... the United States would be prepared to commit air and sea forces and to provide logistic support ... It was recognized that the interests, commitments and responsibilities of the ANZUS partners in the Pacific area require that all parties concerned ... avoid political actions or statements which might lead to precipitate military action involving one or more of the ANZUS partners.[22]

In short, Australia might reasonably expect some logistic support, but no ground forces. Moreover, the United States retained the right to 'opt out', should it have deemed that Australia had brought military action upon itself. Interestingly, the United States adopted the same position in its consideration of its policy towards the International Force East Timor (INTERFET) when it deployed to East Timor in 1999 in the aftermath of the independence vote there.

Ultimately, the scope of application of the ANZUS Treaty will be decided by the US president. The president's decision will be informed by the self-interest of the United States and the domestic political acceptability of the use of US forces, especially ground forces, in distant theatres. No US president will be held to ransom by ANZUS. Its application is by no means automatic. Even less would it be generous. As Dick Woolcott has noted, 'The Kennedy administration declined to support Australia under the ANZUS Treaty.'[23] We may well ask whether any future US administration would act differently.

And even if a future US administration were to wish to provide Australia with direct military assistance in the event of direct military pressure against Australia, one would have to question whether it retains the ability to do so. The logistic capabilities of the United States are in deep trouble. In September 2019 the US military conducted the largest stress test of its wartime sealift fleet in the US Transportation Command's history. Less than 40 per cent of the fleet was mission-capable.[24] And given that any direct threat against Australia would almost inevitably occur in the context of a broader strategic disturbance in the Asia-Pacific region, Australia's chances of standing first in line would be highly doubtful.

Over three decades ago, in 1986, changing strategic circumstances were certainly enough to persuade New Zealand's prime minister, David Lange, that the ANZUS Treaty was less useful as a security guarantee than his country's support for a nuclear-weapons-free zone in the Pacific. New Zealand's participation in the treaty was suspended, and while some aspects of the treaty subsequently resumed in the bilateral New Zealand–United States relationship, New Zealand does not participate in the annual ministerial meeting or in the subordinate ANZUS meetings. For its part, New Zealand does not see itself at all disadvantaged by its suspended membership of ANZUS.

But just how the treaty might be relevant to emergent circumstances, particularly at a time when change is forged through disruption, and whether the treaty can evolve to meet those circumstances, depends in part at least on what the treaty mandates.

What does the ANZUS Treaty require?

At just over 800 words, the body of the ANZUS Treaty consists of five preambular paragraphs (unlike the North Atlantic Treaty, which has none) and eleven articles (the North Atlantic Treaty has fourteen), of which articles 1, 3, 4 and 5 (taken together) constitute the operative parts of the agreement. With its six references to the United Nations, the ANZUS Treaty is a product of its times; the UN Charter itself had been signed only six years before, and the optimism attaching to a new and energetic international mechanism for the maintenance of world peace infuses the document. It certainly stretches the imagination to think that such a treaty could be negotiated in present circumstances.

To appreciate the current effect of the ANZUS Treaty, it is important to understand the treaty within the terms of its drafting – what it says – and with regard to the external and internal messaging contained in the text – what it means. The United States certainly interprets the treaty narrowly, informed as it is by the carefully crafted (and often ambiguous) language of the text. Drafted in terms that are at once high-minded and intentionally imprecise, the treaty affords the Americans enormous amounts of wiggle room. It certainly does not contain or imply a guarantee that the United States will necessarily come to Australia's aid were Australia to be attacked, nor does it require Australia to come to the aid of the US were it attacked or engaged in armed conflict in pursuit of its own interests.

A quick look at the operative paragraphs illustrates the non-binding nature of the treaty. Article 1 requires the parties 'to settle any international dispute in which they may be involved by peaceful means in such a manner that international peace and security and justice are not endangered'. It further requires the parties 'to refrain in their international relations from the threat or use of force in any manner inconsistent with the purposes of the United Nations'. The creative ambiguity evident in this paragraph is a tribute to the drafters' intention to commit to very little. The loftiness generated by terms like 'any', 'peaceful' and 'justice' lend an unrealistic breadth to 'endangered', effectively eviscerating the first part of the paragraph.

The parties are required to refrain from threatening or using 'force' – unqualified in this paragraph – in a way that is inconsistent with the 'purposes' – also unqualified – of the United Nations. What is 'force' and what are 'purposes'? Both terms are so broad in both their denotation and their connotation that they render the clause so unspecific as to be effectively meaningless.

Article 2 is brief: 'In order more effectively to achieve the objective of this Treaty the Parties separately and jointly by means of continuous and effective self-help and mutual aid will maintain and develop their individual and collective capacity to resist armed attack.' This paragraph oscillates between individual and collective action, without any reference to the balance that might be struck between individual, joint or combined preparations and activities. Moreover, it leaves open the question of whether mutual 'aid' is provided by means of support or assistance. There is, of course, a world of difference: 'support' does not imply the provision of combat troops; 'assistance' does.

Whatever the intent of this paragraph in 1950, its interpretation became much clearer with the enunciation of the Guam Doctrine by President Richard Nixon in 1969. The United States sought to ensure that nations expecting US military support in times of tension or conflict at a minimum provided for their own self-defence. Coming as it did during the Vietnam War, when the United States was both stretched and stressed, Nixon's Guam statement made it clear that the United States was not some kind of global saviour. Speaking during a stopover in Guam, the president said his country was 'going to encourage and has the right to expect' that 'military defense … will be handled by, and responsibility for it taken by, the Asian nations themselves'.[25] The message was not lost on either Australia or New Zealand.[26] And, for his part, President Trump drove the message home in his remarks at the NATO Headquarters in Brussels in May 2017, when he upbraided NATO members for not paying 'their fair share' – a situation he saw as being 'not fair to the people and the taxpayers of the United States'.[27]

While US reluctance to continue to fund military forces located in Europe and Asia to provide for the security of allies is understandable, it should be remembered that US global force dispositions were the price the United States was prepared to pay in the post–World War II years to establish the global authority that gave legitimacy to its strategic power.[28] President Trump appeared to regard the NATO partners as 'free-riders', underfunding their national defence budgets as they rely on the United States to provide European security. Europe was, to some extent at least, the battlefield separating the United States and the Soviet Union, and the post–World War II European nations were disinclined to raise the stakes, which might precipitate exactly the outcome they were hoping that US predominance would preclude. NATO members have increased their military spending. But whether that assuages any US sense of grievance or encourages the Americans to reduce their forward deployed forces is unclear. But if, as President Emmanuel Macron of France has said, NATO is 'brain dead',[29] the implicit guarantee that the United States will engage in the defence of Europe on the basis that 'an attack on one is an attack on all' becomes increasingly doubtful. That certainly has implications for the longer-term US approach to the ANZUS Treaty.

Article 3 of ANZUS is equally brief: 'The Parties will consult together whenever in the opinion of any of them the territorial integrity, political independence or security of any of the Parties is threatened in the Pacific.' Consultation is the core requirement of the treaty.

This article has several moving parts, but they do not necessarily move in the same direction. First, it is important to recognise that consultation, without any subsequent commitment of forces, would of itself meet the requirements of the treaty. Then, of course, there are the limits that might apply to whatever 'consultation' is taken to mean. The article specifies that such consultation would take place 'whenever in the opinion of any of [the members]' a threat arises, but without specifying whether the consultation is to be conducted between all the parties or, as has happened at least twice, between only two of them – or, indeed, whether action could be unilateral, without any trilateral or bilateral consultation at all. One could certainly have imagined situations where New Zealand might not have wanted to be dragged into bilateral Australian–US action. Whereas Prime Minister Howard of Australia invoked the ANZUS Treaty in his immediate response to the 9/11 attacks, Prime Minister Clark of New Zealand did not. Nor did New Zealand deploy forces to the Iraq War in 2003.

Finally, Article 3 specifies 'the territorial integrity, political independence or security of any of the Parties ... in the Pacific' as being the target of the threat. How any of these elements might condition each of the other elements is unclear. The article apparently restricts the geographical scope of the treaty to the Pacific. Predating as it does more modern terminology such as 'Asia-Pacific' and 'Indo-Pacific', the term 'Pacific' has attracted considerable exegesis over the decades, particularly in the Australian Department of Defence. While the Radford-Collins Agreement predated the ANZUS Treaty and does not form part of it, this 'gentlemen's agreement' remains in effect, providing the additional confidence to successive Australian governments that ANZUS applies to the defence of the entire Australian continent and the adjacent waters in the Indian Ocean.

Articles 4 and 5, taken together, are the heart of the treaty, addressing specifically the issue of armed attack in the Pacific area on any of the parties. Its terms are particularly open-ended, requiring each party to 'act to meet the common danger in accordance with its constitutional processes' – where those constitutional processes are unspecified and vary significantly between the parties. The article also restricts the application of the treaty to those attacks that might occur 'in the Pacific area', which is construed in Article 5 to mean the entire landmass and island territories of each of the parties. It does not extend to Afghanistan or to the Middle East.

The second part of Article 4 is, in contemporary circumstances, highly problematic. It requires the parties to report 'all measures taken as a result' of an armed attack to the UN Security Council, and then to terminate such measures 'when the Security Council has taken the measures necessary to restore and maintain international peace and security'. In the context of 1951, when the United Nations and its Security Council were new international rule makers deeply dependent on the power and authority of the United States, the provisions of Article 4 made perfect sense. But at a time when the United States displays disregard for the United Nations, and for many of the institutions that manage the international rules-based order that is so critical to the management of Australia's international relations, such recourse to the Security Council is virtually unthinkable. It is just not what the United States does anymore.

The contemporary politics of the ANZUS Treaty

The ANZUS Treaty is a legal text and should be construed as such. It is not poetry. Yet Prime Minister Howard's invocation of the treaty in the aftermath of 11 September 2001 construed Article 4 in broad terms, and the treaty in emotive terms. His speech to the Australian parliament, where he defended his decision to invoke the treaty, was highly oratorical and blatantly rhetorical.

> If that treaty means anything, if our debt as a nation to the people of the United States in the darkest days of World War II means anything, if the comradeship, the friendship and the common bonds of democracy and a belief in liberty, fraternity and justice mean anything, it means that the ANZUS Treaty applies and that the ANZUS Treaty is properly invoked.[30]

In his insightful commentary on Prime Minister Howard's speech, Graeme Dobell described it as 'a speech from the heart as well as the head'. He continued:

> Formally invoking the treaty for the first time, Howard marked another moment in an Australian tradition: Deakin inviting the US Great White Fleet; Curtin turning to the US in the Pacific war free of any pangs for the traditional links to Britain; Spender achieving the ANZUS treaty; Menzies committing to Vietnam with the new great and powerful ally; Holt going all the way with LBJ; Whitlam hanging on to the alliance despite Vietnam and the controversy

> over the US bases in Australia; Hawke incorporating the US bases into the alliance. The course Howard set with his speech and parliamentary resolution took Australia to Afghanistan and Iraq. The commitment Howard made was not just to the alliance but to George W Bush. The Push With Bush was to impose great political costs on Howard and Tony Blair, and significant alliance burdens on their nations.[31]

As was detailed above, Articles 4 and 5 of the ANZUS Treaty were constructed in terms designed to narrow the opportunity for military engagement, not to encourage it. Moreover, it set the resort to military force squarely within the United Nations–based 'international rules-based order' as it existed in 1950 – essentially an artefact of US power and authority resulting from its overwhelming victory in World War II. It is also important to appreciate that Article 4 does not imply automaticity for any party following any other party into armed conflict. Acting 'to meet the common danger' would require policymakers to consider precisely how far the term 'act' extends, what 'common' means and what constitutes 'danger'. The consultation prescribed by Article 3 does not imply commitment of forces under Article 4. When, in 2017, Prime Minister Turnbull said that he would invoke the relevant clauses of the ANZUS Treaty were North Korea to launch an attack on American forces, a former defence minister, Kim Beazley, was quick to point out that the clause 'to consult' does not automatically require the commitment of force.[32]

Beazley, of course, has long been a firm advocate for the ANZUS Treaty. Just days before the 11 September 2001 attacks in the United States, the Australian parliament debated a motion commemorating the fortieth anniversary of the signature of the ANZUS Treaty. Beazley detailed the various evolutions through which the treaty had passed:

> At different points of time the ANZUS Treaty has presided like an umbrella over strategies of forward defence. More recently it has presided over strategies of defence self-reliance, albeit within a framework of an alliance relationship ... As more and more of our

> armed forces rely for their effectiveness, in the region in which we live, on a margin of technical superiority in terms of equipment, on excellent intelligence, the military significance of the alliance to Australia has taken on more of that character.

Beazley recognised clearly that ANZUS was a product of its times, and that to renegotiate the treaty following New Zealand's self-exile from the treaty would be so fraught as to be impossible.

> We discussed the issue of how that relationship should continue in the absence of New Zealand ... Consideration was given to the creation of a separate bilateral treaty. Consideration was given to what we ultimately arrived at: a set of ministerial discussions, albeit under a rubric of a continuation of that treaty [AUSMIN]. At the time we all sat down and talked it through, it was quite evident to us that, to get together the type of treaty that could be sustained through an argument in Congress and through deliberations between our two peoples, with the difficulties that seemed to emerge from that process, the best thing we could do was to stick with what we had.[33]

As touched upon earlier, the 1984 decision by Prime Minister Lange of New Zealand to ban nuclear-powered or nuclear-armed US naval vessels from New Zealand ports was tantamount to a fundamental step back from ANZUS. It caused considerable soul searching, particularly on Beazley's part. He instituted a thorough-going reappraisal of Australia's involvement at the two major joint Australian–US facilities at Pine Gap, in the Northern Territory, and Nurrungar, in South Australia, a review that, paradoxically, had the effect of turning the ANZUS Treaty on its head.

Reflecting on events over a decade later, Beazley spoke guardedly about the fundamental shift in both control and engagement in the joint facilities. He did so in terms of Australia's bilateral relationship with the United States, not its partnership through ANZUS. This was not just a shift in rhetoric. It was a shift in policy, repositioning the defence relationship within the framework of the broader and much deeper bilateral relationship.

> The key elements of the *bilateral relationship* [emphasis added] for Australia were the joint facilities. The Labor government approached the Americans with a new agenda with the following elements. Firstly, we wanted the ability to say more about their functions publicly. This was not only because our party policy demanded it but also because, if we were to win over elements of public opinion that were slightly or, in some cases, massively sceptical, we needed to be able to detail the significance of the joint facilities for a stable nuclear balance and for arms control ... We wanted more day-to-day Australian involvement in the facilities and the ability to utilise those facilities for Australian purposes. As we ... got a deeper and deeper understanding of what the joint facilities did and their levels of capability, which were really quite massive, the more it appeared to us that there was value in those joint facilities for Australian purposes. We wanted Australians running the operations in so far as that was possible ... So there was an effort on our part to get more and more control over those facilities ourselves.[34]

Beazley's 'deeper understanding' and 'more control' had the effect of transforming the common threat basis of the ANZUS Treaty into a common interests-based paradigm for the bilateral relationship.

By the mid-1980s, the ANZUS Treaty had become less of a statement about Australia's place in the strategic affairs of the Pacific than an umbrella under which the Australian Defence Force was able to develop its force structure through increasingly open access to core US defence systems. The treaty moved from providing a strategic assurance to Australia against a remilitarised Japan to providing the underpinnings of Australia's bilateral intelligence and security relationship with the United States. Its effect was to strengthen the bilateral relationship with the United States rather than an open-ended security guarantee against all potentialities. And while, as a core expression of the Australia–United States defence relationship,

ANZUS has some strategic effect, it is far from the strategic panacea that Australian governments have always sought. While remaining an important part of our shared strategic history, ANZUS is no longer the driving force of Australia's strategic security, if it ever was. Its utility as a strategic asset in the direct defence of Australia is a thing of the past.

The announcement of the AUKUS partnership, however, has signalled a significant change in the contemporary purpose of the ANZUS Treaty. Instead of providing Australia with a sense safety in the extreme circumstances of a direct attack on Australian territory, it has morphed into a vehicle for engaging Australia in the strategic activities of the United States. By acquiring hunter-killer nuclear submarines, optimised for destroying an adversary's ballistic missile submarines in order to deny it a nuclear second-strike capability, Australia has acquiesced in an inevitable role in the conduct of nuclear war.

Does ANZUS have any residual value?

Hyperbole, along with its consort hubris, is no basis for strategy. While overblown statements may afford their speaker and their audience a warm inner glow, they seldom represent bankable policy. Prime Minister Morrison, with characteristic confidence and lack of nuance, stated in October 2019 that the ANZUS Treaty with the United States was 'the single most important achievement' of the Liberal Party in its seventy-five years.[35] This may well be a view shared by former foreign minister Julie Bishop, who declared that 'at the heart of the treaty is a commitment to come to one another's aid in the worst of times' – a claim that the ABC's fact-checking unit judged as being, 'like the ANZUS treaty itself', ambiguous.[36] But if the characterisation of the treaty by another former Liberal foreign minister, Alexander Downer, as 'symbolic'[37] retains any currency – and the former defence minister David Johnson appeared to share the non-compulsory and non-automatic interpretation of the treaty[38] – then we must conclude that the Liberal Party has not achieved very much at all in its seventy-five years.

As a kind of security policy rallying point, the ANZUS Treaty may play a role in assuaging the anxiety and insecurity that push Australia to seek a protector. Some find the new world order to be sufficiently destabilising – and anxiety-inducing – as to warrant a significant beefing-up of the ANZUS Treaty. Stephen Kuper asks: 'Is it time for the two parties to renegotiate and expand the scope of the ANZUS Treaty to reflect the "combined arms" economic, political and strategic competition they both find themselves engaged in?'[39] Geoffrey Barker, on the other hand, has posed the opposite question – 'Has ANZUS passed its use-by date?' –arguing that ditching it would have limited security consequences.[40]

So, should Australia defend ANZUS or discard it? Like many of the binaries that masquerade as the terms of political and strategic analysis, this is in fact a confected alternative. It is like asking diners whether they prefer the front or the back half of a potato. The question is meaningless.

ANZUS has always served political purposes for all its parties, even New Zealand. It continues to serve political ends for Australia and the United States. Although some of those political ends are negative – for instance, the constant trumpeting of ANZUS as Australia's ultimate security guarantee, which only serves to draw attention to our dependence and exacerbate our chronic anxiety – others are decidedly positive, such as the annual opportunity for Australian and US foreign and defence ministers to confer (AUSMIN). ANZUS also provides the umbrella agreement under which scores of subsidiary agreements, MOUs, exchanges of letters and other quasi-contractual arrangements that support the development, maintenance and operation of much of Australia's defence capability.

But ANZUS no longer has great strategic utility. It no longer underpins our security. Times have changed. The strategic circumstances that gave birth to ANZUS have changed. The region has changed. The

United States has changed. Australia has changed. The treaty is an historical artefact, not a fundamental principle of national strategic policy. Quite simply, it is not, and cannot be, the basis of Australia's strategic policy or defence planning.

What, then, is the alternative to a faith-based policy that signals dependence and anxiety? If ANZUS is no longer relevant to our contemporary strategic posture and our future strategic options, should we ditch it? Has it passed its use-by date? The answer must be no, since it never had one. What advantage would there be in denouncing an instrument that is strategically irrelevant but remains an important statement of an enduring defence relationship? As Paul Barratt has pointed out, a much sounder response to contemporary circumstances is to return to first principles and conduct 'a really deep stocktake of what is in our vital national interests and what we are prepared to sign up to'.[41] And to this end, ANZUS does not define who Australians are and what Australia is. Our identity and power are determined by how we identify ourselves, who we are and who we want to be, not by some vague proposition that might or might not protect us against real or imagined threats. It was never, and is not now, the 'bedrock of our national security', as Morrison proclaimed. The bedrock of our national security is to be found in who we are and what we stand for, not who might protect us.

In this secular age, marked by discontinuity and disruption, faith-based policies will not prevail, just as hope will not triumph over experience. The hard reality of the global strategic environment demands hard realism as the foundation of effective policy.

Ultimately, Australia's security depends on how clearly we understand who we are and what we stand for. It depends on how we view our identity and our power – in which our national interest consists – and on how we define our national interests: the purposive dimension of our international and strategic policy. It depends on how we maintain a strong economy and underpin the long-term prosperity of the nation. It depends on how we build human and social capital, without which we are unable to maintain an inclusive and resilient community.

To that end, Australia's security relationship with the United States is important, but not determinant. There are not many countries whose constitutional arrangements both promote and protect the rule of law. The United States and Australia are two of them.[42] Our joint future is not in fighting wars, but in securing peace. And that is not the role of ANZUS. It is the role of an active, engaged and properly endowed diplomacy that builds the kind of world we would like to live in while we deal with the world in which we in fact live.

4
China: Our Comprehensive Incomprehension

Courtesy wards off insults; tolerance wins all hearts; good faith inspires the trust of others; diligence ensures success; generosity confers authority on others.

Confucius, *Analects* (translated by Simon Leys)

Insecurity, anxiety and a pervasive fear of abandonment by a great and powerful protector together generate paralysis in establishing an independent foreign policy. This paralysis – something we do not share with New Zealand, for instance – has become increasingly evident since the G20 Brisbane meeting in 2014, when Prime Minister Tony Abbott told German chancellor Angela Merkel that Australia's relations with China were driven by 'greed and fear'.[1] Our greed is increasingly unsatisfied as China imposes trade barriers, while our fear grows inversely. The national conversation on how we should deal with China's rise, and how we should construct a workable long-term relationship with China, has become both polarised and shrill. 'Wolf warriors' in Beijing and 'wolverines' in Canberra amplify real and imagined grievances, employing ever more emotive language to shroud the fundamental problem in the relationship: we just do not understand or trust each other.

Whatever some of Australia's strategic commentators might claim, our fear of China is not simply a function of geopolitics, or the inevitability of China's geostrategic domination of Asia. These factors amplify our fear, of course, but they do not cause it. Rather, it results from a deeper preoccupation with race – with the 'other', whose appearance, culture, language and social mores are alien. 'Otherness' breeds suspicion and mistrust, the incomprehension that manifests itself in antipathy, exclusion and rejection. It is the incomprehension that has distinguished the immigrant settlers' relationship with Australia's

Indigenous peoples since 1788. It is the same incomprehension that has distinguished the immigrant European community's relationship with Chinese immigrants, and consequently with China, ever since Chinese people first appeared in Australia in any numbers.[2] Incomprehension motivates fear.

In Chapter 1, we saw just how potent a force anti-Chinese sentiment had become by the end of the nineteenth century, when the Australian colonies federated to establish the Commonwealth of Australia. Not only did the first federal parliament, led by Prime Minister Edmond Barton, legislate the *Immigration Restriction Act* in 1901, but his successor Alfred Deakin put the White Australia policy at the centre of Australia's national security. There should be no illusions here: concepts of racial purity were very much alive at the beginning of the twentieth century, as they are now.[3]

Racial slurs pepper the Australian idiom, showing up currently in crude attempts at racial profiling. As John Budarick has pointed out, 'person of African appearance' confuses race with identity.[4] The term means 'black', and, anecdotally, has even been used to identify people who are Indigenous Australians. The issue of Indigenous and non-Indigenous 'blackness' came to a head in 2015, however, when the Haitian American author Roxane Gay tweeted the question 'are there Black people in Australia'. This prompted an indignant response from some in the Indigenous community, who felt that the question of 'blackness' was being appropriated, confused and/or denied. Natasha Guantai, who identifies as a black (Kenyan) non-Indigenous Australian, commented:

> This twitter exchange is the result of a collision between two narratives of Blackness. In much of the world, 'Black' refers to Africans, or to members of the African diaspora, often in the context of a country in which whites are dominant. Thus we have Black Americans, Black Canadians, Black British, etc. In the dominant Australian narrative, Blacks are regarded as Aboriginal. This is a narrative with little space for non-Indigenous Black Australians.[5]

Similarly, 'person of Middle Eastern appearance' means 'looks Arabic' (and Muslim), but runs into the problem of including anyone with an 'olive' complexion, including Indians. 'Person of Caucasian appearance' usually refers to people of Anglo-Celtic, Nordic, Germanic and Slavic origins, and may exclude some people from the Iberian Peninsula and Greece, who are sometimes described as 'Middle Eastern', while 'person of Asian appearance' quite offensively includes people from China, Japan, the Korean Peninsula and even Indochina. As Australia's immigration minister Arthur Calwell said in 1947, allegedly in jest but no less offensively, 'Two Wongs do not make a White.'[6]

The Bulletin, that defiant Australian journal of political and social record, was notorious for its racist cartoons during its first forty years (1880–1920). These indiscriminately denigrated Aboriginal, Afghan, Chinese, Japanese, Indian, Jewish and every other non-white race and non-Christian religion. It nourished the instinctive racism of early Australia. But more than creating and polishing the racist lens through which Australians viewed China, *The Bulletin* contributed significantly to a habit that Australians share with people of many other postcolonial countries. We look at 'other' cultures through the lens of our own cultural, historical and social experience. We regard our cultural development and experience as normative, setting the benchmarks by which we judge the cultural and political evolution of other societies. Not only is the keyhole through which we view the world small, but it is also narrow and superior. Other cultures are not comprehensible, so they are dismissible.

The Bulletin ceased publication in 2008. Under its post–World War II editors, it had become less jingoistic and strident, delivering considerably more balance and nuance in its commentary on national and international affairs than it had in its early days. Yet Donald Horne's commentary in 1971 on Gough Whitlam's first encounter with China's Zhou Enlai held overtones of cultural superiority and strategic dependency. Horne was both snide and superior:

> The part of the world in which we are most important is the part of the world in which we live and it is hard to see that it would

> be within any conceivable definition of national interest that we should seem to be so concerned with toadying to whatever great power momentarily takes our fancy that we seem to be looking down on our mates in our own neighbourhood.
>
> Since Malaysia, Singapore and the Philippines are all three of them also showing interest in China, it is to be hoped that Australia is sharing views with them, and with Indonesia. The problem goes beyond that: if any of these nations wish to make military arrangements with Australia that might include the stationing of Australian military forces in their territories, that is simply a matter of agreement between governments. It does not have the same meaning as the idea of foreign forces discussed by Mr. Whitlam and Mr. Chou.[7]

Whenever 'our' and 'mates' appear in the same sentence, condescension is immediately at play. So we see *The Bulletin* blithely supporting the stationing of Australian troops on foreign territories, while failing to see that the stationing of US, Australian and other foreign forces in Japan, the Republic of Korea, Malaysia and Singapore, the Philippines, Thailand and Vietnam might appear inconsistent and problematic to the Chinese government. Horne may not have had to hand David Barnett's transcript of the conversation between Whitlam and Zhou. But the record shows that China's concerns reflected the fact that the deployed US forces seemed far greater than might have been required for the direct defence of the countries in which they were stationed.[8]

In his own report on the meeting with Zhou Enlai, Whitlam captured the tension that underlies the recurrent misunderstanding and mistrust that has long infected Australia's relationship with China:

> One of the great troubles in relations between China and the West is that we expect China to believe the best about our statements of intention while we choose to believe the worst about hers. We expect understanding for our own fears, but we have never tried to understand hers. We have been obsessed by our own historical

> experience, but we scoff at China's obsession with her own experience.[9]

Whitlam's observation is no less true now than it was then: the introspection and self-absorption that has distinguished the Australian character since the convicts and their guards arrived in 1788 continues to blind us to the fact that other societies have rich histories and complex narratives that shape their expectations and behaviours, and perhaps none more so than China and India.

A little history: Pre–World War I

In important but subtle ways, 'China' is a Western construct. The decline and fall of the Qing dynasty and the political and social chaos that ensued brought a small group of intellectuals, reformers and intellectuals into a common but most assuredly contested enterprise of creating a modern nation-state and a contemporary vision of a modern China. Bill Hayton has called this 'the invention of China', and notes:

> The China that presents itself to us in the twenty-first century is more like the West than it, or the West, generally acknowledge. Rather than being a standard bearer of 'Asian values', it is in fact a state in a Western mould complete with missions of identity, sovereignty, nationalism and territorial aggrandisement. This is not surprising when we look at how it emerged: it is, in essence, a foreign construction.[10]

China confounds analysis and understanding, not least because of its inherent schizophrenia: it sees itself in imperial terms, where things like borders are immaterial to the exercise of power. At the same time, it sees itself in Westphalian terms, 'determined to incorporate every scrap of territory, every rock and reef, within the homeland's "sacred" national border'. So China is an enigma, which to a large extent explains why Australia, along with many other countries, found it difficult to come to terms with this dormant but awakening dragon.

So, Whitlam's 1971 visit to China was a radical moment in the chequered history of Australia's official relations with China, which extends back to 1909. It is a history of missteps and missed chances for independent diplomatic manoeuvre.

The evolution of Australia's relationship with China is characterised by fits and starts, ambition unmatched by perseverance, lost opportunities (when or even if they were recognised), cultural incomprehension and arrogance. In the decades after the gold rushes, increasing numbers of Chinese managed to gain residency in Australia, but felt marginalised by the Commonwealth's early race laws. So they looked to China's Qing government for validation and protection. The Chinese communities in Melbourne and Sydney petitioned the Qing government in Peking for official representation.

Following a few years during which prominent members of the Chinese community acted as quasi-honorary consuls, the imperial Qing government of China appointed an experienced diplomat and fluent English speaker, Liang Lanxun (Lan-hsun), as its consul-general in Melbourne (then the seat of the Australian parliament). He arrived 'attired in the picturesque dress of a mandarin' (no sense of 'the other' here!) and announced that his first and chief duties were 'to look after the interests of my countrymen, to promote the friendship of the two countries, and to improve when opportunity offers their commercial relations'.[11]

Halfway through his posting, Liang was recalled, ostensibly because of ill health. But *The Age* reported that he had in fact been promoted, which might suggest that he had carried out his duties to the satisfaction of his bosses at the Wai Wu Pu (Board of Foreign Affairs).[12] He was replaced by Tang Entong, identified variously in the Melbourne press as Tong Ying-ting and Tong Ung Tung.[13]

It was long assumed by Australian historians that the consul-general's role was simply to facilitate trade, and not to represent the interests of the Chinese community to the newly constituted Australian government. More recent research suggests otherwise. Using Chinese records together with Australian-based Chinese-language newspaper resources, 'Tiger' Zhifu Li has argued that 'the White Australia policy, trade and "recognition" (recognition means which regime [the] Australian government regarded as an official and legitimate government in China) were the dominant themes in the [*sic*] Sino-Australian relations, between 1901 and 1921'.[14] As Li's thesis makes clear, the Chinese diplomats worked assiduously to modify the impact of the White Australia policy on the Chinese community in Australia, giving Chinese nationals (especially wives and family relations) greater freedom to enter the nation – perhaps the first examples of 'Chinese political interference' in Australia! Unsurprisingly, they were not successful.

A little more history: Post–World War I

As with so many other things, World War I completely interrupted whatever relationship might have grown between Australia and China. Australia was overwhelmed by the war in Europe and the defence of the British empire, which became the principal international focus of the Australian government. But at the Paris Peace Conference in 1919, Prime Minister Billy Hughes embarked on a set of policies that would have dire consequences. In an astonishing example of short-sighted, racist and divisive diplomacy, Hughes vehemently rejected Japan's suggested amendment to the Treaty of Versailles that would abolish racial discrimination between the five great powers that controlled the Peace Conference – the United Kingdom, France, Italy, Japan and the United States. And as a sop to wounded Japanese pride, he then supported Japan's claim to the former German possessions in China's Shandong Province, as well as mandating the administration of the Mariana, Marshall and Caroline islands in the Pacific.[15] Although Shandong reverted to Chinese control in 1922 because of US mediation during the Washington Naval Conference, the political damage to Australia's standing with both China and Japan was done.[16]

Hughes was so deeply attached to the White Australia policy that he saw any broadening of the post-war power structures to include

Japan as a prelude to an immigration flood from North Asia. He was able to persuade the British prime minister Lloyd George to accommodate Australian, Canadian and New Zealand racial policies to hold the empire together. And he was able to persuade President Wilson of the United States, who had his own race problems in the segregationist South, to go along with keeping Japan out of the 'club' – the price for reaching agreement on the Treaty of Versailles. Robert Kane captures the trade-offs well:

> The uninhibited hostility towards the Japanese proposal of Australian Prime Minister Billy Hughes … allowed the Wilson Administration to leave its own opposition largely unsaid. Upholding the protests of Great Britain and its Dominions, Wilson effectively vetoed the racial equality proposal by requiring a unanimous vote of the Commission on the League of Nations instead of simply the favorable majority that it had received.[17]

This might have looked like successful diplomacy on Hughes' part, but its results were calamitous. There are important lessons to be learned here about the implications of 'decoupling' and marginalisation. As the veteran journalist Max Suich wrote in 2012, 'Struggling as we are today to adjust to another formidable rising Asian economic and military power in China, these policy failures offer a fruitful perspective on present-day policy thinking.'[18]

The crippling reparations bill imposed on Germany, China's disaffection at the loss of the former German concessions in Shandong to Japan, and Japan's anger at the defeat of its equality proposal on race grounds all played into the complex of factors that precipitated World War II.[19] Like so many of his prime ministerial successors, Hughes was playing to the domestic political audience of the day, trading off longer-term political and strategic considerations against his political popularity in Australia. Whenever China refers to its 'century of humiliation', warranted or not, Australia's relatively minor role in the suppression of the Boxer Rebellion and its larger role in the post–World War I transfer of the German concessions in Shandong Province feed into the grievance. China remembers that. We do not.

While some percipient commentators identified the likelihood of adverse strategic consequences for China, Japan and the entire Pacific community stemming from the Paris Peace Conference, Australia was oblivious.[20] The possibility of a complete strategic reorientation by Japan and the collapse of China within two decades was simply ignored. So, in the early post-war years, Australia began to look to Asia for trading opportunities to help offset the economic impacts of World War I. In 1921, Prime Minister Hughes appointed Edward Little as trade commissioner in Shanghai. Little had thirty years' experience in China as a commercial agent, most recently as a representative for a substantial British company (which subsequently became part of the Imperial Chemical Industries group) that produced and marketed agricultural fertilisers. He was well qualified to expand what *The Sydney Morning Herald* described as 'a great market for Australian goods'.[21] His posting was short-lived, however, drowned in 1923 in a flood of allegations of overspending on costs and allowances and poor results. The more substantive reason was the lack of support by British diplomats in Shanghai, who saw themselves as Australia's official representatives in China and cared little for colonial attempts at independence, and dissension within the business community in Melbourne.[22] The Chinese business community was not accustomed to working through a non-Chinese intermediary, the newly emerging 'white' business, commercial and trading companies were looking for quick returns without understanding the nature of the market or how trade was conducted in China, and neither of the communities was accustomed to working with the other. These problems echo today.

In 1922, the Hughes government also appointed Egbert Sheaf as 'Australian Trade Representative in the East', though precisely what that meant was never clear. Sheaf left the China trade to Little, setting up his own office in Singapore. He had a sophisticated understanding of business conditions in Asia, identifying the enormous potential of the 'native' market as well as that of expatriate Europeans.[23] Sheaf's appointment was essentially an exercise in patronage by Hughes, and following Stanley Bruce's landslide victory at the general elections in 1925, Sheaf's appointment was terminated, like Little's before him. For the next ten years, Australia 'relied on British diplomats to look after Australia's interests in China',[24] their efforts being perfunctory at best.

As it had with the Hughes government, in 1932 it dawned upon the Lyons government that trade with China might provide some way out of the Great Depression, which had hit post-war Australia so hard. On the advice of the public service commissioner, and funded by Queensland premier Arthur Moore, Alexander Melbourne, a University of Queensland academic, visited China and Japan to review and report on Australia's economic connections with both countries. Nothing came of his report.

There were, however, the beginnings of progress stemming from the report provided to Prime Minister Lyons by external affairs minister John Latham (later the chief justice of the High Court of Australia), who visited China and Japan in 1934. Latham reported that increased trade with both countries was contingent upon the relaxation of the White Australia policy: Australia's Asian trade prospects were constrained by its race policy. They were also constrained by Australia's dependence on Great Britain for the conduct of its overseas diplomatic relations, even following the passage of the *Statute of Westminster* through the British parliament in 1931. Australia might have gained legislative autonomy from 'the motherland', but it was slow to steer an independent foreign policy. More importantly, Latham recommended the appointment of an official Australian representative in Shanghai, advice acted upon through the 1935 appointment of Vivian Bowden as trade commissioner in Shanghai. Bowden remained there until 1941, when his responsibilities were assumed by the new Australian legation in Chungking, led by Menzies government minister Sir Frederic Eggleston.[25]

Even more history: World War II

Between the two world wars, the management of Australia's relations with China was caught between what Neville Meaney has described as 'the community of culture' – Australia's relentless self-identification with the 'white' Anglophone world (the antecedents of today's 'Five Eyes')[26] – and the 'community of interests' – economic and trade relations with China and Japan. Billy Hughes had fought relentlessly to exclude Japan from the post–World War I global leadership group, setting that country on the path to nationalism and militarism, with profound strategic consequences. World War II put an end to that, though it took nearly three decades for the new reality to reflect itself in Australia's China policy. The popular myth about World War II is that the 'community of culture', essentially Australia, New Zealand and the United States, defeated Japanese aggression – 'white' Anglophones quashing Asian militarism and establishing a new international order. Of course, it is not nearly as simple as that. Nor is it true.

As the US Navy had warned President Wilson, Japan's control of the Mariana Islands (the springboard from which it captured Guam after Pearl Harbor in 1941), the Marshall Islands (where the Battle of Kwajalein took place) and the Caroline Islands (where the Battle of Truk took place) – key strategic footholds across the Pacific – had profound military consequences. But of even greater strategic consequence was the fact that Japan, like Germany, had to fight its war on two fronts. It is worth speculating how much bloodier and more devastating the Pacific War would have been had the United States and its allies faced the ten or so Imperial Japanese Army divisions that were bogged down in China. The Nationalist forces under Chiang Kai-shek and, in the earlier phases of Japan's occupation of China, the Communist forces controlled by Mao Zedong absorbed everything that Japan threw at them. Like Russia in Europe's east, China sustained enormous casualties and unspeakable suffering to deliver strategic success to the Allies. Speaking in 2014, Malcolm Turnbull, then the communications minister in the Abbott government, captured this history poignantly:

> For China the war with Japan had begun in 1937 and for four years she fought alone. Japan had 680,000 troops in China at the time it launched its offensive in the Pacific – four times the number it

> deployed to sweep through Southeast Asia until they were stopped at our doorstep in the jungles of New Guinea.
>
> Had China been defeated and become a collaborating puppet state, like Vichy France, not only would Japan have been able to fling vastly greater resources into the war against Australia, but it would have been able to invade Siberia in 1942, as Hitler asked, when the Red Army was almost smashed by the Nazi offensive in the West.
>
> We may not have succeeded in resisting Japanese aggression without the tenacious heroism of our Chinese ally.
>
> The Soviet Union, reeling in the face of the blitzkrieg, may not have been able to survive a two-front war at its moment of greatest weakness.
>
> The central role of China as our ally in the Second World War is barely remembered in Australia today. But it will never be forgotten in China.
>
> We should never forget that China's war against Japan was not just their war, but our war too – and without China we may not have won it at all.[27]

While most Australians know little and care less about China's contribution to the Allied victory in the Pacific, China remembers the devastation it endured only too well. Sadly, amnesia incurs a high cost: whether forgotten or expunged, there are no lessons from history – everything must be relearned. This applies as much to China as it does to Australia.[28]

And a bit more history: Post–World War II

The immediate post–World War II years marked a return to national introspection for many Australians, as the names of the 40,000 killed in Asia, North Africa and Europe were added to the 60,000 World War

I dead already inscribed on the walls of the Australian War Memorial in Canberra and on community memorials and shrines around Australia. It was a time for healing the emaciated and wounded people who returned from the Japanese labour camps; for coming to terms with the horrors inflicted on the peoples of South-East Asia and the Pacific, especially women; and for addressing the unfathomable evil of the Holocaust. It was a time for post-war reconstruction; for building more robust national institutions; for an imaginative (if racially exclusive) immigration program; and for ambitious national infrastructure schemes like the Snowy Mountains hydroelectric scheme. It was a time for international efforts to establish a world order and a set of international rules to enable an enduring peace and prevent the recurrence of global violence – a project on which Australia's foreign minister, Dr Evatt, embarked energetically.

The Chifley and Menzies governments tackled the tasks of domestic post-war reconstruction with enthusiasm and a measure of bipartisanship. But there were clear differences in perspective between the two governments on questions of foreign and security affairs. Chifley pursued a post-war internationalist-realist approach to the emerging issues of postcolonialism and nationalism, while Menzies adhered to his pre-war imperial preference – a mindset he carried forward into his post-1949 government. Chifley, against the wishes of Evatt, supported the independence of postcolonial Indonesia from the Netherlands, contrary to the wishes of the post-war Dutch government, of course, and of Britain and the United States. But he would not be budged. And from the viewpoint of principle and long-term strategy, and with the advantage of hindsight, he was right.

Reflecting on his government's policy from the opposition benches in 1950, Chifley offered a succinct explanation of his government's immediate post–World War II policy:

> The Labour Government sought to bring about peace and a reasonable degree of harmony in that country. We realized that a revolutionary tendency, which might finally lead to the development of communism in that country, would constitute a grave

> danger to Australia. When I sat on the other side of this House [that is, in government], I said that in the long view – looking 40 or 50 years ahead – it was essential that we should develop reasonably friendly relations with the people of Indonesia. The Good Offices Committee of the United Nations did excellent work in bringing about a settlement of the differences between the Dutch and the Indonesians. As I have said, we did not attempt to take sides in the dispute. We merely tried to bring the parties together under the auspices of the Good Offices Committee. I think that we can reasonably claim that as a result of our initiative the United Nations was able to bring about the degree of harmony that now exists in Indonesia.[29]

But Menzies' opposition, voiced in 1947, when he was not yet in government, captured the race-based foreign policy prescriptions that continue to resonate in contemporary conservative circles in Australia:

> So far as Australia is concerned the nearest problem to us, geographically speaking, is the problem of the Netherlands East Indies [Indonesia]; and if we are to be judged by results, then I want to say plainly that this Government has accepted a policy in relation to the Netherlands East Indies formulated by the Australian Communists, which is a policy of driving the white man out of the Netherlands East Indies just as their policy is to be pliant and complaisant in respect of elements which would drive the white man out of south-east Asia and, indeed, out of the whole Asian continent. If that is our policy, then it represents what a great commentator once described as the very ecstasy of suicide – that we, a country isolated in the world, with a handful of people, a white man's country with all the traditions of our race, should want to set ourselves apart by saying to our friends here and there, as in the case of the Dutch, who have been great colonists and our friends, 'Out with you, we cannot support you'. The moment there is any trouble we automatically say we are in favour of the rebels. If that is to be our policy, then we shall be a very lonely country.[30]

Chifley was advocating acceptance of the reality of Indonesia's postcolonial independence from Holland, and comity with its political leaders. Menzies was in favour of the status quo ante – colonialism and imperialism and the continued domination of Asia by the 'white man'. These contrasting foreign policy views on Indonesian independence, so different in both principle and perspective, together with the very long period for which the Menzies (and successor) Coalition governments held office (1949–72), help to explain Australia's inability to deal with China's political upheavals in the aftermath of World War II. They also go some way towards explaining Australia's ill-judged involvement in the Vietnam War – which, of course, is a quite separate matter.

The end of history: Immediate post–World War II China

At the end of World War II, there were more than a million Japanese servicemen and over half a million Japanese civilians north of the 16th parallel. Their formal surrender in Zhijiang (formerly Chihkiang, in Hunan Province) on 21 August 1945 and in Nanjing (formerly Nanking) on 9 September 1945 brought no peace to China. The on again, off again truce that had obtained between the Nationalist forces under Chiang Kai-shek and the Communist forces under Mao Zedong was replaced by all-out conflict between the two. Notwithstanding his participation at the Potsdam Conference in July 1945 establishing the general terms of Japan's surrender, Chiang's relations with the Japanese occupying forces in China were ambiguous. This was in part a consequence of the training that he and several of his senior generals had undergone at the Shimbu Gakko military academy in Tokyo, established expressly for Chinese officer trainees before World War I, and the Confucian obligation of duty and respect between the students who trained there and their instructors. The instructing staff included several officers who later commanded Japan's military occupation of China until 1945. To understand how Japan's post-war relations with China evolved, it is important to remember that Japan's forces in China were not defeated before they surrendered.[31]

Chiang's Nationalist forces emerged from World War II poorly trained, poorly armed and demoralised. They had generally avoided force-on-force engagements with the superior Japanese occupation force. Instead, they preferred skirmishes on the borders of the Japanese occupied areas, and exploiting Japanese logistic problems closer to Burma, where they could be resupplied across 'The Hump' between India and Chongqing, Chiang's wartime capital, by the US Flying Tigers. The Communist forces were even less well equipped than the Nationalists, but had developed their ability to conduct guerrilla warfare against the Japanese main force, and to organise civil opposition and sabotage. They were particularly skilful in their propaganda war, enlisting the rural peasantry as both fighters and, equally critically, providers of logistic support.

In the months following World War II, considerable numbers of Japanese troops joined the Nationalist forces fighting the Communists, supplying skills, weapons and tactical expertise. While some Japanese troops, freely or coerced, joined the Communist side, its real windfall was an arsenal of weapons and munitions, along with the Japanese artificers who could maintain them, handed over by the Soviet troops in Manchuria. So the scene was set for a military resolution of the tensions that had festered between Chiang and Mao since Chiang assumed the leadership of the Nationalist government in 1943.

The civil war that ensued was bitter and bloody, though the urban civilian population largely escaped the massive deprivations experienced during the decade leading up to World War II. The Nationalists' superiority in troop numbers and, initially at least, firepower was ultimately defeated by a combination of three irresistible forces: the political power of the Chinese Communist Party (CCP), especially its advocacy of land reform, which proved so attractive to the farmers and workers in the rural areas; the unity of command displayed by the Communist leadership under Mao Zedong; and the tactical superiority of the Communist forces in conducting guerrilla warfare. The CCP's political superiority in rural areas was reinforced by the lack of support for the Nationalist government in the urban areas, where it was notorious for its corruption and venality. In short, the CCP was able to mobilise, and in rural areas weaponise, massive popular discontent.

Ambiguity and vacillation in US policy further contributed to the Nationalists' defeat. Exhausted by the Pacific War, the United States was in no position to fight a protracted land war in China as it set about creating a new world order through the United Nations.[32] It did, however, provide considerable materiel and logistic support to the Nationalists, airlifting Chiang's troops from central to northern China, providing surplus military stores, cash loans and grants.[33] Altogether, it backed the wrong side to the tune of US$3.5 billion, congruent and consolidated advice from experienced State Department officers notwithstanding.[34] In immediate post–World War II China at least, an ideological commitment to capitalism, democratic idealism, faith in US exceptionalism and a profound confidence in the universalism of America's political institutions prevented US policymakers from taking into account the cultural and social dynamics of an alien but ancient civilisation. *Plus ça change, plus c'est la même chose.*

The People's Republic of China

On 1 October 1949, Mao proclaimed the People's Republic of China (PRC) and established its capital in Beijing. Following the advance of People's Liberation Army (PLA) forces into Sichuan Province, the Nationalists retreated to Taiwan, where Chiang proclaimed Taipei to be the capital of the Republic of China. Thus began the 'two Chinas' phenomenon – not quite a 'policy' at that stage, but rather a profound political division, as were West and East Germany, and North and South Korea. Chiang's forces were effectively routed, though his anti-communist credentials, especially given the growing tensions of the Cold War, and his assiduous pursuit of legitimacy in Washington won him a seat on the UN Security Council for the next two decades and ensured a sustained US rejection of Mao's claims to the leadership of China.

Mao's assumption of power in Beijing took the Australian government by surprise. It was Chifley's instinct to move quickly to recognise the People's Republic of China as a fait accompli, and to get on with the business of diplomacy. But with an election looming, and growing anti-communist sentiment within his own Labor ranks, Chifley hesitated. The hesitation quickly became a significant stumble and a diplomatic standoff that lasted over two decades. The incoming prime minister, Menzies, and his cabinet decided to follow the US lead, while both fomenting anti-communist sentiment in the broader Australian community and then responding to it by keeping China at arm's length.

Australia's transfer of dependency from the United Kingdom to the United States became even clearer in Menzies' rejection of Prime Minister Clement Atlee's suggestion that Australia, along with other Commonwealth partners India, Pakistan and Ceylon, should join the United Kingdom in accepting the inevitable. Foreign Minister Percy Spender also advocated recognition. In early 1951, for instance, he advised the Menzies cabinet:

> I think it is permissible to reconsider whether it is desirable to take some action which, while not necessarily according full diplomatic recognition to Mao Tse-tung's Government, would nevertheless make it clear that we do not propose to bolster up Chiang Kai-shek's regime, that we have no expectation of Chiang Kai-shek ever controlling the mainland of China again and no desire that Chiang Kai-shek's forces should become associated with the United Nations forces in military operations in Korea or on the mainland of China.

Spender went on to say:

> I have taken the utmost care during the past few months to maintain a common front with the United States ... While it is my firm conviction that the American point of view in international affairs must be given the fullest possible weight, at the same time, it is obviously necessary for countries like Australia to ensure

> that they are consulted before important steps are taken likely to commit them to political or military action. In addition it is necessary that we should bring a degree of public pressure to bear upon the United States in order to try to prevent their pursuing policies which, in our opinion, might be seriously disadvantageous both to them and to us. I feel that the continued recognition of the Chiang Kai-shek regime is a matter of sufficient importance for Australia to take an independent line, provided Australian action is taken at a point of time carefully chosen so as not to prejudice the fundamentally friendly relationships which exist between the United States and ourselves.[35]

Menzies toyed with the idea, but inertia prevailed. As Colin Mackerras has pointed out, during this period 'Australian policy on China and Asian communism tended strongly to follow an American lead'.[36] And for its part, as the Cold War intensified, the United States had its own interests to pursue, painting all things communist with the same brush, positioning itself and its close partners for a series of strategic disasters.

Spender's successor, Richard Casey, who shared Menzies's fear of Chinese communist control over South East Asia, pressed hard for recognition, as much an acceptance of the inevitable as an avenue for negotiation and the exercise of a measure of influence in the conduct of regional affairs.[37] Casey pressed for recognition several times between 1953 and 1955,[38] but, as Allan Gyngell has noted, 'Cabinet only wanted to move if Washington approved, and that was not going to happen.'[39] So Australian foreign policy was already subordinated to that of the United States.

The world of the early 1950s was a confusing and threatening one. The early political alignment between the Soviet Union and China, amplified by the Soviet Union's oppression of the Eastern European nations and China's 'Seventeen Point Agreement for the Peaceful Liberation of Tibet', which put Tibet squarely under Chinese domination, appeared to signal communist expansionism. China's entry into the Korean War, its brutal suppression of the 1959 Tibetan

Uprising and its 1962 border war with India made the Menzies government even more cautious on the question of recognition. Casey's successors – Menzies himself, Garfield Barwick and Paul Hasluck – became progressively more hardline as they conflated postcolonial nationalism in South-East Asia with Beijing-inspired expansionary communism. In an extraordinary (and embarrassingly naive) exchange of views with Soviet foreign minister Andrei Gromyko in 1964, Hasluck set out his and the Menzies government's views on China:

> Mr. Hasluck ... explain[ed] that Australia's anxieties in South East Asia were mainly connected with the threat of Chinese aggression in this area ... He himself had recently concluded a visit to South East Asian countries. Australia was represented throughout the area and had close contact with event[s] there. His own view, which was also the view of the Australian Government, was that *the fear of Chinese aggression* [emphasis added] represented the greatest threat to the peace of the region and the political stability of countries in South East Asia. The small, recently liberated, countries of the area had a real fear of China. The leaders of these countries had read the aggressive statements by Chinese leaders and had seen the actions of the Chinese in Tibet and against India. This fear of China threatened the territorial integrity of all the newly independent countries, and prevented stability in South East Asia.
>
> From the narrower and national point of view of self-interest, Australia would not like to see a situation where one power was dominating the whole of Asia. Asian countries should be free to develop freely their economies and societies, and Australia wanted to see independent national states develop without being subjected to pressure from one dominant power.
>
> Mr. Hasluck continued that he was not talking about a dominant power simply in the ideological field. The question of ideological domination was less prominent in his mind that the question of the new imperialism of China – the questions of power and

> nationalism. The emergence of a dominant power in Asia such as China represented a threat to the rest of the world.[40]

Australia's fear of China and its insistence on remaining in lockstep with US policy was tempered by hopes of economic advantage when, in 1960, Australia increased wheat sales to China, where people were literally starving because of Mao's misguided agricultural policies. From 16,000 tons in the 1950s, it grew to almost 2 million tons in 1961–62, only to come crashing down when Canada recognised the People's Republic of China in 1970 – the harbinger of later instances of economic retaliation against Australia.[41]

Gough Whitlam's unannounced visit to China in July 1971 was greeted with outrage by the government of Prime Minister William McMahon. Speaking at a Young Liberals rally, McMahon described Whitlam's 'excursion into "instant coffee" diplomacy as [the most] damaging and irresponsible series of declarations by any political leader in all my time in politics in Australia'.[42] He went on to say:

> Chou En-Lai had Mr. Whitlam on a hook and he played him as a fisherman plays a trout. It was done in public and in a way that guaranteed a world-wide coverage ... Mr. Whitlam went far beyond what was necessary in responding to his hosts when sensitive matters were raised. In the process he managed to insult just about most of our friends and allies in Asia and the Pacific. Chou En-Lai set out to denigrate the United States and Japan the first being our greatest ally in Asia and the Pacific and the other being our best customer in trade. He even told Mr. Nixon how to run his Administration or get thrown out. What an impertinence to the Leader of the United States, and it is not likely to be forgotten by the American Administration.[43]

This was strong and colourful rhetoric to a crowd of party faithful. He ate his words only four days later, when President Nixon's announced his own visit to China, scheduled for early 1972. This followed immediately upon US secretary of state Henry Kissinger's visit to Beijing just days after Whitlam's meeting with Zhou Enlai. McMahon's backdown was as toadying as it was embarrassing.

> I welcome without reservation President Nixon's statement concerning United States relationships with the People's Republic of China and his intention to visit China early next year. I was informed of the purport of his statement in advance. The President's purpose of normalising relationships with China has been the publicly announced policy of the Australian Government for some time [*sic!*]. Indeed, President Nixon's anxiety to 'seek normalisation of relations and exchange views on questions of concern' precisely describes what we ourselves have been seeking to do by our approaches through diplomatic channels in Paris [*sic*]. In particular, I want to draw the attention of the Australian people to President Nixon's statement that the action he is taking will 'not be at the expense of old friends'. In the future, Australia's policies and actions will be guided by these principles as they have been in the past [*sic*]. I share wholeheartedly the President's view that all will gain from a reduction of tension between the United States and the People's Republic of China. I wish him good fortune in an initiative that has the full support of Australia.[44]

It is possible that McMahon had in mind cabinet's earlier discussion of his submission on Australia's foreign policy options regarding the PRC and the need for a review of the recognition question – a submission that ultimately favoured Australia's continuing to hide behind the strategic skirts of the United States.[45]

Whitlam's election as prime minister on 2 December 1972 and the installation of his government on 5 December 1972 precipitated the announcement of Australia's formal recognition of the PRC on 21 December 1972 and the decision to establish an embassy in Beijing. Things moved quickly. In the destructive confusion of the Cultural Revolution, China lacked direction. The death of Lin Biao, Mao's nominated 'successor', just over a year earlier intensified the competition between various military and party factions as they jostled for position to replace the ailing Zhou Enlai and Mao. Mao sought to impose a measure of control on the turmoil surrounding him by appointing Deng Xiaoping as vice premier to balance the PLA faction loyal to Lin Biao and the 'Gang of Four', led by Mao's wife, Jiang Qing.

This was exactly the environment in which a group of talented and enterprising young diplomats, led by Australia's first ambassador to the PRC, Dr Stephen FitzGerald, could make their mark. They did. Their arrival coincided with Deng's return to power. The timing could not have been better. Their innovative and unconventional analyses of the cultural and political forces at play within China afforded the new government – and particularly their main backer, Prime Minister Whitlam – an on-the-spot view of the political and economic opportunities that China might eventually offer.

Whitlam's instructions to the newly appointed ambassador were clear:

> We seek a relationship with China based on friendship, co-operation and mutual trust, comparable with that which we have, or seek, with other major powers ... We ... need to measure our actions carefully so that we do not give the Chinese the impression that we are careless of our own interests. They are themselves hard-headed realists, and it would be unnatural of them not to take advantage of us or hold us in contempt for apparent weakness.[46]

The importance of this initial 'getting to know you' period, for both China and Australia, was crucial. As FitzGerald later wrote:

> We had a relationship of goodwill on both sides, symbolised by the cordial reception in Peking last year (1976) of a Liberal Party Prime Minister. We had a relationship which had successfully navigated the transition between the Labor and the conservative governments. We had a bipartisan China policy. We had a situation where, at the time of Chairman Mao's death in September 1976, both sides of the national Parliament joined in tribute to his contribution to mankind, a situation which, as Whitlam pointed out, would have been unthinkable a few years ago. We were back in business with China. That had been our objective.[47]

FitzGerald also commented on his embassy's diplomatic modus operandi – relationship management practice that has apparently eluded the governments of prime ministers Abbott, Turnbull and Morrison:

> In these first two years we were also learning how to handle our differences and disagreements ... In foreign relations goodwill develops best through mutual respect and that the more important we believe a relationship to be, the more important it is that we should not blink at what is unacceptable, bend to the wishes of the other party or be uncritical or over-accommodating where our own principles and national interests are at stake. The Chinese have this view. I am pleased to say that on a number of issues, Australia took a similar view.

But new brooms are generally unwelcome in staid and risk-averse institutions like the Department of Foreign Affairs, as it was then called. So it was for FitzGerald and his team as they argued that a quite different kind of China would emerge from the Cultural Revolution under Deng – more pragmatic and less ideologically dependent on the Soviet Union. The department held a contrary view. This policy tension came to a head during Prime Minister Fraser's 1976 visit to Beijing. Fraser endorsed the views of the embassy against those of the Department of Foreign Affairs' secretary, Alan Renouf, and, without first seeking the agreement of the United States, proceeded to discuss informally with Premier Hua Guofeng the feasibility of a China–Japan–United States–Australia grouping to counter Soviet aggression. This was anathema to the Canberra diehards, who brought the proposal crashing down via a 'leak' to the Melbourne *Herald*. Interestingly, Renouf resigned soon after.[48] To this day, no one is sure whether Renouf inspired or initiated the leak.

It remains the view of many that the Department of Foreign Affairs and Trade continues to wear the fusty mantle of its predecessors, maintaining a generally conservative view of faithful allegiance to and dependence on the United States, and sustained suspicion of China and its motives.

1989: Things become tricky

The relationship matured relatively slowly, as might have been anticipated between a slowly emerging great power and a smaller, semi-interesting regional state occupying a continent at the bottom of the world. Landmass has always mattered to China. It is important to recognise that central to this maturation of the relationship was the role of Deng Xiaoping, China's paramount leader from 1977 to 1989, and his protégé Premier Zhao Ziyang (who developed a constructive relationship with Prime Minister Bob Hawke). Following Mao's death, Deng took China out of the Cultural Revolution and into a period of radical economic reform, which would produce astonishing economic growth. The opening of China to the global market, the progressive reduction in bureaucratic controls on planning and investment, and, most importantly, the creation of a new and increasingly better-off middle class provided Australia with opportunities that have underpinned the economic relationship for the best part of four decades.

One of the more significant developments was the growth of people-to-people links, especially in education and scientific exchanges. By 1989, there were more than 27,000 Chinese students in Australia, and increasing numbers of young Australians studying in Chinese universities.[49] But rapid economic and social reform, exacerbated by rising expectations, accelerating inflation and growing official corruption, precipitated widespread public protest, ostensibly following the death of Hu Yaobang in April 1989. The enormous Tiananmen Square became the focal point of public mourning for Hu, which gradually morphed into what Deng Xiaoping saw as a challenge to his and the CCP's leadership. The protests in Beijing and other major centres were forcibly suppressed on 4 June 1989, following the declaration of martial law. The dead and injured numbered in the thousands.

In Australia, Hawke's response was immediate. He spoke with characteristic passion, ending his memorial service speech with a statement of hope:

> We all pray that moderation will eventually prevail, so that a new and better China can rise from this carnage, a China that befits the courage and determination of its people. I call on the Chinese Government to withdraw its troops from deployment against unarmed civilians, and to respect the will of its people. To crush the spirit and body of youth is to crush the very future of China itself.[50]

A week later, without consulting cabinet or his colleagues, Hawke announced the extension of all temporary entry permits for Chinese students legally in Australia, thereby opening the door to permanent residence.[51] Some 42,000 Chinese students, and their dependents, took up the offer.[52] In response, the Chinese government banned ministerial visits, though the economic relationship continued apace.

1996: Things become trickier

Normal relations resumed slowly, though without personal dynamic that Hawke, who retired from parliament in 1992, and Zhao, who was put under house arrest for the rest of his life following the violent suppression of the Tiananmen protests, brought to the relationship. In the months following the election of the Howard government in 1996, several events converged to destabilise the bilateral relationship once again: strong Australian statements in support of the United States following a deterioration in China–Taiwan relations;[53] the cancellation of Australia's Development Import Finance Facility (DIFF), which effectively cut development assistance to China; an increase in Australia–United States defence cooperation following the 1996 AUSMIN talks; and Howard's decision to meet the Dalai Lama during the latter's September 1996 visit to Australia (to which Beijing also objected).

Of these irritants, two combined in 1996 to constrain the relationship with China: Australia's habit of falling in behind US actions regarding Taiwan; and the 1996 AUSMIN Communique, which emphasised the regional security role of the Australia–United States alliance and signalled a major combined military exercise for March 1997.[54] To the Chinese government, the Howard government appeared to be going back thirty years, reverting to a less independent and internationalist foreign policy. A renewed emphasis on the broad regional role of the ANZUS alliance and a more outspoken position on China's Tibet and Taiwan policies were seen as inconsistent and provocative.[55]

The years of the Howard government (1996–2007) saw a spectacular growth in the bilateral economic relationship between Australia and China, but this was shadowed by uncertainty and timidity in the conduct of the political relationship.[56] In important respects, the prospects for a more constructive political relationship were a casualty of Howard's hubris following both Australia's successful leadership of the 1999 UN peacekeeping operation in East Timor, and the 9/11 attacks in the United States. Howard's instincts, generally reactive rather than creative and forward-looking, were to reinforce the defence and security links with the United States, even to the extent of invoking the ANZUS Treaty as a way of offering succour and support to President George W. Bush in the days immediately following 9/11.

Howard allowed himself to be lulled into a comfortable complacency when an article by *The Bulletin*'s Fred Brenchley described him as the US 'Deputy Sheriff' in Asia – a characterisation that Howard rather enjoyed, but which riled the leaders of key South-East Asian nations, especially Indonesia and Malaysia.[57] It certainly demeaned him, and Australia, in China's eyes. This overreach was compounded when, in May 2003, President Bush described Howard as a 'man of steel' for his full-throated support of the United States' war in Iraq. (President Trump's promotion in 2019 of Prime Minister Morrison as 'a man of titanium' – an embarrassing inducement for Australian support for the United States against both China and Iran – completed the trifecta.[58])

Consistent with a century of lost opportunities and missteps, the Howard decade marked a return to the ambivalence, hesitancy and insecurity of the Menzies years. The security relationship was the fulcrum on which the relationship with China balanced: the relationship was highly sensitive to changes in US policy settings, with Australia always happy to play 'the lamb' to America's 'Mary'. Foreign Minister Alexander Downer's enthusiastic support for the US decision to deploy two carrier battle groups to Taiwan in 1996 delighted the United States. His apparently off-the-cuff remarks in 2004 that ANZUS was 'symbolic', with the implication that the ANZUS Treaty did not apply automatically to the security of Taiwan, did not.[59] The 'clarifications' and back-pedalling were almost immediate. Downer's advocacy of a 'strategic relationship' with China notwithstanding, Howard went to considerable pains to assuage the feelings of the Bush administration. The problem that Howard faced was the intrinsic difficulty of reconciling a deep and historical security relationship with a new and expanding economic relationship. And because he viewed them through the lens of a reductionist binary, he could not reconcile them.

Language is always problematic. For Howard, no matter how hard or how often he tried, he could not use the term 'strategic' in the same sense when referring to China and the United States. The problem has endured, with the Morrison government inheriting the confected expression 'comprehensive strategic relationship' to describe Australia's dealings with China. It was a relationship built on confusion about objectives and insecurity about consequences.

2007: Along came Rudd

The arrival of Prime Minister Kevin Rudd, a Mandarin-speaking former diplomat, was seen by many as the harbinger of a return to a more constructive and personality-driven way of doing business. It was not. Rudd not only inherited the Howard government's baggage but generated some of his own. Sensitivities relating to Chinese direct foreign investment in the agriculture and mining industries, the Rio Tinto bribery and espionage case (involving four of its employees based in Shanghai), ongoing human rights issues involving the Islamic Uighur minority in Xinjiang Province, and the visit of the Uighur activist Rebiya Kadeer were all made more difficult by the 'own goal' of Australia's 2009 Defence White Paper. This was a clumsily written and unnuanced effort at representing difficult international issues in the argot of domestic political spin. Its treatment of China's military expansion was symptomatic of the problem it caused for Rudd:

> 4.26 China will also be the strongest Asian military power, by a considerable margin. Its military modernisation will be increasingly characterised by the development of power projection capabilities. A major power of China's stature can be expected to develop a globally significant military capability befitting its size. But the pace, scope and structure of China's military modernisation have the potential to give its neighbours cause for concern if not carefully explained, and if China does not reach out to others to build confidence regarding its military plans.
>
> 4.27 China has begun to do this in recent years, but needs to do more. If it does not, there is likely to be a question in the minds of regional states about the long-term strategic purpose of its force development plans, particularly as the modernisation appears potentially to be beyond the scope of what would be required for a conflict over Taiwan.

As I pointed out at the time, no single sentence in this excerpt is untrue: 'The problem is that, when assembled in this way, they convey a linear, superficial and alarmist view of China's military growth.'[60] China's response to the Defence White Paper was swift and extremely negative.

Hugh White summarised Rudd's China problem well:

> [Rudd] ... fears that, because he knows China so well, he will be seen as too close to it. He fears being accused of being on China's side. This means that for Rudd, speaking Chinese turns out to be a liability. It may turn out to be irrelevant as well. As China's power grows, managing the relationship will be less and less about explaining to the Chinese what we want, and more and more about deciding how to respond when they tell us what they want. That means that Rudd's most important contribution will not be to

> explain Western perspectives to the Chinese in elegant Mandarin, but to explain the new realities of power to Australians in plain English.[61]

Following his loss of the prime ministership in June 2010, Rudd served as foreign minister and found himself caught, as had Howard been before him, in the crossfire between keeping the Americans happy and maintaining an expanding economic relationship with China. For all his skill as a linguist, Rudd could not speak in two languages out of both sides of his mouth at the same time. His legacy was disappointing.

The way things are

The election of the Abbott government in September 2013 coincided with the beginning of a precipitate decline in the Australia–China relationship. This was less due to Abbott's foreign policy approach, exemplified by his pugnacious offer to 'shirtfront' Russian president Vladimir Putin, than to the growing insecurity and unease in Australian policy circles about China's accelerating growth in political and strategic power, and uncertainty about how to deal with that. A brief overview of the main events will help to set the scene. This is not an exhaustive listing of the factors that have come to define a soured bilateral relationship. Some of the issues, such as the South China Sea, have festered away, returning to prominence as circumstances or media interest dictate. But the overview does illustrate what happens when relationships lose control, direction and purpose.

November 2014

- Australia and China sign a free trade agreement.
- President Xi Jinping addresses a joint sitting of the Australian parliament.

May 2015

- Defence Minister Kevin Andrews criticises China's land reclamation and military base expansion in the South China Sea at the Shangrila Security Dialogue in Singapore.

April 2016

- Prime Minister Turnbull visits Beijing (the last prime minister to do so).

October 2016

- President Xi claims leadership parity with Mao Zedong and Deng Xiaoping.

March 2017

- Foreign Minister Julie Bishop delivers a speech in Singapore in which she criticises China's political system.

December 2017

- Senator Sam Dastyari resigns from parliament as a result of his long-term dealings with political donor Chinese businessman Huang Xiangao and doubtful donations and payments.

December 2017

- Prime Minister Turnbull introduces new 'foreign interference' laws and delivers a provocative speech (quoting a phrase attributed to Mao Zedong), saying, in Mandarin, that Australia will 'stand up' against Chinese political interference.

August 2018

- The federal government bans China's Huawei telecommunications company from participating in the construction of Australia's 5G mobile network.

October 2018

- Victorian premier Daniel Andrews signs an agreement with China to cooperate in its Belt and Road Initiative (BRI).

June 2019

- Political demonstrations and riots begin in Hong Kong.

September 2019

- Prime Minister Morrison, speaking in Chicago in support of President Trump's position on China's trading status, questions China's developing country status under international trade rules.

April 2020

- Foreign Minister Marise Payne calls for an independent international inquiry into the origins of the COVID-19 virus in Wuhan, China, and its subsequent management by China.

May 2020

- China imposes tariffs on Australian barley and beef.

June 2020

- ASIO and the AFP raid the residence of Shaoquett Moselmane, a Labor member of the New South Wales Legislative Council, over allegations of links to the Chinese government and its attempts to interfere in the state's politics.

August 2020

- Treasurer Josh Frydenberg blocks the proposed sale of Lion Dairy & Drinks to Chinese interests.

- Chinese-born Australian journalist Cheng Lei, an employee of a Chinese TV broadcaster in Beijing, is arrested by the Chinese authorities.

- Prime Minister Morrison visits Tokyo for talks with new Japanese prime minister Yoshihide Suga, ostensibly to sign a reciprocal access agreement to cover bilateral troop deployments, but they also discuss North Asian security matters.

November 2020

- China imposes steep tariff increases on Australian wine.

- Prime Minister Morrison demands a formal apology from China after an offensive digitally altered image was tweeted by a junior Chinese foreign ministry spokesman as comment on allegations of war crimes committed by Australian special forces in Afghanistan.

- The Chinese embassy in Canberra issues a list of fourteen 'grievances' against Australia.

December 2020

- The Australian government legislates to cancel or proactively block agreements entered into by states, territories, local governments and public universities with foreign governments if they are deemed to compromise Australia's national interests.

March 2021

- Australia's ambassador to China, Graham Fletcher, describes Chinese diplomatic behaviour as 'unreliable' and 'vindictive'.

It is not the purpose of this chapter to analyse these incidents in detail. Rather, it is important to understand what lies behind this remarkable deterioration of the relationship. There are five major forces at play, each of them compounding the effects of the others.

First, China's power – economic, political, social and strategic – has grown inexorably since diplomatic relations were established in 1973. Then, Australia's economy was larger than China's. In 2021, China's economy is ten times larger than Australia's, and its defence spending is also ten times bigger. China is increasingly confident in asserting its power, building enormous diplomatic and influence networks and taking on an ever-increasing number of international leadership roles. What's more, China is increasingly confident in asserting its power and status with respect to the United States. It no longer sees itself as a second-class global citizen, or as subordinate to the United States in Asia.

Second, the role of the United States is also changing. Its relationship with China is highly dynamic, and the balance between the two behemoths is constantly adjusting. The United States, particularly during the Trump presidency, has been slow to adjust to the rise of China, continuing to see itself as the natural leader of the global community, as 'exceptional' and as 'pre-eminent'. In fact, the authority and credibility of the United States was significantly diminished during the Trump presidency. Without a comprehensive diplomatic and economic plan, it is difficult to see how America will be able to restore its prestige, both by differentiating its power from that of China and by leveraging the assets, particularly longstanding alliances, that China so evidently lacks.

Third, Australia has not been able to accept or understand China's rise as an inevitability, or to adjust its diplomacy to the new power realities. Australia has preferred to retreat into 'containment and constrainment' models of relationship management rather than build engagement channels with China and develop its cooperative linkages with its regional neighbours. At a fundamental level, Australia has been unable to adjust its thinking to the fact that we have become a multiracial and highly diverse society. The lens of 'race' still colours our attitudes to China and our region, as it continues to prevent us from crossing the divide between Indigenous Australia and settler communities.

Fourth, Australia has fallen into the trap of trying to advance its major economic, foreign and strategic policy interests through the filter of domestic political acceptability. Key international policy objectives have become grist to the mill of domestic politics. Political leaders have mistaken assertion for assuredness, imagining that ephemeral advantage in political polls is proof of substance and success. What has in fact happened is that short-term political contests, largely devoid of analysis and argument, have generated confusion and exacerbated the insecurity that is at the centre of Australia's political culture and national identity.

This feeds directly into the final factor that lies behind Australia's diminished relationship with China: the absence of leadership and vision on the part of our political leaders. While several of Australia's prime ministers have been skilful transactional and retail politicians, few have shown an instinct for the transformational leadership that capitalises on opportunity and coalesces the electorate's enthusiasm and support. Whitlam had vision and created hope, though his government proved to be woeful at delivering it. Fraser had glimpses of a better world, and kept some of that hope alive. His visit to China and meeting with Zhao Ziyang in 1982, for instance, built a sound, though prudent, personal relationship, which enabled Hawke, who became prime minister the following year, to turn Zhao's reciprocal visit into a relationship management triumph.[62] Between them, Hawke and Keating expanded the relationship with China while maintaining the defence partnership with the United States. But in the past twenty-five years, Australia has paid a price for our leaders' lack of leadership and vision.

It is easy, of course, to blame China as primarily responsible for the continuing deterioration in the relationship.[63] As I have said elsewhere, China is certainly capable of self-defeating ham-fistedness.[64] But the problem is more multidimensional and multifaceted than that. Australia's political leaders have been much given to hysteria and hyperventilation in their commentary about China. As I commented, 'Bloviation and stridency are not signs of strength, any more than deliberation and measure are signs of weakness.'[65] And for its part, China knows only too well that it loses no skin in South-East Asia by beating up on Australia. We have managed to squander our diplomatic capital in the region as recklessly as we have in China, and no one is disappointed to see arrogance reap its own reward. Moreover, by using Australia as a whipping boy, China delivers a strong lesson to its Asian neighbours about what they might expect, were they to imitate Australia's approach. As one great Australian diplomat once said, 'Modesty much becomes us.'[66]

So, where to?

In important respects, Australia has found itself caught up in the surprisingly sentimental view espoused by the neo-cons at the beginning of this century: that the integration of China into the global economic and trade system would inevitably lay the groundwork for a new liberal world order. The march of history and a globalised economy would bring a new democratic dawn that would force China's leadership to democratise China's political system. In her bumbling Fullerton Lecture in Singapore in March 2017, Julie Bishop rehearsed the view that 'democracy and democratic institutions are essential for nations if they are to reach their economic potential'.[67] As Graham Allison and Fred Hu pointed out recently, these expectations were illusions. What the United States needs to do is to put its vital interests first and deal with China as it is – the biggest player in the history of the world.[68] So too Australia. The task for both Australia and China is to seek to align core interests as far as possible – economic growth, long-term economic prosperity and social stability, regional stability and national security.

Values are of course important, because they define who we are. Our values do not, however, define who anyone else is. The values that ground Australia as a robust democracy do not align with those that ground China as a strong centrally controlled state. And while respectful discussion of differences in values is critical in building mutual understanding, alignment of values is not a determinant of a stable region or a peaceful world. Stability is a consequence of the ability to manoeuvre around difference, and that is a skill that is absent on both sides of the Australia–China relationship. That skill is called diplomacy.

The relationship with China is broken – perhaps not irreparably so, but certainly to the point that its restoration is not possible while China and Australia continue to pursue finger-pointing and name-calling as an alternative to diplomacy. Indeed, the AUKUS partnership announced in September 2021 has made the restoration of the relationship even more difficult, a task compounded by the fact, as Bill Hayton has pointed out, that 'Xi's China is not a happy place. It is dogmatic and coercive, anxious and unsure, fearful that its unity may come unzipped at any moment. The myths will hold it together for a while, but the fracture lines within the *Zhonghua minzu* were there from the start.'[69]

And given how habituated the Morrison government is in its pursuit of boisterous overstatements and oversimplifications, the remedy may not be found before the current Australian cast has left the stage. That makes the creation of a new way of doing business on Australia's part dependent on the electoral cycle and political change. That does not necessarily mean a change of government. But it does mean a change of thinking and a change in diplomatic management. The key to that change is a return to a calibrated, confident, managed and purposive foreign policy that focuses on the alignment of interests rather than the drama of differences.

5
Australia's Pacific Problem

Australia is an island continent completely surrounded by sea.

From a Royal Australian Navy submission to the
Defence Operational Requirements Committee, 1983

Pedestrian governments and their leaders are distinguished by the unconscious irony that provides political context for their key policy pronouncements. In 2018, by which time the Black Lives Matter movement was already five years old and growing in resonance around the world, Prime Minister Morrison's major Pacific policy statement was delivered at the Lavarack Army Barracks in Townsville, Queensland.[1] Even the slightest familiarity with Australia's history in the Pacific might have suggested that anywhere else but Townsville would have been a better location for his 'Pacific Step-up' speech, excepting perhaps Mackay in the same state. If the prime minister himself was not aware of Townsville's Pacific past, his advisers should have been. Insouciance is no excuse for unconscious irony.

Morrison's rhetorical flourishes – Australia's 'step-up' in the Pacific, which is 'our' home and a region in which 'we' have 'natural advantages in terms of history, proximity and shared values', and where Australia is 'a force for good' and the Pacific nations are 'our family' – were also completely oblivious to a past built on arrogance, condescension, disparagement, exploitation (including sexual exploitation) and neglect. This lent a grim tinge to the unconsciousness of his irony.

The vacuousness of this attempt at a contemporary Pacific policy was compounded eighteen months later when Morrison, now making a foray into history, proclaimed that 'there was no slavery in Australia'.[2] It was inexcusable for any Australian prime minister to be ignorant of the fact that Australia's early (and failed) cotton and subsequent (and supremely successful) sugar industries were built on the illegal immigration and exploitation of Pacific islanders, and that groups of Indigenous Australians were still being confined together by neck-chains in Western Australia as late as 1958.[3]

Australia's hidden history of human trafficking

The Australian slave trade is another dark secret hidden in Australia's colonial past. Like the alienation and dispossession of Indigenous peoples, the sexual subjugation of women for at least the first fifty years of colonisation, and the racism extended to Chinese and other Asian immigrants, the forced immigration of 'indentured labourers' – also known by the grim euphemism 'blackbirding' – imposed unspeakable misery on unsuspecting peoples from the archipelagic chain extending from Papua New Guinea to New Caledonia.

In modern times, slavery has been the most diabolical expression of racism. Reflecting pseudo-scientific acclimatisation theories that were popular in the nineteenth century, black people were deemed more suitable than their white counterparts for strenuous manual labour in extreme conditions. But, as Alex McKinnon has written, 'backbreaking labour, heat exhaustion, disease, mistreatment and malnutrition killed Islanders in their thousands'.[4]

Trafficking in 'indentured' labour began in 1847 when Benjamin Boyd, a squatter with enormous landholdings in Victoria and southern New South Wales, shipped sixty-five people from New Caledonia and Vanuatu to Boydtown, on the southern shore of Twofold Bay, near today's Eden. Understandably, the islanders refused to work, whereupon Boyd abandoned them. Thus began Australia's unhappy experiment with slavery.

Colonial Australia displayed almost no interest in the Pacific, and even less curiosity. The focus was on 'the motherland', and it was for the motherland to extend its empire into the Pacific on its terms.

Indeed, any Australian colonial interest, such as Queensland's plan to annex Papua as part of its jurisdiction in 1883, was decisively squashed by the Colonial Office.[5] But what did stir the imaginations of some Queensland landholders was the promise of 'cheap' labour. This cemented a disgraceful period in pre-Federation Australia's exploitation of the peoples of the Pacific – the capture and enforced transportation of Pacific islanders to Queensland. And deeply involved in Australia's practice of 'indentured labour' – a British euphemism for slavery, as practised in Malaysia and Fiji, for instance – were Captain Robert Towns,[6] after whom Townsville was named, and John Mackay,[7] after whom Mackay was named. Prime Minister Morrison's advisers should have known this.

Burns Philp, a trading conglomerate that created Australia's biggest commercial footprint in the Pacific for eighty years, was an enthusiastic early supplier of shipping to the blackbirders.[8] With strong connections to the colonial Queensland government (Robert Philp was twice premier of Queensland), Burns Philp began the transportation of fraudulently recruited and criminally abducted labourers in 1881, withdrawing from human trafficking in 1885 when it diversified into the more profitable sandalwood trade. The company later established its own plantations in various South Pacific islands, continuing its involvement in schemes dependent on low-cost labour.

Around 60,000 people were either tricked or forced to work on the canefields and pastoral leases of northern Australia. With companies such as Colonial Sugar Refining (CSR) a major beneficiary, it is reasonable to argue that Queensland's early economic growth was built on human servitude. CSR held a monopoly on sugar refining in Queensland and Fiji for the best part of a century, even after diversifying into building products during World War II. And for its part, Burns Philp was inducted into the Queensland Business Leaders Hall of Fame in 2009 'for its significant contributions made to the development of Queensland and its economy'.[9]

The exploitation of Pacific islands labour ended as ignominiously as it began. It is important to recall that race policy was a consuming preoccupation of Australians at that time. As Chad Cooper has noted, 'At the time of Federation ... federal parliamentarians managed the complex and arguably contradictory task of fostering a national ideology based on racial exclusivity whilst remaining a civilised member of a diverse British Empire.'[10] Among the first enactments of the new Commonwealth parliament were the *Pacific Island Labourers Act 1901* and the *Immigration Restriction Act 1901*, both giving legislative expression to the White Australia policy. Section 8 of the *Pacific Island Labourers Act 1901* was particularly harsh. It provided for the deportation of Pacific islands labourers who had been unemployed for a month or more, their repatriation being paid from the funds held in trust but which had not been paid to the 15,000 or so who had died while working on the canefields. It was the largest mass deportation in Australian history. And, as McKinnon records, 'for those who escaped deportation, and their descendants, decades of segregation, ostracisation and official erasure created a cycle of inherited disadvantage and trauma'.[11]

Memories of the Pacific labour trade, however described, linger in both the descendent communities in Australia and in the originating communities throughout the Pacific. Almost 120 years after blackbirding was prohibited, Pacific islander families are still discovering links between themselves and other families along the Australian coastline and across the Coral Sea.

Historians may argue over whether the exploitation of Pacific islander labour was slavery or not. The Australian Human Rights Commission certainly regards Australia's early experimentation with forced labour between 1863 and 1904 as racist, discriminatory, exploitative and tantamount to slavery.[12] Some Pacific islanders signed up freely, though whether they exercised informed consent is moot. Some were kidnapped, and many were hoodwinked. But the core issue is that 'cheap', usually underpaid labour was the central premise on which blackbirding was conducted and condoned by many who rose to positions of political and judicial pre-eminence. One constitutional founding father, the former premier of Queensland and High Court chief justice Samuel Griffith, presided over the 1906 High Court case that upheld the deportation of islanders – the 'illegal immigrants' of the day. The chief justice did not recuse himself on the grounds of a perceived conflict of interest.

This problematic history in Australia's relationship with the peoples of the Pacific is made worse by the practice of the early postcolonial state governments to lump islander problems in with Indigenous ones. As McKinnon puts it:

> Complicating matters are the extensive historical, cultural and familial ties between Islander and Indigenous communities. Roughly half of Australian South Sea Islanders today also have Aboriginal or Torres Strait Islander heritage. The uniqueness of their circumstances, and the unwillingness of authorities to grapple with its complexity, has often resulted in a double erasure of the Islander identity – cast out of white societies and lumped in with Indigenous ones. Islanders were herded into Aboriginal missions or non-white parts of town. Many governments, confronted with non-white people who defied simplistic identification, simply classed them as Aboriginal.[13]

Like so many issues attaching to Australia's racist past, our long-term relationship with the Pacific demands both an acknowledgement of past wrongs and an apology to the affected communities. It would not, however, be advisable for anyone to hold their breath awaiting either. While Australian governments remain ignorant of this sordid period of our Pacific history, or in denial about it, our inability to come to terms with our past seriously compromises our ability to create a better future in the Pacific. More than acknowledgement and apology, Australia needs to embark on an effective program of economic, political and social engagement and interaction with the nations of the Pacific – engagements in which we listen rather than preach, contribute rather than control.

World War I and conduct unbecoming

Australia basks in the confected and reflected glory of heroism and sacrifice, the blood of young men cut down in their prime as they defended king and country. Through war memorials and shrines, our cities and suburbs, towns and villages bear witness to those who served and died in the defence of freedom and the Australian way of life. At least, that is how the Anzac mythology would have it.

The ugly reality of war, however, sometimes reveals a less gilded story. Australia's early military action in German New Guinea and the occupation of Rabaul is another facet of our Pacific history that provides an inglorious foil to the hubris and rhetoric of Prime Minister Morrison's 'step-up' speech.

Germany's imperial ambitions in the Pacific did not amount to much – New Guinea and its north-eastern islands, extending to Nauru in the north and Samoa in the south, and including present-day Palau, the Federated States of Micronesia, the northern Mariana Islands and the Marshall Islands. And, quite distinct from its practice in Africa, Germany retained no troops or armed forces in the Pacific, 'defence' being the responsibility of the small naval detachment at Qingdao, the German concession in China. There were small 'native police' units in Samoa, though these were disbanded in January 1914 after some members had run amok. German New Guinea boasted a formation of 'police soldiers', equipped with old Mauser rifles but with virtually no military training.

Australia, nonetheless, was deeply exercised by Germany's presence in the Pacific, with companies such as Burns Philp agitating against a German trading company monopoly, leading to compensation payments and its acquisition of 10,000 hectares for plantations in the German Solomon Islands.[14] So, with the outbreak of World War I, Australia and New Zealand moved quickly to capture the German outposts. On 29 August 1914, New Zealand occupied Apia, in Samoa, without resistance and without loss. Strict surrender terms were imposed on the hapless Germans, most of whom spent the next four years interned on cold, damp and uncomfortable islands off Auckland and Wellington.[15]

Australia's military preparations and conduct of operations to take German New Guinea were a fiasco. A battle group consisting of HMAS *Australia*, *Melbourne*, *Sydney* and *Encounter*, together with the submarines *AE1* and *AE2*, the 11,000-ton troopship HMAS *Berrima*, and coal and supply ships, was dispatched to Rabaul carrying a ragtag force of ill-equipped and untrained troops. Hermann Hiery sets the scene:

> The force itself contained many completely unsuitable men. A large number of those who had volunteered in the hope of adventure were young greenhorns who had obviously never held a gun before in their lives. There were also men with highly dubious pasts, and many former convicts. The Queenslanders were the worst behaved.[16]

The civilian vessel SS *Kanowna* was requisitioned to transport a thousand members of the Australian Naval and Military Expeditionary Force (ANMEF) to New Guinea. In transit from Port Moresby to Rabaul, hearing that they were on their way to a war zone, the stokers mutinied, necessitating the ship's return to Australia.

On 11 September 1914, the Australian force finally arrived in Blanche Bay, near Rabaul, to take the wireless station. After an unopposed landing, the force met unexpected resistance from a group of German colonial officials and untrained Melanesian police. After a day of fighting, the German force surrendered, and the wireless station was taken and destroyed. But the skirmish was far from the walkover that the Australians had expected. Six Australians, including two officers, were killed, along with thirty Melanesians and one German. Four Australians, one German and ten Melanesians were injured.[17] Unlike the terms of surrender negotiated by the New Zealand force commander in Samoa, the terms of surrender settled in Rabaul on 17 September 1914 by the force commander, Colonel William Holmes, were extremely favourable to the Germans – a marker of Australian inexperience and trepidation.

The terms of surrender were strongly criticised in Australia, which perhaps persuaded Holmes to contravene the normal application of the laws of armed conflict by having recalcitrant German civilian prisoners publicly flogged. While the legality of Holmes' actions was highly questionable, the floggings were seen as an appropriate balance to soft surrender terms, and secured his later career.[18]

What occurred in the ensuing weeks and months was a national disgrace: undisciplined Australian soldiers looted and pillaged, officers engaged in larceny, and officers opportunistically embezzled over-printed postage stamps, with rarity philatelic status, for private gain. In the words of the administrator at Rabaul, quoted in a report to the Commonwealth parliament by Attorney-General Billy Hughes, 'the troops returning to Australia had left an unenviable reputation as champion looters'.[19] More than a century later, that reputation survives in local folklore.

Australia's poor reputation in post-surrender New Guinea was exacerbated by an occupation administration that was predatory, corrupt and unprofessional at worst and ramshackle at best. Burns Philp exercised a monopoly on trade and logistics, effectively profiteering from Australia's military occupation, with initial help from Colonel Holmes and his family members, who held officer commissions in his headquarters. Whether in New Britain, New Ireland, Bougainville or on the mainland from Finschhafen to the Sepik, Australian administrators condoned the illegal hunting of protected species (particularly birds of paradise, the feathers of which were in demand in the fashion industry), the felling of native forests, lawlessness and tribal fighting among the indigenous peoples (which the German administration had managed to control), and the withdrawal of any effective administrative infrastructure, leading to anarchy. Police patrols undertook punitive expeditions against local communities, summarily executing suspects and mutilating their corpses.[20]

Australia's administrative policy foundations were deeply racist, remaining so throughout the period of the League of Nations mandate and into World War II. The racist antecedents of Australia's early-twentieth-century administration coloured its post–World War II administration. As Hermann Hiery comments:

> [T]he Australians … accepted that the 'otherness' of the Melanesians was an obstacle to their assimilation to European-dominated modernity … [They] equated the otherness of the Melanesians with a serious congenital defect. They believed that, if it could be eliminated at all, it would be only with the greatest difficulty. The otherness of the Melanesians, like that of the Australian Aborigines, was regarded not as having any intrinsic value but merely as a stain. Thus the Australian view of Melanesians oscillated between absolute condemnation of them as nonhuman (and thus unreformable) and the belief that they must be quickly and rigorously assimiliated [*sic*]—if necessary, by force.[21]

Racism was reinforced by misogyny and sexual exploitation. Just as the arrival of the women transportees of the First Fleet was 'celebrated' by debauchery and rape on an industrial scale, so too the arrival of Australian troops in German New Guinea was marked by 'sexual attacks and the raping of local women'.[22] So predatory and vicious were the Australian district officers that local women ran into the jungle screaming whenever they caught sight of a white man.[23] Echoes of this period linger not only in the collective memories of the Papua New Guinea population but also in the significant numbers of people with both indigenous and white ancestry in the local communities.

Pacific memories of World War II

Like World War I, World War II has become deeply embedded in Australia's national mythology, reinforcing images of gallantry, heroism and sacrifice. Yet those are not the memories of the peoples of the Pacific. Australia's theatre of operations did not extend far beyond Papua New Guinea – it was for the US service personnel, especially those of the US Navy and the Marines, to meet the Japanese on the atolls and islands of the Pacific archipelagos. In those micro-polities, the Pacific War is remembered as a time of death and destruction, fear and servitude, rusting wrecks, pollution and unexploded ordnance. In Papua New Guinea, World War II is remembered as 'the white man's war' – without any discrimination between the allies or Japan. To the peoples of Port Moresby's hinterland, Milne Bay, Madang and Rabaul, the combatants all looked the same, and their presence was painful and unwelcome. Australian troops may have used 'fuzzy-wuzzy angels' as a term of affection, though it would not meet contemporary standards, rightly sensitive to its condescending, patronising and racist overtones. But as Monash University's Seumas Spark has written, 'What histories of the war tend not to mention is that many, perhaps most, of the "fuzzy-wuzzy angels" didn't serve willingly. In the area around Port Moresby, from where Australian authorities recruited carriers for the Kokoda Trail, male villagers hid to avoid being pressed into service.'[24]

It was not their war. Pacific memories are not focused on valiant colonisers freeing them from people who themselves wanted to be colonisers, whether Australian or Japanese, or heroic defenders against yet another set of invaders. Rather, they remember atrocities committed by combatants of all stripes, mango trees that provided food and fun transformed into gallows for hanging Japanese (as happened in Salamaua), and indiscriminate death. As Spark commented:

> Most Australian histories of the war relegate New Guineans to the edge of the story. We read little about the massive disruption and suffering visited on New Guinea from 1942–45. About 1.5 million foreigners descended on the country in those years, around one foreigner for every New Guinean. That statistic is worth dwelling on. One person came into New Guinea for every one of its 1.5 million or so inhabitants. New Guineans served Australians, Americans and Japanese, sometimes willingly, sometimes not. In

parts of the Sepik, Bougainville and New Britain, around one quarter of the local population died.

All of this remains deeply ingrained in 'our' Pacific legacy.

The beginnings of a Pacific community

The end of World War II, and the establishment of a professional Department of External Affairs, set the scene for a considerably more engaged Australian approach to the Pacific. The responsibilities of post-war reconstruction and redevelopment persuaded Australia and New Zealand, along with the Pacific colonial powers – the United Kingdom, the Netherlands, France and the United States – to recognise the need to align their development assistance policies and, where they could, their post-colonisation policies. In 1947, the Canberra Agreement established the South Pacific Commission (SPC), comprising Australia, France, the Netherlands, New Zealand, the United Kingdom and the United States. None of the Pacific states, all colonies, was a member, giving the SPC a decidedly white, colonialist look. Still, it was a start. Yet it took twenty-five years for all twenty-two Pacific islands countries and territories to be recognised as full members of the SPC, beginning with Samoa in 1965. And it took a full half-century for the SPC to reconstitute itself as the Pacific Community (PC), with a twenty-six-nation membership – the twenty-two Pacific nations and four of the founding members (the Netherlands and the United Kingdom withdrew in 1962 and 2004, respectively, when their colonial responsibilities ended).

An Australian has held the position of secretary-general/director-general of the SPC/PC four times. But despite the efforts of William Forsyth (who was secretary-general twice), Robert Dun and most recently Stuart Minchin, Australia's role in the organisation has been patchy. Why? The PC has not been accorded sustained strategic and political priority by successive Australian governments. This is due to a lack of policy interest by some governments and ministers, fluctuating development assistance funding, a lack of continuity in development priorities (as if by whim, focus shifts back and forth from direct health and education funding, health worker and teacher education, infrastructure investment, addressing women's and children's disadvantage, institution building, policy advisory services and, of course, interminable consultancies), and Australia's longstanding view that the Pacific is what separates the east coast of Australia from the west coast of the United States. And what clearer indication is there that the Pacific is accorded second-class policy status and importance than the Abbott government's decision to abolish the Australian Agency for International Development (AUSAID), or DFAT's historical practice of overlooking anyone with sustained Pacific experience for promotion to the department's top leadership executive?

Where are we now?

In 2019, according to the World Bank, Australia ranked fourteenth by gross domestic product (GDP), and sixteenth by GDP per capita. If the funds management outliers (Monaco, Liechtenstein, Luxembourg, Bermuda, the Cayman Islands, Macao and the Isle of Man) are excluded, Australia ranked ninth by GDP per capita, after Switzerland, Ireland, Iceland, Singapore, the United States, Qatar, Denmark and the Faroe Islands (which are more about fishing than funds management). By any measure, Australia is a rich and well-endowed country.

In the mid-1970s, Australia spent more than 2 per cent of the federal budget on overseas aid.[25] Yet the generosity that distinguished Australia as an aid donor in earlier decades has given way to parsimony as we transfer official development assistance (ODA) funding allocations to refugee detention centre management and other overseas budget demands. Australia's overseas aid has fallen by almost a third since the Abbott government assumed office in 2013. In 2019–20, Australia's total aid expenditure was just over $4 billion, a fall of nearly $120 million on the previous year, and the sixth consecutive year in which aid funding had been cut in real terms.[26]

Australia's ODA as a percentage of gross national income (GNI) has fallen from 0.32 percent in 2014–15 to an estimated 0.21 per cent in 2019–20. By the end of this decade, ODA's share is estimated to fall to 0.17 per cent.[27] The ANU's Development Policy Centre estimates that aid spending has been cut by 27 per cent since 2012–13.[28]

It is especially sobering to analyse Australia's overseas aid spending as a proportion of Australia's defence spending. The two are rapidly diverging, with the defence spend estimated to reach almost sixteen times that of the aid spend by the end of the present decade. This divergence suggests that, far from having a comprehensive national security policy that incorporates regional human security, we are prepared to trade off regional human security investment in favour of higher defence (as distinct from security) spending. This divergence also suggests a failure on the part of the agencies that assess the regional security environment. There are two critical features of the current regional security environment that, if left unaddressed, will generate exactly the kinds of problems that will be amenable only to military interventions and solutions.

First, the accelerating effects of climate change on the smaller Pacific nations will generate the humanitarian emergencies for which the Australian Defence Force is the only available remedy. And in the absence of any clear plan for the safety and welfare of the communities subject to such threats, what might happen to climate refugees is currently unknown. The eyes of the world will be on Australia and, to a lesser extent, New Zealand. Australia's record on refugee settlement and evident unwillingness to plan for the human security consequences of climate change in the Pacific do not augur well for a constructive outcome.

It is important to recognise the global nature of the rising sea level problem. The Pacific micro-states, especially those that comprise atolls (Kiribati, Tuvalu and the Marshall Islands), are already suffering tidal inundation, and have moved to purchase land in other Pacific states such as Fiji to relocate their populations.[29] Small uninhabited islands in the Solomon Islands archipelago disappeared five years ago.[30] But the micro-states of the Indian Ocean, along with the Andaman and Nicobar, Indonesian and Philippines archipelagos, are also subject to inundation and, consequently, the displacement of local populations. This is compounded by the vulnerability of Bangladesh, Burma and Vietnam to flooding of the great Asian riverine deltas and the displacement of large populations. For Bangladesh and India, which together control the giant Ganges–Brahmaputra–Meghna basin, the risk of global sea-level rise threatens the lives and livelihoods of 200 million people.[31] The world faces a refugee catastrophe by the end of this century.

Second, Papua New Guinea's economic and social problems are both accelerating and deepening. With a current population of just under 9 million that is growing by almost 2 per cent each year, Papua New Guinea will have more than 14 million citizens by 2050.[32] Three-quarters of its population is under thirty-five years of age, and 40 per cent of its population are under the age of fifteen.[33] With some 80–85 per cent of Papua New Guinea's people dependent on subsistence farming and small cash-crop agriculture,[34] the nation's official jobless figures mask high levels of youth unemployment and underemployment. This provides a significant reservoir of popular alienation and disaffection, generating high levels of crime and violence throughout the country. Corruption at senior levels and growing economic inequality render Papua New Guinea increasingly vulnerable to civil unrest.[35] As with the effects of climate change, this may impose challenges for the ADF that a more strategic overseas aid program could mitigate.

The fundamental problem facing Australia's ODA policy is its highly transactional character. Since the abolition of AUSAID and its incorporation into DFAT – a frontal attack on ODA as a key element in Australia's foreign policy – Australia's foreign aid has been framed in terms of 'things to do' rather than 'objectives to be achieved'. Reliance on action-man slogans such as 'Pacific step-up' is indicative of a transactional approach to the development tasks in the Pacific, as distinct from a transformational approach that identifies strategic goals and disciplined priorities. The transactional nature of

Australia's approach to development assistance is further illustrated by the reliance on contractors and subcontractors to undertake both the planning and delivery of programs, the emphasis being on getting the money out the door rather than on the uses to which funding might be put.

Australia's current ODA performance

The policy foundations of Australia's current development assistance program are set out in the 2017 Foreign Policy White Paper.[36] Unsurprisingly, aid policy is relegated to the more marginal part of the white paper, after consideration of Antarctica. Altogether, the white paper is a lengthy meditation on China's growing influence and role in the Pacific, one that reveals heightened concern without being unnecessarily alarmist. But the newfound emphasis on security cooperation and infrastructure funding takes Australian policy in a new direction.[37]

The centrepiece of the new Pacific policy direction is the Australian Infrastructure Financing Facility for the Pacific, a funding mechanism launched by Foreign Minister Marise Payne on 1 July 2019. It describes its role as providing 'financing for transformational energy, water, transport, telecommunications and other projects that are socially inclusive, resilient and create lasting prosperity for Pacific citizens'.[38] It is a four-year financing mechanism that consists of $500 million in grants and $1.5 billion in loans. The loans are non-concessional, so they will not be ODA-eligible and hence will not draw down on the aid budget. The grants will be drawn from the aid budget.

The economies of most small Pacific nations are substantially dependent on remittances from Australia. Accordingly, the aid program encompasses a $70-million Pacific Labour Scheme running until 2022/23. It enables Pacific islands workers to take up unskilled and semi-skilled jobs in rural and regional Australia for periods of up to three years, and extends to citizens of Fiji, Kiribati, Nauru, Papua New Guinea, Samoa, the Solomon Islands, Tonga, Tuvalu, Vanuatu and Timor Leste.

While the Morrison government has maintained aid funding to the Pacific, it has not increased the overall level of ODA. It has actually robbed Peter to pay Paul by cutting development assistance in Asia by almost $120 million. The Australian Parliamentary Library's 2019–20 budget analysis paints a dismal picture.[39]

Non-governmental organisations (NGOs) have sustained their criticism of the government's approach to ODA. Oxfam described the policy as 'blind to [the] dual crises of inequality and climate change ... a selfish, narrow-minded Budget that does nothing to position Australia as a nation which does its fair share in our region, or the world'.[40] The Australian Council for International Development labelled it 'a "strategic blackhole" and a demonstration of the incoherence of [the government's] foreign policy'.[41]

To support its strategic interests in the Pacific, Australia has long invested in a Defence Cooperation Program in the Pacific that focuses on providing law-enforcement capabilities such as patrol boats and personnel training. The ODA program has never managed to sustain a focus on broader strategic issues, which are understandably sidelined by the more immediate demands of health, education and infrastructure. To undertake such a sweeping realignment of the ODA program requires a fundamental change in strategic mindset – a difficult task for a department the principal business of which is diplomacy, itself marginalised by a government that mistakes bluster and slogans for policy. Jonathan Pearlman captured the problem well when he described the government's response to strategic change in the Pacific as a 'pitiful'. He continued:

> Many of the problems that the nation and region face will not be solved by spending measures but by careful, creative diplomacy. This would include handling alliances and partnerships shrewdly, and demonstrating a commitment to active and humane global cooperation that can serve as an international example and ensure that Australia has a credible voice when it demands that other nations do more. Yet, when it comes to funding, the budget

indicates that the government is unwilling to commit to long-term solutions to the challenges it outlined.[42]

The fundamental problem faced by successive Australian governments is that, for all their maudlin and sentimental guff about 'our' Pacific family, they prefer to place short-term budget management interests (such as the fabled 'return to surplus') ahead of long-term political, economic and strategic interests – playing Uncle Scrooge rather than the Ghost of Christmas Present (to strain Charles Dickens' *A Christmas Carol*).

Recalibrating the development assistance program

Australia's development assistance program is presently constructed around a set of confused and conflicting activities and projects. It is a case of 'no-one's in charge and everyone's in charge'. It is what happens when slogans replace policy. Even DFAT's website on the Pacific cannot escape the slogan – Pacific Step-up.[43]

'Pacific Step-up' is itself the linear descendent of a slogan. In 2016, Prime Minister Turnbull coined the expression "step-change" to signal his new Pacific strategy,[44] though "change" was seen by DFAT as discontinuity and accordingly was quickly amended to "step-up". To improve the policy's marketability, Prime Minister Morrison announced the 'Pacific Step-up' as a "new chapter in relations with our Pacific family",[45] thereby providing just enough sentimentality and condescension to signal the triumph of spin over substance. By describing the Pacific as "not just our region, or our neighbourhood", but "our home", Morrison implicitly ties the security of the Pacific community to that of Australia. Whether the nations that comprise the Pacific community welcome the idea that they are living in Australia's "home" is moot. But the ambit of Australia's political claim suggests hubris and hyperbole rather than strategic sensitivity. And the hubris is only heightened by the equally condescending claim that the peoples of the Pacific are "our family". It is nonsense.

It is particularly revealing that Morrison chose to announce his new Pacific 'step-up' at Lavarack Barracks, the home of the Australian Army's 3rd Brigade. The delivery of a major Pacific aid announcement at an ADF base is consistent with the Morrison government's predilection for securitising policy matters to give them a sense of gravity and urgency. The deeper securitisation of Australia's Pacific aid policy means that ODA becomes an instrument of strategic positioning, and aid programs become artefacts of a regional security policy in the traditional sense: the competition between states for position and power. In other words, Australia's approach to development assistance is more a product of raw political interest than it is of cooperating with Pacific nations to enhance their interests.

This, sadly, is consistent with the findings of a recent Pew Research Center report entitled *International Cooperation Welcomed Across 14 Advanced Economies*,[46] which reflects poorly on Australia. While almost 60 per cent of those surveyed in the fourteen most advanced economies thought that their country should take other countries' interests into account when dealing with major international issues (like climate change, aid, global health), almost 60 per cent of Australians thought that Australia should pursue its own interests rather than supporting international compromise. Ominously, this is consistent with the Pew Research Center's comment that, 'in every *European* country surveyed, those with favourable views of right-wing populist parties are much more likely to say their country should follow its own interests even when other nations disagree'.[47]

And, of course, by situating a new Pacific aid policy in a defence and national security context, the prime minister's emphasis on Australia's 'abiding interest in the Southwest Pacific that is secure strategically, stable economically and sovereign politically' (whatever all of that is intended to mean) played the China card without mentioning China.

The centrality of Australia's fear and mistrust of China in the further development of the 'step-up' program was nowhere clearer than in Prime Minister Morrison's address to the Aspen Security Forum in August 2020, where he described the Pacific as 'the epicentre of strategic competition'.[48] That statement has no meaning if it does not comprehend current tensions between the United States and China.

Australia has long sat on the sidelines of the competition between China and Taiwan in the Pacific, happy enough, it would seem, to see Pacific countries test the credibility of the 'one China' policy as they sell diplomatic recognition to the higher bidder, but disconcerted to find China gradually gaining the upper hand, both muscling Taiwan out and cementing new relationships with cash and development assistance projects. And with China now well and truly a player in the South Pacific, Australia is belatedly attempting to limit its access and influence by means of a security-inspired ODA policy. As Graeme Dobell has pointed out, the 2020 Defence Strategic Update mentions the 'step-up' seven times – the same number of times China is named.[49]

The plain fact is, however, that worry as it might about China's growing influence in the Pacific, there is little Australia can do to contain or constrain China. Cash-strapped and poor, the countries of the Pacific will accept money with or without conditions. A competitive relationship with China in the Pacific may make some strategic sense for the United States (though one cannot be sure about that), but it makes no strategic sense for Australia. The economic and military power imbalance, together with the disparity of interests, suggests that Australia may be better advised to pursue a more nuanced and subtle policy in the Pacific that plays to Australia's strengths rather than to China's. Should China wish to outspend Australia in the Pacific, it probably can. And should it want to outmuscle Australia in the Pacific, it certainly can.

So, where does Australia have comparative advantage in the Pacific, if not in cash and weaponry? The answer is: almost everywhere else.

First and foremost, as the leading aid donor in the Pacific, Australia enjoys considerable agency, authority and legitimacy in the realisation of its interests in the Pacific. And as a thriving and prosperous democracy in a community that needs leadership, Australia is well positioned to take on a leadership role – on the basis, of course, of consultation, respect and transparency. With so many disconnected and competing programs underway in the Pacific, an early initiative for Australia to consider would be to propose improved coordination and planning among the major donors.

And that certainly includes China. Rather than seeking to constrain or contain China, Australia would be better advised to encourage China into habits of cooperation that are easier, cheaper and more effective than competition. China may well be attempting to expand its strategic influence in the Pacific. But it needs to recognise that influence is a consequence of cooperation and collaboration, not a cause of development. So, instead of contesting China's wish for influence, Australia should seek to guide it. Australia should also be aware that China's exercise of influence faces substantial obstacles in the Pacific. As a communist country in a largely evangelical Christian Pacific community, China's values are not shared, and the Pacific's experience of Chinese entrepreneurialism has not always been a happy one. Consequently, trust is in short supply. Without common ground and trust, influence is difficult to exercise.

To this end, it would suit Australia's purposes in the Pacific to convene a broad-based Pacific Donors' Conference, bringing together the major ODA donors to align and coordinate programs and projects. It would certainly play to the preference of Pacific countries for collaborative problem solving, at the same time enhancing accountability on the part of both donors and recipients. Unsurprisingly, when this proposal was put to DFAT, it was unable to say whether it supported the annual convening of a donor experts conference. Rather, all it could do was to fall back on the annual Pacific Leaders' Conference ritual, 'which brings together Pacific leaders including our Prime Minister'.[50] Development problems in the Pacific will not be resolved through political talk-fests. Rather, the professional involvement of experts is needed.

Second, Australia has a history of mostly constructive engagement with the nations of the Pacific, especially since the end of World War II. While, for the past two decades, the effectiveness of Australia's development assistance programs has flatlined, and political relations have had their ups and downs, especially with Fiji, Australia has for the most part been a good neighbour. Due in part to the British colonial legacy and the British Commonwealth, Australia's values are largely consistent with those of the Pacific nations and, outbursts of arrogance and condescension notwithstanding, Australians are largely welcome in the Pacific and generally trusted.

But if Australia is to capitalise on its natural political advantage in the Pacific, it must eschew one of the few constants in its approach to the nations of the Pacific: mixed messaging. We seem to have a natural propensity to speak out of both sides of our mouth, talking 'family' and 'step-up' at one moment, then announcing an exclusive and decidedly 'white' security partnership, AUKUS, at the next – a throwback to the imperialist and colonialist habits of the past. AUKUS is an unwelcome development in the Pacific. As the president of Kiribati, Taneti Maamau, has said:

> [AUKUS] puts the region at risk and raises some troubling memories. The people of Kiribati recall when the UK and US tested nuclear weapons there. Then the islands were part of colonial Britain and between 1957 and 1962 more than 30 nuclear tests were carried out. Our people were victims of nuclear testing ... we still have trauma ... with that in mind, with anything to do with nuclear, we thought it would be a courtesy to raise it, to discuss it with your neighbours.[51]

Australia must conduct a much more calibrated and considered policy in the Pacific if it is to allay the fears and suspicions of its neighbours.

Third, many of the inhabitants of the Pacific, especially the young, would, if Australian laws so permitted, migrate to Australia. Australia is a popular destination, and the opportunity to provide remittances to their families and villages is a strong inducement for many to avail themselves of the Pacific Labour Scheme and the Seasonal Worker Program. Labour mobility is a strategic asset that is not currently available to China, but one that Australia needs to refine and improve if it is to derive the relationship advantages and economic effects that the programs could deliver.[52] Education and training in Australia (and New Zealand) also provide strategic opportunities for the Pacific nations.

The medical services available to the nations of the Pacific are well below an acceptable international standard and are chronically under-resourced. Refugees housed in Australia's offshore detention centres enjoy higher standards of medical care than many Pacific islanders, yet even they need to be transferred to Australian hospitals for medical issues requiring treatment. Broadening accessibility to Australian (and New Zealand) medical services to the peoples of the Pacific is a high priority, at least until adequate services are available locally. To some it may appear cynical to use a term like 'family' when parsimony prevents any display of care, compassion or kindness.

The welfare systems that Australians enjoy are absent in most of the Pacific. Yet if Australia's 'step-up' is to be anything more than 'tough love', we need to discover avenues for improving the long-term health outcomes of the peoples of the Pacific. This, in turn, demands a change in our development assistance mindset, from scattered transactions to targeted transformation. The question is: how do we do that?

The key to transformation: Human security

If the global community has learned anything from its experience with the coronavirus, it is this: human security is fragile. It the citizen cannot be safe, the nation cannot be safe. Yet the jostling for position and power in the Pacific does not deliver human security for the peoples of the Pacific. To the contrary, power competition undermines the wellbeing and security of the peoples of the Pacific because it distracts attention from key health, education and economic issues, and subtracts from the funding levels available for non-defence investment. Remember, the ratio between Australia's defence and development assistance spending is trending to 16:1.

In April 2020, I released a discussion paper entitled *Re-thinking National Security in the Age of Pandemics and Climate Change Catastrophe*.[53] In it, I argued that social inclusion, the protection of rights, the promotion of values and resilience – all of them supported by a strong economic base – are fundamental elements of security policy. In a way, this turns conventional security thinking on its head: far from being the starting point for any consideration of human wellbeing, happiness and security, the security of the state is a consequence of social harmony, happiness, inclusion and wellbeing.

As we have seen, terms like 'Pacific step-up' and 'Pacific family' may represent a measure of rhetorical flourish. But unless they intend outcomes that are properly strategic and transformational, they are merely sanctimonious labels for the kinds of transactional programs that have left the Pacific where it currently is: poor and disconnected. As an objective describing a long-term development strategy for the Pacific, human security goes to the heart of the Pacific's problems – economic, physical, political and social. Climate change, economic collapse due to the pandemic, declining health standards among women and children, poor educational outcomes – each of these is a pressing human security matter.

A human security mindset would reform Australia's ODA policy in fundamental ways. Not only would it provide the key to improved coordination among the major donors, but it would also create innovative ways of addressing the consequences of absent health and social security measures. For example, while continuing to invest in preventive medical programs and medical extension services, Australia could consider admitting those Pacific communities that are without a basic level of healthcare to Australia's Medicare program for life-saving medical procedures. And lest anyone think that this would be prohibitively expensive, just remember that 16:1 ratio of defence spending to aid spending.

For many Australians, it is a matter of national shame that the medical infrastructure of Papua New Guinea is so precarious, and that the basic medical procedures that Australians take for granted – oncological services, for example – are inaccessible to most Papua New Guineans. The same applies to dialysis, diabetes treatments and basic obstetric services. And while the shortfalls are massive, and cannot be rectified overnight, a targeted approach in conjunction with other major donors offers some hope of improvement, especially if enhanced child health and welfare are also prioritised.

It is time to dispense with platitudes. It is time to address the core issues affecting the wellbeing of the peoples of the Asia-Pacific region. And this means not only coming to terms with Australia's place in the Pacific, but also establishing where we fit with Asia, and where Asia fits with us.

6
Asia Incognita

Asia is the place you fly over on the way to Europe.

Misattributed to Paul Keating
by Bob Hawke in *The Hawke Memoirs*

Australia knows little about Asia and appreciates it even less. It is as though we look at Asia through trick binoculars, one side the telescope of apprehension and the other side the microscope of anxiety. Our fears are enlarged while our stress points are revealed in intricate detail. What we see is confused, distorted and confronting. It is little wonder that we deal with the incomprehensibility of Asia by resorting to a standard default position: look the other way, reach for the dog whistle of race, drum up a bit of fear and deny that we have a problem. Some of our best friends are Asian, of course! That approach is, after all, well-practised. It is how Australia has dealt with the country's Indigenous heritage, the ecological uniqueness of the continent, and the inability of the immigrant majority to come to terms with its own 'whiteness' in a nation that is increasingly diverse and multicultural.

The White Australia policy was, in important ways, the most significant of the colonial legacies, deeply etched in the mindset of the early Federation and resonating still in the latent racism that informs Australian attitudes. Well into the twentieth century, many young Australians grew up memorising the imperialistic, soppy lines of Rudyard Kipling – poems such as 'If' and 'The Road to Mandalay'. It was doggerel like this that was printed, framed and hung on the walls of Australian classrooms, reminding us as children of the 'White Man's Burden' (another Kipling poem) – brown people, 'sullen peoples, half-devil and half-child'. It also served to cement the superiority that always accompanies racial dominance, whether it is white

Anglo-Saxon dominance in Australia or ethnic Han dominance in China. And lest there be any mistake, China's current resurgence and determination to redress what it calls the 'century of humiliation' at the hands of various Western powers reveals strong ethnic and racial overtones. 'A Song of the White Men' is a Kipling poem first published in 1899; it decorated a classroom wall at the school I attended in Brisbane in 1951. We were required to recite it by heart.

> Now, this is the cup the White Men drink
> When they go to right a wrong,
> And this is the cup of the old world's hate –
> Cruel and strained and strong.
> We have drunk that cup – and a bitter, bitter cup –
> And tossed the dregs away.
> But well for the world when the White Men drink
> To the dawn of the White Man's day!
>
> Now, this is the road that the White Men tread
> When they go to clean a land –
> Iron underfoot and levin[1] overhead
> And the deep on either hand.
> We have trod that road – and a wet and windy road –
> Our chosen star for guide.
> Oh, well for the world when the White Men tread
> Their highway side by side!
>
> Now, this is the faith the White Men hold
> When they build their homes afar –
> 'Freedom for ourselves and freedom for our sons
> And, failing freedom, War.'
> We have proved our faith – bear witness to our faith,
> Dear souls of freemen slain!
> Oh, well for the world when the White Men join
> To prove their faith again.

Far from simply extolling racist triumphalism, these lines are emblematic of the arrogant and superior stance adopted for instance by *The Bulletin* in its early years, as noted when we looked at Australia's historical problems with China. But identification with the Anglophone world and feelings of racial superiority do not explain Australia's disdain for and disengagement from Asia. It runs far deeper than that. It stems from a fear of difference, an inability to come to terms with deep cultural 'otherness' often revealed in 'culture shock', customs that seem confronting – the *Naga Sadhus* in India, the amplified pre-dawn call to prayer in Muslim countries, unusual foods such as toads in China, dog soup in Korea or duck embryos in the Philippines, or public theatre such as the *wayang* in Indonesia or *khon* dancing in Thailand.

Until World War II, as we have seen, much of Australia's diplomacy in Asia was conducted by British diplomats, with little official or formal contact between the Australian government and the non-colonial governments of Asia. Much like the Pacific, Asia was for adventurers and eccentrics. Serious Australians went to Britain. For most of the twentieth century, Australians felt comfortable in Britain. The British spoke the same language, ate the same food, played the same sports, listened to the same music, went to the same churches and delivered just the right amount of condescension. The landscape conformed with the picture books and Dorothea Mackellar's 'love of field and coppice, of green and shaded lanes'. The feelings of alienation in an alien land felt by most immigrant Australians were assuaged in Britain, but exacerbated in Asia.

If Asia excited anything, it was 'greed and fear', as Prime Minister Abbott put it. While Japan waged its undeclared war in China in the late 1930s, Australia continued to export pig iron and scrap to Japanese steel mills. This eventually led to the SS *Dalfram* dispute in November 1938, when waterside workers walked off the job in Port Kembla. The attorney-general in the Lyons government, Robert Menzies, intervened. The issue was finally resolved after a ten-week strike with the assurance that no more pig iron would be sent to Japan. But the affair earned Menzies the nickname 'Pig Iron Bob', a sobriquet he retained well into the 1950s.[2]

World War II confirmed the suspicion that Asia was a dangerous place, home to wars and warlike people. Japan's defeat of Malaya and Singapore, its occupation of Indochina, Burma, Thailand, the Philippines and Indonesia, and the atrocities committed against both civilians and combatants reinforced this view. And the fact that some people in South-East Asia, mostly under duress, collaborated with the Japanese further cemented Australian views of the peoples of Asia as reeds bending to the prevailing wind. In the post–World War II years, the processes of decolonisation did nothing to change the overall impression of instability and anti-imperial agitation. Nationalist political movements were dubbed 'communist', lazily misrepresenting Asian nationalism as a facsimile of Eastern European communism. Indonesia's quest for independence from the Dutch, the Malayan insurgency, the anti-French movement in Vietnam (leading inexorably to the Vietnam War), the Korean War, the Huk insurgency in the Philippines, military coups in Burma and Thailand, and President Suharto's post-1965 autocracy in Indonesia all confirmed Australia's anxiety and apprehension towards Asia.

How to think about Asia

Geopolitical analysis is a way of interpreting the relationships between neighbouring and regional states through the lenses of geography, history and culture, as well as day-to-day political, economic and strategic events.[3] It helps economic and foreign policy analysts, defence and security planners and strategic commentators to track the shifting sands of international relationships and alignments both to build understanding and to reduce the scope for misapprehension and misadventure. Geopolitics is what happens behind the 'arras' that is the shimmer and distraction at the surface of the twenty-four-hour news cycle.

History has shaped the geopolitical contours of Asia. Yet most Australians, indeed most Westerners, know little of the political and cultural history of Asia, least of all South-East Asia. The geopolitical contours of Asia have evolved significantly since the end of World

War II, with decolonisation and the quest for a defined national identity being key drivers. The historical ability of most South-East Asian nations to assimilate diverse ethnic groups and, generally, to accommodate racial diversity also provides a singular dimension to the geopolitics of the South-East Asian region. And even in South and North Asia, cultural and racial accommodation are the more typical consequences of economic and political expansion, periodic instances of armed conflict notwithstanding. The Cold War gave rise to several assumptions about the geopolitics of Asia. Some continue to colour Western, particularly American, understandings of the political dynamics of Asia. Concepts of the 'red menace', 'yellow peril' and 'domino theory' underpinned the formation of the Southeast Asia Treaty Organization, which ultimately fizzled, and the disastrous US foray into Vietnam.

Any overview of the currents and trends that have distinguished the political and cultural history of South-East Asia, particularly the members of the Association of Southeast Asian Nations (ASEAN), risks stereotypes, reductionism and oversimplification. Instances abound of the exceptions that prove the rule: individuals are always able to ignore cultural, political and social conventions, and do. But ignorance doesn't validate error. Noting these risks, however, it is possible to discern, at least broadly, six consistent themes in the geopolitical dynamics of South-East Asia. These are different in significant ways from 'Western' conventions. Yet while they do not constitute a single or singular 'Asian' way of international relationship management, they are, in various combinations, evident in how that South-East Asian countries deal with one another, and with China (and to a lesser extent India). As vectors of South-East Asian social coordination, they intersect in surprising ways. The six themes are:

- An acceptance of diversity.
- A tendency towards harmony and inclusion, manifest in the Javanese practice of communal cooperation (*gotong-royong*), notwithstanding sporadic outbursts of inter-communal conflict.

- A general tolerance towards and acceptance of differences in religious belief and practice, not to be confused with syncretism, except where difference can be exploited for political advantage, as it has been in Myanmar.

- For those countries that derive from the Buddhist tradition, a deep cultural acceptance of the doctrine of non-injury (*ahiṃsā*), which manifests itself in a practice of neither hurting nor being hurt (bearing in mind the preceding caveat).

- A preference for consultation and consensus for problem solving and the maintenance of communal harmony (*musyawara* [conversation] and *mufakat* [agreement], in Indonesia and Malaysia).

- A deep and subtle appreciation of the cultural and political dynamics of accommodation (as distinct from the Western concept of appeasement).

Many Western commentators, educated in the more muscular and less conciliatory Western tradition of logical binaries and confrontation, dismiss the Asian approach as appeasement, compromise, vacillation and weakness.[4] Yet modern Asian nation-states – China, Japan and Korea in North Asia, and Vietnam, Cambodia, Laos, Thailand, Myanmar and Indonesia in South-East Asia – are the identifiable successors (even in name, in some cases) of political entities that pre-existed most modern European states, sometimes by a millennium. Their endurance and longevity reflect, to some extent at least, the dynamics of their geopolitical culture. That is not to be dismissed offhandedly, especially when disparagement is due to arrogance and incomprehension.

Acceptance of diversity

Tribal groups, generally identified by language and culture, have ebbed and flowed across Asia since prehistoric times. It is important, however, to recognise that the term 'race' has an extensive Western usage, bringing with it largely Western preconceptions of 'otherness'. It is a less traditional descriptor of difference between people in Asian countries. 'Race' and 'ethnicity', as linguistic tools for categorising and classifying people, have a relatively short history, and are essentially cultural and political artefacts of European exploration and colonisation dating from the fifteenth century CE. Indeed, it was not until the second half of the seventeenth century CE that François Bernier gave wider currency to the term 'race'.[5] The superficial phenomena that are generally used to describe 'race' – skin colour, eye shape, hair types, facial features, physical taxonomy and 'phenotypes' – have no genetic or biological validity.[6] Rather than describing and identifying people, 'race' is a term that divides and stratifies. And that was how colonising powers employed racial classification politically.

In classical Indian societies of the pre-Christian period, for instance, people were classified according to birth (*jāti*) and colour (*varna*), terms that are both translated as 'caste'. Because the concept of 'race' was foreign to classical Indian thought, there are many Sanskrit words (for example, *abhijana, gotra, nidhana, upajātiḥ*) that can be translated as 'race', though their meaning, both by derivation and by usage, is significantly more local and restricted than the term 'race' would suggest.

Similarly, its lexicographical richness notwithstanding, Mandarin does not recognise the concept of race. Many names are used to describe non-Chinese people, and they are often derogatory. The specific names for various minority groups generally had an uncomplimentary radical (the semantic element, as distinct from the phonetic, in the relevant character) attached to them, such as 'snake' or 'dog' or, in the case of the Japanese, 'dwarf'. Following the Opium Wars, this was a practice that the British insisted that the Chinese discontinue – yet another grievance contributing to the 'century of humiliation'.[7]

In modern-day Indonesia and Malaysia, the term 'race' is variously translated as *orang* ('man'), *bangsa* ('tribe' or 'nation'), *kaum* ('group' or 'tribe'), *keluarga* ('family' or 'kin') or *masyarakat* ('community'). Even the word 'international' fails in translation, mainly because 'nation' and 'race' become conflated: *antarabangsa*, which was formerly used in Indonesia, has given way to *internasional* in common usage.

The point that needs to be understood here is that diversity among peoples in Asia is not seen through the lens of 'race', as the term is understood in the West, but much more through the joint lenses of language, cultural and credal practices, and habit – what in Malaysia is called *adat*. Diversity was less about difference than it was about identification: where one comes from, one's family, one's history, one's religious beliefs and cultural practices. This is not to suggest that issues of communal ascendancy, cultural superiority and customary dominance (meaning that one group exercises primacy with respect to communal customs) are not commonplace. They are, right across Asia. The important thing is that they coexist, whether it is Parsee custom coexisting with Hinduism in Mumbai, the animistic elements of Javanese court custom accommodating Islam in Central Java (or vice versa, in the *abangan* form of Indonesian Islam) or Singapore's pluralism in celebrating the festivals of all its constituent communities.

Interactions between peoples became progressively denser and more frequent during the past two millennia, resulting in what the West would see as extensive transcultural blending. Group identity, however, was maintained through language and cultural adaptation, while 'national' identity (in the Western sense) was progressively forged through a common language (the lingua franca!), the preservation of cultural artefacts and practice, music and dance, and above all the inclusive representation of diversity in the conduct of national pageantry and rituals. Symbolism is a powerful tool in Asia that at once maintains diversity and creates unity.

There are many examples of transculturation across Asia. One of the more interesting is evidenced by the Peranakan people of Sumatra, the Malay Peninsula, southern Thailand and parts of the Indonesian archipelago. They are the descendants of waves of migrants from southern China arriving between the fifteenth and seventeenth centuries CE, following the Ming emperor's reopening of trade links in South-East Asia. These immigrants intermarried with the local Malay groups, giving rise to distinctive housing styles, cultural forms and cuisine (commonly described as *nyonya* in Malaysia and Singapore). The first prime minister of Singapore, Lee Kuan Yew, was of Peranakan descent.

While the acceptance of diversity might have been the default position of South-East Asian communities, communal harmony could and did break down from time to time. Communal discord was more often a product of economic inequality, political difference and the perennial problem of land rights and land reform. Until the postcolonial period, it was rarely a consequence of racism.

Inclusion

Intra- and inter-communal harmony and inclusion have long been practised in South-East Asia. For many generations, people have been able to maintain communal harmony, preserving their cultural and linguistic identity while speaking a common language (usually the language of the culturally dominant community, or a simplified 'market' [*pasar*], pidgin or creole language). In the centuries before European colonisation, immigrant communities tended to assimilate into local communities, sometimes maintaining their cultural and linguistic identity and sometimes not. But so long as there was mutual advantage – usually economic – harmony was maintained and patterns of inclusion, if not of assimilation and integration, prevailed.

Generally, the European colonial administrations tended to maintain racial separation as a 'divide and rule' tactic to maintain a firm hold on power: better to have the separate racial groups worrying about each other than worrying about the coloniser! As Kua Kia Soong has written:

> Racism and racial politics came about during British colonial rule. In the circumstances of the time, it suited British colonialism to legitimise their dominance by a divide and rule strategy that viewed

minorities as 'non-indigenous' (or 'immigrants') who required assimilation. It was also the strategy of the colonial power to segregate the various ethnic groups according to both occupation and domicile.[8]

During British, Dutch and French rule in South-East Asia, there was remarkably little inter-communal tension reported. The colonisers in the eighteenth-century Dutch East Indies encouraged substantial immigration from southern China to provide labour for the sugar mills and coffee plantations, and, like the British in Malaya in the nineteenth century, practised racial separation as a means of social and political control. Marc Rerceretnam summarises this practice succinctly: 'Colonial governments cleverly worked on separating the interests of local Asian communities to ensure their grip on power.'[9]

There were incidents that have been variously described as 'race riots', such as the insurrection by Chinese mill labourers in Batavia (modern-day Jakarta) in 1740. This was in fact less about 'race' than it was about changing labour conditions in the wake of a slump in the sugar price, leading the Dutch troops in Batavia to suppress worker demonstrations with maximum force, slaughtering upwards of 10,000 Chinese workers. The Dutch governor was subsequently recalled to The Hague, where he was charged with crimes related to the massacre.

But as South-East Asia decolonised, 'race' in the Western sense became both a political and economic rallying point, leading to a breakdown of the traditional acceptance and inclusion that had long distinguished social practice in the region. The rise of Islam-inspired nationalism during Sukarno's presidency saw the introduction of anti-Chinese legislation and, tragically, the slaughter of many ethnic Chinese citizens in the wake of the 1965 Thirtieth of September Movement (*Gestapu*), an abortive coup d'état. Similarly, the race riots of 13 May 1969 in Kuala Lumpur led to the suspension of the Malaysian parliament and direct rule by the National Operations Council from 1969 to 1971. It also precipitated the resignation of Malaysia's first prime minister, Tunku Abdul Rahman, his succession by Tun Razak, and the introduction of clear economic preferences for the Malay community under the New Economic Policy.

The imposition of Western concepts of race resulting from colonial rule in South-East Asia continues to affect the conduct of political discourse, where race-based political parties and governments exploit confected racial sensitivities for political purposes. This is nowhere clearer than in the political manipulation of the 'overseas Chinese' question. Permeating much Western consideration of the geopolitics of South-East Asia has been the belief that historical Chinese migration created a 'fifth column' that opened the gates to subversion throughout South-East Asia by the People's Republic of China.[10] While that assumption has been largely discredited, it continues to inform the commentary of the more nationalistic commentators throughout South-East Asia and the more ideological commentators in Australia and the United States.[11] Given China's growing importance as a regional and global power, this is understandable. It is also wrong. The default inter-communal disposition remains one of inclusion, as the formation of new political groups and parties (extending across various communities) demonstrates, and as the effects of transculturation practices slowly take hold.

China's continuing influence in and over the region, however, is part of the geopolitical fabric of North and South-East Asia. How the nations of Asia accommodate ethnic, racial and religious diversity offers some insight into the future geopolitics of a region on which Australia's economic, political and strategic future depends.

Tolerance

As with ethnicity and race, so with religion: Western views are often an artefact of Western historical experience and philosophical mindset. Lindsay Falvey puts the problem well:

> Religious and scholarly studies about the region often reflect a narrow Western understanding that imagines religion to be separable from other aspects of life. Such a concept of secularity in personal life or politics is alien to regional worldviews ... Western works continue to define Confucianism as a moral philosophy, yet

> its origins and its continuing serious practice treat the secular as sacred ... A further example ... is an apparent Western refusal to acknowledge the indissolubility of religion and governance in Islam.[12]

Belief systems and religions have coexisted peacefully across Asia for millennia. Buddhist and Hindu cults have lived side by side, sometimes adopting local practices syncretically (as Christianity did in Europe, adopting fertility rituals and 'Christianising' various Germanic gods and goddesses such as Eostre – thereby giving us Easter), sometimes merging and sometimes representing themselves as defiantly separate. The great Buddhist temple at Borobudur (Central Java), dating from the Sailendra period (ninth century CE) was constructed at the same time as the remarkable Hindu temple at Prambanan, barely 50 kilometres away, dating from the Sanjaya dynasty. And Bali remains Hindu to this day.

The ancient belief systems of Asia coalesced around animism, remnants of which continue to inhere in the practice of the 'imported' religions – Hinduism, Buddhism, Islam, Sikhism and Christianity – as they do in the practice of Confucianism and Taoism. Indonesia, for instance, has long promoted a kind of syncretic mysticism called *Kejawèn* or *Kebatinan*, a blend of Buddhist, Hindu and animist beliefs and practices overlaid with the observance of Islamic rituals, especially in Java. President Suharto was particularly drawn to Javanese mysticism as he sought to legitimise his presidency through association with the royal courts (*kratons*) of Central Java. But the heterodox or syncretic (*abangan*) form of Islam continues to coexist with the orthodox (*santri*) tradition, especially outside the large population centres.[13]

In recent decades, Wahhabism – a fundamentalist form of orthodox Islam sponsored by Saudi Arabia – has slowly infiltrated the practice of Islam in Indonesia and Malaysia, replacing a broad-based tradition of tolerance with a more 'fundamentalist' form of Islam. Whereas Islam is the established religion of Malaysia, Indonesia is constitutionally a secular state, though the Pancasila (the 'Five Principles' – the constitutionally expressed state values of Indonesia) prescribes 'belief in the one and only God', though quite how Hinduism meets this criterion is moot. Six religions are afforded constitutional recognition – Islam, Protestantism (Christianity), Roman Catholicism, Buddhism, Hinduism and Confucianism. Judaism is tolerated. Atheists, however, are commonly regarded as weird (*aneh*) and evil (*jahat*).

While Indonesia and Malaysia are largely tolerant of the non-Islamic religions, including Judaism (there is a synagogue in Penang and another in Manado), and there are institutions that encourage inter-faith dialogue, sectarian violence occasionally manifests itself when political and economic differences between ethnic communities are inflamed. The governments of Indonesia and Malaysia, however, have demonstrated concern at the exploitation of youth groups, often uneducated and unemployed, by fundamentalist Islamic preachers and political extremists. In 2002, Singapore asked the United Nations to add Jemaah Islamiyah (JI, an Indonesian Islamic activist group) to its list of terrorist organisations.

Traditional Buddhist tolerance of other religions is under stress in Myanmar, as the Tatmadaw military forces continue to suppress the political activities of the Rohingya peoples on the Bangladesh border and forcibly expel them from Burmese territory. There is no doubt that the Rohingya are subject to a form of ethnic cleansing under the guise of 'counterterrorist operations'. But the underlying issues are essentially political rather than racial.

The origins of the problem are twofold. First, substantial numbers of people from modern-day Bangladesh (previously East Pakistan and British India) migrated into north-western Burma in the late nineteenth and early twentieth centuries, and, as with migrations from Tamil Nadu to Malaya, immigrants were undocumented and unregistered. Second, there was a deep political schism between the Rohingya and Buddhist communities in north-western Burma during World War II, when the Rohingya supported and fought with the British forces, while the Buddhist Burmese tended to be collaborationist, supporting and fighting with the Japanese forces (driven partly by the beginnings of anti-British decolonisation sentiments). So the Rohingya have sought political autonomy within Myanmar (as a minimum) or, more generally, political independence and the creation of an independent state. Various Rohingya military and paramilitary organisations have formed over the past seven decades, having been more recently infiltrated by Islamic extremist organisations. The problem has become intractable, and the outlook for the Rohingya people is bleak.

Not harming, and staying out of harm's way (*ahiṃsā*)

It is not the purpose of this book to explore the ethical or philosophical bases of Buddhism, any more than it is to evaluate the Golden Rule (act towards other people as you would have them act towards you) or Kant's 'categorical imperative' (act as you would have all other people act towards all other people). Suffice it to say that violence and war is endemic to all societies, whatever their ethical and moral foundations, and that all societies grapple with the fact of defence and offence as intrinsic elements of the art of war.

In Buddhist societies, the default position is *ahiṃsā*, the avoidance of harm, and consequently the avoidance of war. This contrasts with many other societies, including Christian societies, where the sanctity of human life and 'thou shalt not kill' is tempered by the casuistry and legalism of the 'just war' theory, whereby offensive action in pursuit of a higher good[14] is as defensible as protective action against an aggressor.[15] The Buddhist tradition, far from being blind to armed conflict and its causes, emphasises the avoidance of war and the renunciation of violence as a means of acquiring power, not of defence against armed aggression. Nor is it pacifism, the repudiation of violence as intrinsically immoral. Rather, *ahiṃsā* is the recognition that dependence on violence or the threat of violence will fail in the long term because it generates a self-perpetuating cycle where injury and suffering eventually force the combatants to desist. It offers an ethical alternative to annihilation in a philosophical framework that transcends the binaries of peace and war, victory and defeat, power and servitude to advocate a world the elements of which are synthesised into a harmonious resolution that creates mutual advantage – much like the 'win-win' strategies of contemporary management theory.

Ahiṃsā is an ideal that informs the fundamental statecraft of Buddhist societies and governments. While, as a principle, it is inviolable, it is evidently ignored when circumstances appear to warrant military action. Of course, governments that are ostensibly Buddhist, such as those of Cambodia, Laos, Myanmar and Thailand, are not alone in acting against their intrinsic values from time to time. The covert actions of great powers, extending to extra-legal operations and extrajudicial assassinations, bear witness to that fact. But the underlying fact is that *ahiṃsā* informs the governmental culture of Buddhist leaders and Buddhist governments. As Lindsay Falvey puts it:

> The regional concept of harmony or conflict avoidance may also be interpreted in practical terms, such as avoidance of possible personal harm from taking a contentious position. This observation is supported by the distinction between Southeast Asian societies continuing to operate according to customary law, while Westernized societies rely on statutory law ... The difference is often described in terms of face in regional languages.[16]

Customary law, also called consuetudinary law, derives from social practice and agreed behavioural norms. As the term 'consuetudinary' suggests, communities habituate themselves to social behaviours that establish tradition, whether expressed in oral histories, folklore or storytelling, that consolidates values, norms and codes (such as rules of consanguinity). The effect of customary law and tradition is the maintenance of social harmony and stability – the state of *ahiṃsā*.

Community consultation and consensus building

If *ahiṃsā* is the main goal of a peaceful society, consensus building is the instrument that delivers it. Asian societies have long practised community consultation and collaboration as a central means of maintaining harmony and resilience. From Thailand to the Philippines, from Indonesia to Indochina, community consultation remains a basic tool in public administration and national governance, even if the results are often less than the community might have desired. Of course, the experience of colonialism and the arrival of the mass media have had an impact on traditional ways of doing business. And central governments have tended to become more dominant, not to say autocratic. Yet engagement with and by the community remains pivotal to the management of any form of national consensus. At the same time, community consultation and the consensus formed are subject to considerations of social hierarchy, status and elites.[17]

Social organisation and dynamics in Thailand are subject to *krengjai* – literally, the fear of giving offence. When added to a general preference for collectivism and the avoidance of uncertainty, *krengjai* might appear to be a formula for conservatism and social stasis. In fact, however, Thai social organisation remains remarkably dynamic, reflecting an apparent paradox embedded in *krengjai*: it operates up and down the social hierarchy, with individuals retaining agency through their ability to create social indebtedness and to exploit the management of 'face'.

The operation of conversation (*musyawarah*) and consensus (*mufakat*) in Indonesia and Malaysia has been well documented. As Citra Anggita and Tsuyoshi Hatori explain:

> Musyawarah and Mufakat (deliberation and consensus) are a customary basic decision-making procedure in Indonesia, which has regularly been recognized in village gatherings. Musyawarah Mufakat terms (together with terms Koperasi and Gotong Royong) has to do with the obligations of the individual toward the community, the compatibility of power, and the relation of state authority to traditional social and political systems.[18]

In Indonesia, theorists are grappling with the relationship between the deliberative approach of traditional Indonesian decision-making and the more adversarial and argumentative approach that informs modern democratic practice. Indeed, some Indonesian thinkers see the more overtly democratic form of national decision-making that has characterised the post-Suharto era as a logical evolution of traditional Indonesian approaches to consultation and consensus-building. Of course, the arrival of political parties, political campaigning, media manipulation and political corruption does not sit well with the less combative style of traditional Indonesian policymaking. Yet *musyawarah* and *mufakat* are the necessary precursors of South-East Asia's forms of democracy.[19]

The place of consultation and consensus within the broader ASEAN organisation was elegantly expressed by the Sultan of Perak (Malaysia) in his address to the ASEAN–Australia Dialogue in 2018:

> ASEAN's culture of peace-building also draws inspiration from the Indonesian principles of *musyawarah* (consultation) and *muafakat* (consensus). These indigenous principles have become ASEAN's own. The emphasis is thus on mutual consultation and consensus building as the preferred methods for managing disputes and moderating differences. This has made a preference for pacific and consultative approaches to peace-building, rather than adversarial approaches, a distinct characteristic of ASEAN's response to conflicts in the region.
>
> ASEAN members view security as being comprehensive in nature. It covers domestic and external threats, along with challenges to security of the person, society, economy, state and environment. Long before the term 'non-traditional security' was added to the lexicon of security, to cover the so-called 'new' threats such as terrorism and piracy, it was already a part of the comprehensive security perspective of the ASEAN countries. Terrorism or piracy is not something new to them. Many of them lived with terrorism for many decades in the last century. Piracy is ancient.[20]

The Sultan might have added that the communities and civilisations of South-East Asia have been practising collective approaches to development, prosperity and security for centuries. And, in what might have been a subtle shot across the bows of the United States and its allies (including Australia), the Sultan added:

> I am sure that ASEAN's approach is not perfect, and nor will it be able to solve all problems quickly and neatly. But it is far preferable to coercive diplomacy, and hasty resort to military force. The latter has only brought utter destruction and profound misery, at colossal cost, to other parts of the world.[21]

The ASEAN member countries are sensitive to accusations that their association is little more than a 'talk shop', a 'toothless tiger' or a 'road to nowhere'.[22] Yet, as a multi-level forum for discussion, including discussion with external parties (such as the ASEAN Regional Forum provides), the association is a critical component of South-East Asia's way of doing business. Indeed, the habit of consultation and conversation offers a critical method for issue and problem resolution in a time of disruption and uncertainty.[23] Even if concrete results are difficult to negotiate, the fact that foreign ministers are in the same place discussing the same things is a necessary precursor to action. Impetuosity is less the enemy of patience than it is the enemy of progress.

Accommodation, not appeasement

For over two millennia, Asian communities, states and empires have developed an across-border (or in contemporary parlance, international) statecraft that has simultaneously maintained their independence and identity while at the same time it acknowledged the authority and status of a powerful neighbour. The patterns of accommodation reflect varying engagement strategies, ranging from the exchange of envoys, the creation and maintenance of military forces (usually through a levy system), the engagement of proxies, collaboration with neighbours to provide a united front to the payment of tribute – or a mix of each. The so-called 'tribute system' – itself a Western description of a distinctly Confucian approach to legitimacy and alignment – was not a form of taxation or the exaction of dues, but rather a form of mutual legitimisation, cultural alignment and trade facilitation. In most cases, tribute took the form of gifts from foreign rulers to the emperor of China. The gifts often included precious stones, rare birds and animals, as well as people such as dancers, cooks, concubines and courtesans, and eunuchs – some of whom rose to high office – to attend upon the emperor.

It is incorrect to view the Chinese tributary system as the creation of vassal states – or political subordination to the emperor by foreign rulers. There was much political display and theatre in the conduct of official relations with the Chinese court. Often, the gifts provided in return by the emperor to the tribute-bearing envoys significantly exceeded the value of the gifts given to the emperor, thereby reinforcing his superior status. At the heart of the tribute system was a particularly Asian approach to mutual accommodation. In return for a foreign leader's acknowledgement of the legitimacy of the Chinese emperor and the primacy of Chinese culture, the emperor recognised the political legitimacy of the foreign ruler.

The economic and cultural benefits of this system of mutual accommodation were considerable. The large-scale commercial trading links delivered superior Chinese goods to the world market while transforming China – during the Ming dynasty, at least – into the dominant global economy, with almost 30 per cent of global wealth.[24] Accommodation worked to everyone's advantage.

The tributary nature of relationships across Asia in some ways presaged the way NATO operates, where the leadership of the United States is accepted and assumed, and NATO members contribute to the maintenance of peace and stability according to their means. As Richard Rigby has pointed out, Vietnam offers a fascinating example. Following the collapse of the Ming suzerainty there in the seventeenth century CE, Ming officials settled in Vietnam, no longer representing 'China'. With the advent of the Qing dynasty in China, Vietnam's later Lê dynasty resumed tribute payments to the Qing court, and because, like the Koreans, they had a recognisably Confucian monarchy, their status was regularised. This lasted until the arrival of the French, at about the same time the Japanese ended the Korean tributary relationship with Beijing. There are interesting accounts of the Vietnamese and Korean tribute missions to Beijing swapping notes, literally, as they, along with the Japanese, wrote their formal documents and communications in literary Chinese. That was the regional order that finally came to an end at the close of the nineteenth century CE.[25]

For well over a millennium, the peoples of North and South-East Asia learned to deal with China, and vice versa. It was not appeasement, because there was no loss of agency or identity on the part of the so-called tributary states. In fact, China's neighbours saw benefit in a mutually reinforcing system of relationships built around Confucian values, broadly applied, and the centrality of Chinese culture. At the same time, they maintained their own distinct cultural identities. It is not so very different from the US cultural domination of the English-speaking world in the twentieth and twenty-first centuries.

Where to for Australia?

To fix a problem, first the problem must be recognised. The economic, political and strategic world in which Australia now lives is dominated by Asia. By 2030, China, India, Indonesia and Japan will rank in the world's top ten economies, with Thailand and Pakistan outranking Australia in twenty-third place by purchasing power parity (PPP). By 2050, the Philippines, Vietnam, Bangladesh and Malaysia will overtake Australia, which is projected to be in twenty-eighth place.[26] In per capita terms, Australia will remain a wealthy and well-endowed country. But the national power relativities will change, and with that change there will be no place for complacency and condescension. Writing in 2001, Mark Beeson observed:

> At a time when the East Asian region is in the throes of profound and potentially far-reaching change, [Australia's] anachronistic and complacent attitude looks short-sighted ... The risk for Australia is that by not playing an active part in any emergent

> trans-regional institutional architecture, Australia inevitably becomes less able to influence the course of regional development. For all the claims about not having to choose between geography and history, Australia's future will clearly be profoundly influenced by the region to which it is geographically adjacent. By not having a clearly defined strategy for encouraging closer relationships with its neighbours, one which allows it to play a more effective and influential role in regional affairs, Australia may be increasingly marginalised from a region upon which its long-term military and economic security depends.[27]

In more than two decades, not much has changed. For all the talk by governments over the decades about the need for Australians to learn Asian languages, their teaching continues to decline, with four universities (La Trobe, Swinburne, Murdoch and Western Sydney) withdrawing from teaching major Asian languages in 2021 due to funding cuts.[28] It is as though Australia wishes wilfully to compound its ignorance of Asia. Yet in a world where the old order of US strategic leadership has already given way to new patterns of cooperation and competition, with a new rivalry for strategic dominance emerging between China and the United States – to the advantage of neither, it might be added – Australia must navigate an uncharted course. And it will remain uncharted until we explore the political and strategic topology of Asia, become familiar with Asian ways of doing business, recognise the skill of our neighbours in managing their affairs and, most importantly, learn from them.

In South-East Asia and the Pacific, the Australian government's announcement of the AUKUS partnership and its nuclear-propelled submarine objective simultaneously reinforced its reputation for diplomatic ineptitude and its cavalier disregard for the interests of its regional neighbours. Australia's friends in Indonesia, Singapore, Malaysia, Thailand and the Philippines – countries with which we have had the kinds of vacillating relationships more typical of adolescents – are often dismayed at our inconsistency. As the ASEAN nations grow in confidence and economic clout, Australia's retreat into imperial nostalgia and the pseudo-comfort of a 'white man's club' can only convince them of our pusillanimity and irrelevance. It is as though we have regressed a century or so to the sanctimonious sentimentality of Kipling's 'faith the White Men hold'.

The nations of South-East Asia, especially the ASEAN members, are only too aware of their history, and are not inclined to align themselves one way or the other in a contest between China and the United States. Prime Minister Morrison may have become the 'man of titanium', replacing Prime Minister Howard as the 'man of steel', but pretensions to the position of the United States' deputy sheriff in Asia simply cannot withstand the test of reality as Australia's relative position in Asia declines. This fact does not require Australia to appease anyone. But it does require us to accommodate ourselves to the emerging realities of Asia. And to do that, we need to know Asia: how it works and how it navigates changing power balances.

7
The Four Horsemen of the New Apocalypse

I am death. I have been walking by your side
for a long time. Are you prepared?

Ingmar Bergman, *The Seventh Seal*

'She'll be right, mate' is a distinctly Australian way of expressing confidence that a difficult problem will be resolved satisfactorily. More an expression of hope than of conviction, it sums up the laconic optimism that helps us muddle through impending disasters, exploiting our penchant for improvisation rather than innovation. Interestingly, it captures elements of misogyny and racism in the one phrase. Australia is not the only country that has an expression turning quiet resignation into a kind of feckless buoyancy. Indonesians say *'tidak apa-apa'* ('no worries') and the Thais move on with *'mai pen rai, krap'* ('no matter'). Māori people console themselves with *'kei te pai, kei te tiakina tatou e te Atua'* ('God's with us') – though by the time those words are out calamity has probably struck, which may explain why *'ka tika tana hoa wahine'* ('she'll be right') buys a bit more time!

While being laid-back and quietly confident may be an endearing aspect of the Australian character, it is not a sound starting point for dealing with the existential threats that, in combination, may well affect humanity in general in the coming decades, and the Australian community in particular. Indeed, complacency and dependence on others to fix the problems facing Australia can only lead to our own marginalisation at best, and serious decline at worst.

The four horsemen of the Apocalypse are war, famine, plague and death. Given its historical experience with famine, disease, war and, in the nuclear age, potential annihilation, it is curious that Australia has become so blasé about the big threats that face the global community. The food shortage and hardship of first two years of colonisation at Sydney Cove were etched into the consciousness of the early settlers. The First Fleet and its contingent of convicts and their guards quickly faced starvation, which was made worse by the arrival of the Second Fleet in June 1790 – more people, but no more food. It was not until the arrival of the Third Fleet, in April 1791, that food supplies became more secure. Similarly, from the moment of settlement, communicable and infectious diseases were commonplace, especially cholera, dysentery, smallpox and typhoid, along with venereal diseases, requiring the establishment of quarantine facilities. In 1789, barely a year after the arrival of the First Fleet, smallpox decimated the Cadigal Indigenous community (the traditional owners of the lands around Sydney Cove) and spread into central and south-western New South Wales.

War, of course, cast an enduring pall over the twentieth century, as much for Australia as for any other nation. During World War I, some 60,000 Australian service personnel died, with over 200,000 others experiencing mental or physical injuries – and this from a population of fewer than 5 million. World War II added another 30,000 to the tally of dead, and the same number of physical and psychological casualties. In various theatres, Australian forces were deployed abroad for forty years during the twentieth century, and have been deployed continuously during the twenty-first century. Australia saw the destructive power of atomic weapons when twelve were detonated in the Monte Bello and Maralinga nuclear tests between 1952 and 1957, with minor component tests continuing until 1963. Quite apart from moral and strategic considerations, popular opposition to the atmospheric tests conducted in Australia persuaded governments from the mid-1960s through to the mid-1990s to pursue nuclear disarmament negotiations actively. That, sadly, is no longer the case.

In different though related guises, more virulent and more dangerous, the four traditional horsemen populate a new apocalypse: the threat of regional and global conflict (especially a contest between the United States and China, triggered perhaps by China's asserting its claim to Taiwan, as a new and unpredictable power balance is struck between the two superpowers); climate change and its impacts on water availability, food production and the mass migration of peoples; pandemics such as COVID-19; and nuclear annihilation. On each of these matters, Australia has retreated from any role commensurate with our broader global interests or our ability to contribute to constructive global outcomes. The energy that accompanied 'good international citizenship' in the 1980s has given way to a passivity grounded in complacency and, even more dangerously, cynicism.

But it was not always thus. While our enthusiasm for moderating and defusing regional conflicts has never been great – we were enthusiastic participants in the Malayan Emergency, the *Konfrontasi* between Indonesia and Malaysia, the Vietnam War, the ill-judged adventurism in Iraq and the failed counterterrorism intervention in Afghanistan – we played a significant role in establishing the Multinational Force and Observers in the Sinai, contributing to international peacekeeping efforts in both Bougainville and Solomon Islands, and a substantial leadership role in the UN-sponsored force that oversaw Timor Leste's separation from Indonesia in 1999. Indeed, Australia has an enviable record in its support for UN-sponsored peacekeeping.

Taiwan: A trigger for a United States–China conflict and the harbinger of war?

The past few years have witnessed a precipitous decline in the relationship between the United States and China, and, partly in consequence, in the relationship between Australia and China. Politicians who should know better, and former senior military officers who probably do not know better, talk up the prospects of war. Public commentators amplify what they deem to be the drumbeats of war, normalising anxiety and apprehension. More than that, governments are investing in weapons systems of greater destructive power and lethality. Foreign policy is increasingly securitised as governments emphasise the value and effectiveness of military alliances over the persuasive capacities of diplomacy. Unelected senior US military officers, and even Australian public servants, proffer their views on tension and war, with their governments apparently nodding their heads in agreement. And the business of national foreign, defence and security policy is increasingly conducted by intelligence agencies without much evident involvement by the policy departments or even their ministers. Governments increasingly pay heed to their senior intelligence officials without appreciating that intelligence is but one component of sound international and security policy. For intelligence collection and analysis is intrinsically reactive, focusing on what has already happened and what might happen, rather than proactively and pre-emptively steering a path to security and prosperity. That, of course, is the business of diplomacy.

In recent years, it has become fashionable among some international relations commentators to view the position of Taiwan, as part of 'one China', simply as a question of reunification through peaceful or military means in the aftermath of an ongoing civil war that has never been resolved. But it is not just a matter of ending a domestic dispute, whether by negotiation or armed force. It is not just Taiwan's future that hangs in the balance: because the interests and prestige of both China and the United States are engaged, Taiwan's future may well engage the futures of both nations, and the neighbouring North Asian states of Japan and the Republic of Korea. And, of course, as a determined and vociferous barracker from the geographic bleachers, Australia is willing itself into the consequential dimension of Taiwan's political future. Were headbutting between China and the United States to lead to war between them, many in Australia see no option but to become a belligerent ourselves in support of the latter. But what kind of war would it be, and what would be its consequences? Hugh White's answer is sobering:

> It would be a war the US and its allies would have no clear chance of winning. Indeed, it is not even clear what winning a war with a country such as China means. And it would very likely become a nuclear war. The consequences for Australia, the region and the world would be devastating and it would fail to achieve the objective of preserving US leadership in Asia.[1]

What country in its right mind would embark upon an unwinnable war?

Misunderstanding begets miscalculation. Because of its proximity and the fact that China's political, strategic and territorial interests are all deeply involved, China enjoys overwhelming military advantages that afford it a wide range of options for selective military pressure against Taiwan and any neighbour that might offer basing rights to the United States. John Culver captures this fact well:

> China can, early in a conflict, use long-range strikes to destroy all of Taiwan's key military and leadership facilities, power generation and telecommunications. It can embargo all of Taiwan's oil imports and cut or compromise via cyber all high-bandwidth connectivity to the outside world. And it likely can sustain this indefinitely. It can seize all Taiwan-held offshore islands, including the Penghus and Pratas, and use these as mobilisation and embarkation bases for future landing operations on Taiwan, and as chokepoints against US intervention, while burnishing nationalist domestic support early in the conflict. And perhaps most importantly, it can seek the right time and conditions to demonstrate to the people of Taiwan – and Japan, Australia and the US – that the US military cannot prevent or undo China's actions, and either will not put its major military assets into harm's way, or having done so, will suffer surprising and politically devastating losses. Beijing would strive to portray the US position as analogous to victoryless wars in Vietnam, Iraq, Afghanistan, albeit at far higher potential human and financial costs for the US and its allies.[2]

Taiwan presents a set of wicked problems, the negotiation of which will require extreme care on Australia's part. There are five major components, and it is important that each is understood, both in itself and in its relationships with the other four.

1. Taiwan is part of China

Culturally and geographically, this may appear obvious. But apart from a short period between 1945 and 1949 when the Nationalist forces retreated from the Chinese mainland to Taiwan, Taiwan has not been under Beijing's direct jurisdiction since 1895.[3] The 1972 Joint Communiqué establishing diplomatic relations between Australia and China makes Taiwan's legal status crystal clear: 'The Australian Government recognises the Government of the People's Republic of China as the sole legal Government of China, acknowledges the position of the Chinese Government that Taiwan is a province of the People's Republic of China.'[4]

Nonetheless, Taiwan presents as an anomaly, deprived of the status of independent state and membership of the United Nations, yet boasting a thriving economy and an energetic, if dwindling, international diplomacy. Currently, only fifteen states recognise Taiwan as the Republic of China (and, accordingly, do not recognise the People's Republic of China); they include the Marshall Islands, Nauru, Palau and Tuvalu in the Pacific. For reasons of religious freedom and its opposition to any form of state control over its appointments to the episcopacy, the Vatican continues to recognise Taipei as the seat of China's government. The remainder of the international community recognises the legitimacy of China's claim to Taiwan and the People's Republic of China as the rightful representative of China in the United Nations.

The strategic role of Taiwan has evolved since the outbreak of the Korean War in 1950. Given the massive imbalance between the military might of the United States and China, the Americans were easily able to turn the Taiwan issue, even during the dictatorship of Chiang Kai-shek, into a cat's paw, invoking the protection of rights of self-determination, and democratic rights in more recent decades, as the trigger for armed intervention. China's possible invasion of Taiwan has morphed from 'unfinished business' (from China's point of view) into a casus belli (from the point of view of many US strategists). Yet much uncertainty attaches to whether a direct military assault by

China on Taiwan would afford sufficient legal, political or strategic justification for the United States either to intervene militarily in defence of Taiwan or to initiate offensive operations against China. The fact that many US officials address the Taiwan issue in terms of 'strategic ambiguity'[5] suggests two major considerations: the United States is far from certain that it would wish to put itself at risk of an all-out war with China, possibly extending into a nuclear exchange; and that both China and the United States are engaged in a game of strategic bluff, the motivating force of deterrence.

Yet deterrence is the fatal flaw in the strategic logic currently applied to the Taiwan issue. That is what, fundamentally, the 'hawks' who wish to lend 'strategic clarity' in the face of Chinese 'bellicosity' have recognised: deterrence only works when one side (the deterring party) has the ability to impose catastrophic penalties on the other (the deterred party), by virtue of its overwhelming military power. But when the two potential adversaries enjoy parity, more or less, catastrophic sanctions run both ways.

It is evident that the United States is becoming ever more convinced that the balance on the Taiwan issue is shifting. It has pursued a long-term policy of signalling to China that the forced integration of Taiwan into the People's Republic of China would be provocative. At the same time, it has impressed upon successive Taiwanese governments that any moves towards declarations of independence from China would be both provocative and destabilising. And to that end, the United States has resisted pressure to give Taiwan any guarantee of automatic military support in the event of armed conflict.

The simple fact is that the strategic position in North Asia has changed irretrievably for the United States: it can no longer deter China. That is not to suggest that China can defeat the United States in a one-on-one military contest. But in a contest over Taiwan, China can prevail in the same way that Vietnam prevailed in 1975: the Chinese nation has 'skin in the game', while the United States does not. In a war over Taiwan, the Americans would be engaged in an expeditionary war, as in Vietnam, Iraq and Afghanistan, where their own direct and vital interests are simply not at stake. But for China, its vital interests – the unity of the nation and the credibility of its government – are.

Finally, it is important to guard against reducing the strategic complexity of the Taiwan issue to a simplistic values argument focused on the imperative that 'democracy' must be defended everywhere and at all times. While it is beyond the scope of this book to mount the argument that democracy is not a 'value' per se (it is a political practice that enshrines a value – the right of people to participate in their government), it should be noted that generalised assertions are not a sufficient basis for any decision to go to war. Some might advocate direct intervention in the defence of Taiwan against possible Chinese military force to secure its incorporation into China on the grounds of 'humanitarian intervention' or 'defence of democracy'. But the same advocates are unlikely to justify intervention in Catalonia to defend the rights of Catalonians in their contest with the government of Spain, or to intervene on behalf of the Scots were they to vote for the dissolution of the union with England, Wales and Northern Ireland. Prime Minister Tony Blair's declaration that humanitarian intervention justified NATO's use of military force in the Balkans was more a statement of hubris than the articulation of a universally agreed and universally applicable principle. 'This is a just war, based not on any territorial ambitions but on values,' he declaimed.[6] Yet no one seriously thought about invoking the doctrine when Russia annexed the Crimean Peninsula in 2014, or when China extended its control over the internal security affairs of Hong Kong, effectively curtailing the powers of Hong Kong's legislature.

2. Taiwan is not an ally of the United States

When the United States established diplomatic relations with Beijing on 1 January 1979, the Mutual Defense Treaty between the United States of America and the Republic of China, which had been in force since 1955, was abrogated by President Jimmy Carter, the abrogation itself being subject to legal challenge in the US Supreme Court. In its place, the US Congress enacted the *Taiwan Relations Act* (TRA), which President Carter signed into law on 10 April 1979. The TRA explicitly recognises that any effort to determine the future of Taiwan by other than peaceful means would be a threat to the peace and security of the Western Pacific area. It authorises the provision of arms 'of a defensive character' and declares an explicit policy of the United States 'to resist any resort to force or other forms of coercion that would jeopardise the security, or the social and economic system, of the people on Taiwan'.[7] The TRA does not provide for automatic military engagement by the United States in defence of Taiwan; nor does it preclude such military assistance. Ambiguity is maintained, bearing in mind, of course, that a positive cannot be proved from a negative.

The United States does, of course, provide significant military support to Taiwan through its military sales and training for Taiwanese military personnel. Taiwan has expressed interest in the acquisition (by purchase or lease) of the F-35 stealth fighter, and Taiwanese F-16 pilots train in the United States. In late 2020, US Marines conducted training exercises with Taiwanese forces, the first time in forty years that such training had been publicly acknowledged.[8] The Biden administration then upped the ante in its strategic signalling to China by authorising a 'semi-official' visit to Taipei by senior former US officials.[9]

The people of Taiwan find themselves caught between the power of China and the lure of independence. The two major political parties reflect that divide, with the Kuomintang (KMT) party, the heirs of Chiang Kai-shek, favouring eventual unification with China, and the Democratic Progressive Party (DPP) supporting eventual independence from China to reflect a separate Taiwanese identity. The latter position is anathema to the government of President Xi Jinping. But domestic support for the DPP has been growing steadily over the past decade or so, putting the government of Taiwan in a difficult position, and perhaps on a path to direct confrontation with China. It either represents Taiwanese nationalist aspirations, thereby generating Chinese ire, or it risks electoral defeat by failing to press for independence. The DPP president of Taiwan, Tsai Ing-wen, walks a particularly fine line in supporting her constituents' pursuit of identity while minimising the potential for political provocation of Beijing.

Ultimately, it is for the people of Taiwan to determine their status, though they will not do so without China's involvement. Some Taiwanese see the question 'are we Chinese or Taiwanese' as a binary, while others comfortably accept that they can be both – a necessary precondition for a 'one country, two systems' solution to the dilemma. But for as long as Taiwan relies on the ambiguity of US support to permit a postponement of a resolution to its status, the more difficult that resolution will become. Given its clear preference for prosperity as a reasonable reward for maintenance of the status quo, Taiwan has little to gain from heightened tension between China and the United States – and much to lose, were it to become a tripwire on the path to armed confrontation between two great powers.[10]

3. *Taiwan is not an ally of Australia*

It is thoroughly specious to suggest that, because Australia is an ally of the United States, American actions to uphold the security interests of Taiwan would necessarily involve Australia. It is entirely possible that Australia and the United States would consult in any situation in which China were to threaten or use military force against Taiwan. But such consultations would not reflect any obligation to Taiwan pursuant to the ANZUS Treaty. Rather, they reflect the fact that Australia and the United States share a common interest in the stability and security of North Asia. Such consultations might well extend to Japan and the Republic of Korea, but not for reasons of alliance obligations.

4. *The ANZUS Treaty does not address the situation of Taiwan*

Nor does the treaty address the relationship between Taiwan and the United States. It is critically important that people who invoke the ANZUS Treaty actually read and understand it, and appreciate its deep historical background. The treaty does refer to contemporary political and force dispositions of the United States, particularly in respect of Japan, the Philippines and the Ryukyu Islands, which stretch from Japan to Taiwan. The United States occupied those islands at the time that the ANZUS Treaty was negotiated and entered into force. It also refers to the contemporary fact that Australia and New Zealand, as members of the British Commonwealth, had military obligations 'outside as well as within the Pacific Area'. While those contemporary facts might have imposed a measure of conditionality, and therefore constraint, on the availability and use of military forces at the time of signature, they have long since faded into the mists of history.

5. *Australia's direct strategic interests are not engaged in Taiwan*

Most important is the fact that Australia and Taiwan do not share a strategic relationship, nor do they share deep strategic interests relating to individual or mutual defence. Australia clearly benefits, both economically and strategically, from the continued prosperity, stability and security of Taiwan, just as Taiwan benefits from Australia's economic strength and security. And the fact that both are thriving democracies does not necessitate military support, should one or the other come under threat. Sentiment should never drive strategy. But that being said, a decision by China to integrate Taiwan into China forcibly, to abrogate its parliament and to enforce Chinese law would have profound implications for Asia, its cohesion and its security. The use of force always has such implications.

Australia was right to express its concern and take offence at China's suppression of human and political rights in Hong Kong in 2020, just as the European democracies expressed their concern at Russia's annexation of the Crimean Peninsula in 2014. But, as offensive as the suppression of human rights might be in any circumstance short of a direct assault on an independent state and its people, it does not constitute a casus belli. This reflects the fact that while security interests are engaged, strategic interests are not. Former foreign minister Gareth Evans put this position well when he wrote that:

> Taiwan is a special case. Whether comfortable to acknowledge or not, it is not a sovereign independent state like any other. For most of its history it has been, and has been seen to be – including by itself – part of a single China. It prefers now to be independent, but does not formally claim to be, and is not recognised as such by more than a handful of states. It would be morally repugnant and reputationally destructive for China to reunify by force this freestanding, thriving democracy. But if it does, the issues are not, and will not seem to most of the world, identical to those involved in, say, Iraq's invasion of sovereign Kuwait.[11]

War, particularly one that tends towards nuclear annihilation, is not a credible or rational option. Australia's national interests – which at the very least include the security of the nation, the prosperity of our people, the stability of the region in which we live and the pursuit of constructive internationalism as a means of maintaining global stability – are not served by clarion calls to war. Like the United States, Australia is in the enviable position of deep and long-term associations with a large group of like-minded nations whose democratic practice is deeply anchored in a fundamental respect for the dignity and worth of human beings by virtue of our shared humanity. Our diplomatic efforts need to be directed towards building consensus around shared interests, and shared values where possible. That will be the subject for a later chapter in this book.

Climate change: The harbinger of famine?

On the ABC TV program *Q&A* broadcast on 9 December 2019, former prime minister Malcolm Turnbull declared that climate change was a national security concern.[12] The panel did not demur. The intensity of the fire season in south-eastern Australia that month and the next was catastrophic, impacting on the personal, financial, physical and mental health security of hundreds of thousands of Australians. But the catastrophic fires of 2019–20 were not a singular event. They were part of an enduring pattern of climate change–induced events that will continue to impact on Australia and the globe for centuries to come. That is why climate change and all its associated effects – drought, desertification, soil salinity, declining crop production, famine, rising sea levels, oceanic acidification, rising sea and land temperatures – constitutes a threat to the nation's long-term security and that of the entire global community. But in both the short and long term, the greatest impact of climate change on human security is likely to be famine and starvation.

In one of the most detailed and meticulously researched publications to emanate from an international organisation, the Intergovernmental Panel on Climate Change (IPCC), in its 2019 report *Climate Change and Land*, identified famine as an inevitable consequence of global warming.[13] Addressing 'climate change, desertification, land degradation, sustainable land management, food security, and greenhouse gas fluxes in terrestrial ecosystems', the report sounds the alarm on the threat of widespread famine, starvation and the consequent deaths of hundreds of millions of people, most of them living in abject poverty – more than the victims of wars and pandemics combined. The report also reveals one of the most appalling paradoxes in a world where climate effects will impact on the lives and livelihoods of so many of the poorest people: there are at present more obese adults in the world than underweight adults.[14] For the more than 800 million undernourished people in the world, there are 2 billion who are overweight.[15]

In its 'Summary for Policymakers', the IPCC report delineates the major factors that impact on both food production and food availability. While famine is not, of itself, an existential threat to humanity, climate change, with its multiplicity of consequences that may combine in unpredictable ways, is. Climate change can generate perverse consequences, such as uncontrolled competition for food and water that may lead to armed conflict. As the World Hunger Education Service has commented, how climate change contributes to conflict is not well understood.[16] But it is clear that in countries such as Eritrea, Mali, Nigeria, South Sudan, Syria and Yemen, climate change–induced drought and ethnic conflict intersect to destroy entire communities.

What the scientific data so clearly demonstrates is that climate change, including increases in frequency and intensity of extremes, has adversely impacted food security and terrestrial ecosystems, as well as having contributed to desertification and land degradation in many regions. Climate change has exacerbated land degradation, particularly in low-lying coastal areas, river deltas, drylands and permafrost areas. Paradoxically, the melting of the permafrost has also increased global methane levels. Over the fifty years to 2013, the annual area of drylands in drought increased, on average, by more than 1 per cent per year. In 2015, about 500 million people lived in areas subject to increasing desertification, the majority in South Asia and East Asia, the Sahara region (including North Africa), and the Middle East (including the Arabian Peninsula). Other dryland regions have also experienced desertification. People living in already degraded or desertified areas are increasingly negatively affected by climate change.

Climate change has already affected food security due to warming, changing precipitation patterns and greater frequency of some extreme events. Studies that separate out climate change from other factors affecting crop yields have shown that yields of some crops (maize and wheat, for instance) in many lower-latitude regions have fallen due to observed climate changes. Perversely, in many higher-latitude regions, yields of some crops (such as maize, wheat and sugar beets) have increased over recent decades. With increases in global temperatures, the frequency, intensity and duration of heat-related events, including heatwaves, are projected to continue to increase through the twenty-first century. The frequency and intensity of droughts are also projected to increase, particularly in the Mediterranean region and southern Africa, while the frequency and intensity of extreme rainfall events are projected to increase in many regions.[17] Increased warming will also shift climate zones poleward in the middle and high latitudes. In high-latitude regions, warming is projected to increase disturbance in boreal forests, including drought, wildfire and pest infestations. In tropical regions, under medium and high greenhouse-gas-emissions scenarios, warming is projected to result in the emergence of unprecedented climatic conditions by the mid to late twenty-first century.[18]

The pathway to climate disaster and serious famine is becoming ever clearer. Current levels of global warming are associated with moderate risks from increased dryland water scarcity, soil erosion, vegetation loss, wildfire damage, permafrost thawing, coastal degradation and tropical crop yield decline. As temperatures increase further, risks, including cascading risks, are projected to become even more severe. At an increase of around 1.5 degrees Celsius, the risks from dryland water scarcity, wildfire damage, permafrost degradation and food supply instabilities are projected to be high. With a rise of around 2 degrees Celsius, the risk from permafrost degradation and food supply instabilities are projected to be very high. Additionally, at around 3 degrees Celsius, risks from vegetation loss, wildfire damage and dryland water scarcity are also projected to be very high.[19]

The stability of food supply will decrease as the magnitude and frequency of extreme weather events that disrupt food chains increases. In drylands, crop and livestock productivity will decline, with consequent changes to the plant species mix and reduced biodiversity. Moreover, changes in climate can amplify environmentally induced migration both within countries and across borders, reflecting multiple drivers of mobility and available adaptation measures. Extreme weather and climate or slow-onset events may lead to increased displacement, disrupted food chains and threatened livelihoods, and contribute to exacerbated stresses for conflict.[20]

In its most recent report,[21] the IPCC has endorsed the findings of the 2019 report *Climate Change and Land*. It is noteworthy that the 2021 report adduces even stronger scientific evidence for the increasing danger in which the world finds itself as a consequence of global warming. Water flows and water quality, groundwater levels, soil moisture content and soil temperatures, among other issues, have become critical risk factors threatening reliable food supplies across the globe. For a country such as Australia, the fact that the 2021 report mentions the word 'drought' almost 3,000 times should be a wakeup call, especially for the National Party that pretends to represent the nation's farmers but in fact is more interested in protecting commercial mining interests, particularly the coal and gas industries.

Famine has afflicted humanity since prehistoric times. It is a profound irony that the globe has been able to produce increasing amounts of carbohydrate and protein, ever increasing amounts of food waste and increasing obesity, while the number of hungry and malnourished people continues to grow. The economic, political and structural problems that have led to global warming were and are remediable, just as food shortages are amenable to resolution. But just as the global community, and particularly well-endowed countries like Australia, remain incapable to demonstrating the political will to address the issues associated with climate change, so the spectre of famine will continue to haunt humanity. This is nothing short of a national and global disgrace, particularly for the Group of Seven countries – Canada, France, Germany, Italy, Japan, the United Kingdom and the United States – which represent the world's largest advanced economies and wealthiest liberal democracies.

The coronavirus: The harbinger of pestilence?

As the world continues to increase its carbon emissions, fell more tropical rainforests for plantation plantings, clear ever more land for agriculture and livestock, accelerate the decline of biodiversity and bring human populations ever closer to wild animal populations (thereby forcing animal species to seek refuge in conurbations for their very survival), human beings are exposed to unheralded forms of zoonotic disease. Desertification and deforestation cause habitat loss that forces species not previously in contact with each other to migrate to shared refuges around new food resources. Anthropogenic changes to the global landscape and atmospheric warming are not only affecting weather patterns but also generating global health threats. Climate change is a risk multiplier. It affects the wellbeing of populations, the availability of food resources, the security of communities and ultimately the stability of governments, all of which establish the preconditions for war.

The sudden appearance of the Ebola virus in 1976, and the emergence of the coronaviruses causing severe acute respiratory syndrome

(SARS) in 2002 and Middle East respiratory syndrome (MERS) in 2012, prompted the international scientific and epidemiological community to warn governments of the constant threat of epidemics. A British medical microbiologist wrote in mid-2020:

> Only through robust science and the study of the natural world will we be able to truly understand the natural history and origins of zoonotic diseases like COVID-19. This is pertinent because our ever-changing relationship and increasing contact with wildlife is raising the risk of new deadly zoonotic diseases emerging in humans. SARS-CoV-2 is not the first virus that we have acquired from animals and certainly will not be the last.[22]

Warnings like this increased over the past decade as scientists became more concerned at the mutability and transmissibility of coronaviruses in particular. But just as climate scientists and nuclear scientists have continued to warn about existential threats to humanity, governments everywhere have chosen to ignore the warnings of biologists. For its part, Australia conducted its last national epidemic exercise in 2008.[23]

That complacency changed in early 2020, when the world found itself confronted by a new and lethal coronavirus respiratory disease pandemic. Governments panicked: some nations, like Australia, New Zealand, Singapore and Taiwan, acted quickly to lock their populations down; others, like Italy and Spain, simply froze, allowing the pandemic to take its course; yet others, like the United Kingdom, the United States and Sweden, went into denial, advocating 'herd immunity' as the goal, notwithstanding the death toll. And some, like Brazil and India, pursued totally cynical policies combining quackery, political spin and distortion, and complete disregard for public health, which resulted in the catastrophic collapse of their public health systems. And as the pandemic developed during 2020, the critical faultline between success and failure in managing the population health effects of COVID-19 lay between protecting the health of the citizens and keeping the national economy functioning. Those that chose the former managed the problem. Those that chose the latter succumbed to the problem, and their economies were severely impacted anyway.

To put it starkly, the contest was between the economic wellbeing of the state and the physical wellbeing of the people who constitute the community.

When, in early 2020, the epidemic in Wuhan, China, transformed itself into a global pandemic, forcing many countries into social and economic lockdown, politicians and commentators talked up the 'new normal' that awaited everyone 'on the other side' of the pandemic. What the global community has discovered is that, far from being 'on the other side', the 'new normal' is a world in which viral mutation and variants threaten rolling infection cycles, where waves of illness and death afflict populations unpredictably. Global vaccination may be able to control this pandemic, but may not eradicate it.

This brings us to the hydra-headed nature of the pandemic threat to humanity. It is not simply a complex scientific problem engaging biological research across many disciplines and medical treatment ranging from outpatient services to intensive care. It is also a complex societal problem, impacting on the quality of government and political leadership, national morale, community resilience and the mental health of individual citizens. As the global community's experience with COVID-19 demonstrated so clearly, pandemics can bring out the worst in people (for instance, President Trump's cynical manipulation of the pandemic for divisive political ends, both domestically and internationally), just as it can encourage individual acts of compassion and generosity (the nursing staff of Britain's NHS). The deeply nationalistic approach by the world's wealthy nations to vaccine development, supply and acquisition may appear to meet the challenge of protecting the lives and wellbeing of their citizens. But to ignore the needs and suffering of the world's poor, and effectively to deny them access to vaccines, is ultimately self-defeating. For it keeps the virus alive and mutating in large human population pools, presenting the entire global community with the risk of reinfection by even more virulent and vaccine-resistant strains.

Coinciding as they have, climate change and the coronavirus pandemic have together induced a potentially fatal paralysis in many world leaders. This has mirrored a fatalistic inertia in many of the world's communities – and for the same basic reason. As a species, it appears, human beings are unable to accept the systemic interdependence between people, other animal species and the natural world in general. In the most morbid of senses, then, the global community is currently facing two catastrophes for the price of one, with nuclear annihilation as an add-on. What is more, the interconnectedness of planetary systems places the three most pressing threats to human existence – climate change, pandemics and nuclear weapons – in the same decision space. Each is a 'wicked problem' where solutions are 'messy', iterative and constantly morphing. Solutions do not lie in the hands of individual world leaders, but in the global multilateral councils where consensus is forged and remedies enacted in the interests of humanity's survival rather than national political advantage.

Nuclear weaponry: The harbinger of death?

Western governments, including successive Australian governments, have promoted the 'international rules-based order' as a panacea for global problems. An artefact of allied victories in Europe and the Pacific, the United States–inspired international rules-based order is perhaps best represented by the United Nations and the many institutions that are responsible for managing the international rules that have generally served the interests of Western governments. But the memories of many Western governments are selective: the 'rules' have generally supported the West's economic and political interests, but they failed dismally in the immediate aftermath of World War II to secure humanity's long-term future by bringing nuclear weapons under international control.

The nations in Africa and Asia that have emerged from colonialism (which some of the Allied victors of World War II tried to preserve), the Eastern European nations that escaped the Soviet yoke following the collapse of the Soviet Union, the reinvigorated Russia that has succeeded the Soviet Union, the nations of Central America and South America, and, most significantly, China are not such strong advocates of the 'international rules-based order'. They see it as a vehicle for maintaining the global pre-eminence of the United States and, more importantly, as a system that constrains their prospects while preserving the status of the major beneficiaries of the post–World War II distribution of power and political spoils.

As far as nuclear weapons are concerned, the horse has already bolted – and no one is quite sure where the stable is, whether there is a door to be shut and, if so, whether anyone is able to shut it. Early international agreement was essential if the few nuclear weapons that existed at the time were to be accounted for, held securely and dismantled under appropriate supervision. In important respects, the subsequent proliferation of nuclear weapons is a testament to the inability of the international rules-based order to contain and then eliminate humanity's exposure to the threat of nuclear annihilation.

But it was not necessarily thus. In the immediate aftermath of World War II, the Conference of Foreign Ministers, representing the United States, the United Kingdom and the Soviet Union, met in Moscow to establish a United Nations commission to oversee the destruction of existing nuclear weapons and to redirect nuclear research towards peaceful purposes. The first resolution of the United Nations General Assembly, on 24 January 1946, was to create the United Nations Atomic Energy Commission (UNAEC) with six permanent members: the United States, the United Kingdom, the Soviet Union, China, France and Canada.

To give effect to this resolution, the US Secretary of State formed an advisory committee, consisting of Under-Secretary of State Dean Acheson and Chair of the Tennessee Valley Authority David Lilienthal to prepare the US government's submission to the UNAEC. Its principal drafter was Robert Oppenheimer, one of the 'fathers of the atomic bomb', a brilliant scientist, an idealist and a visionary but a novice in the game of bureaucratic politics. His early leftist sympathies, however, did not prevent his taking a leading role in the

Manhattan Project. Like Albert Einstein, he considered that it was essential for the United States to develop an atomic bomb against the prospect that Nazi Germany succeeded in its atomic bomb ambitions. But the success of the Trinity test and the subsequent destruction of Hiroshima and Nagasaki left him with serious remorse and a conviction that atomic weapons should be banned. He certainly shared Einstein's view that 'atomic war ... is likely to bring destruction on a scale never before held possible and even now hardly conceived, and that little civilization would survive it'.[24]

Oppenheimer's submission called for 'the creation of the Atomic Development Authority to oversee the mining and use of fissile materials, the operation of all nuclear facilities that could produce weaponry, and the right to dispense licenses to those countries wishing to pursue peaceful nuclear research.[25] The submission recognised that, to become effective, the plan required the cooperation of the Soviet Union, given that it was unlikely to accept the repudiation of its veto power in the UN Security Council on any issue. Oppenheimer might have been the right person to draft the United States' submission. He was the wrong person to negotiate it. The day before the submission was due for delivery to the UN, President Truman appointed Bernard Baruch as the principal negotiator in the UNAEC: Truman was not prepared to accept any deal that required the United States to abandon its nuclear weapons program without assurances that the Soviet Union would not embark on its own program. And Baruch shared Truman's fundamental mistrust of Stalin.

So the plan proposed by Baruch differed in small but significant details from that prepared by Oppenheimer. It enhanced the powers of the Atomic Development Agency, making it responsible only to the UN Security Council and revoking the veto powers of council members where the United Nations might wish to impose sanctions against countries that undertook prohibited activities. Only after the plan was fully implemented would the United States begin the destruction of its nuclear arsenal.[26] Given the breakdown of trust between the United States and the Soviet Union, the plan fell over at the first hurdle. The Soviet Union totally rejected any proposal that would see the United States retain its atomic weapons monopoly for any length of time, that would mandate intrusive inspection of Soviet facilities, and that would relieve the Soviet Union of its veto power in the UN Security Council. The vote in the UNAEC failed the unanimity test, with the Soviet Union and Poland abstaining.

It might be argued that the US negotiators engineered the failure of their own plan: the negotiating position of the Soviet Union was quite foreseeable. But the failure of the Baruch Plan owed more to two irresistible forces: the growing contention, supported particularly by the US Air Force, that the United States had no strategic alternative but to persevere with atomic weapons; and the accelerating mistrust between the US leaders and their Soviet counterparts. These two forces – nuclear weapons nationalism, pushed largely by the military, and deep political mistrust – have only intensified in the seven decades since the hopes generated by the Baruch Plan evaporated. Instead, we have a world in which the possession of nuclear weapons has become normalised and proliferation is tolerated. Indeed, reputable defence commentators in countries, including Australia, that have traditionally been supporters of global non-proliferation efforts have begun to advocate consideration of nuclear weapons acquisition.

The normalisation of nuclear weapons possession and toleration of proliferation is the kind of development that could encourage security 'realists' in Germany, Japan, the Republic of Korea and Australia to follow the path chosen by Israel, India, Pakistan, North Korea and potentially Iran: the development of a nuclear weapons capability. We have already seen glimmerings of this malaise. Paul Dibb, one of Australia's best-known defence commentators, coyly raised the question in late 2018, neither advocating the development of a nuclear weapon nor dismissing it on either moral or strategic grounds. While the subliminal strategic concern was China's massive expansion of its conventional military capabilities to 'threaten us seriously' (invoking a kind of antipodean *force de frappe*),[27] Dibb surprisingly puts the question in terms of our alliance with the United States:

> We face a stark dilemma: increasing uncertainty about US extended nuclear deterrence versus the daunting alternative of acquiring our own nuclear deterrent. The other alternative is to simply accept (as we did in the Cold War) that we are a nuclear target and take our chances. My view is that Australia should at least be looking at options and lead times. Doing so doesn't commit us to proliferating.[28]

Another leading Australian defence commentator, Hugh White, is no less adamant that the nuclear weapons question is one 'we will not be able to avoid over the decades to come'.[29] The fact that two of Australia's leading defence thinkers should revisit an issue that Australia's ratification of the Treaty on the Non-Proliferation of Nuclear Weapons might have been thought to have resolved is noteworthy. And that their doing so caused barely a ripple, except for an elegant rebuttal by Ramesh Thakur, is also noteworthy.[30] But these developments are not simply a sign of the uncertainty that distinguishes the contemporary world. They are emblematic of a catastrophic failure in global political leadership, an abandonment of the hope and optimism that persuaded those who negotiated the UN treaty, and the ever-growing influence of military leaders in the formulation of national security policy.

The return to consideration of the acquisition of nuclear weapons by states that do not already possess them is also a sign that defence commentators are more inclined to view the nuclear weapons issue through the lens of military force, rather than through the lens of securing and maintaining the peace.

The Bulletin of the Atomic Scientists has set its 2021 doomsday clock at 100 seconds to midnight. Explaining its decision, the editor said:

> The [COVID-19] pandemic revealed just how unprepared and unwilling countries and the international system are to handle global emergencies properly. In this time of genuine crisis, governments too often abdicated responsibility, ignored scientific advice, did not cooperate or communicate effectively, and consequently

> failed to protect the health and welfare of their citizens … [T]he pandemic serves as a historic wake-up call, a vivid illustration that national governments and international organizations are unprepared to manage nuclear weapons and climate change, which currently pose existential threats to humanity, or the other dangers – including more virulent pandemics and next-generation warfare – that could threaten civilization in the near future.[31]

This is a bleak outlook. States with nuclear weapons continue to invest enormous sums on weapons modernisation programs. Their delivery systems are becoming more accurate, faster and less detectable. The normalisation of nuclear weapons possession has progressively lowered inhibitions about their use, thereby legitimising their deployment in conventional conflict. At the same time, these states have allowed international and bilateral constraints on nuclear weapons use to atrophy, and appear to be blithely indifferent to the potential for accidental use.

Although the Treaty on the Prohibition of Nuclear Weapons continues to gather momentum, no state possessing nuclear weapons is a signatory. The Nuclear Non-Proliferation Treaty continues to stagger along, with none of the nuclear-weapon states party to the treaty taking a single step to honour their obligations under Article VI of the treaty, which requires them to 'pursue negotiations in good faith on effective measures relating to cessation of the nuclear arms race at an early date and to nuclear disarmament, and on a treaty on general and complete disarmament under strict and effective international control'. As an increasing number of states become disgruntled at the imbalance between the substantial obligations imposed on the non-nuclear-weapon states and the absence of any obligations on the nuclear-weapon states, confidence in the Non-Proliferation Treaty will decline. The treaty is often described as 'the cornerstone of the global non-proliferation regime'.[32] The problem is that the non-proliferation edifice is essentially a façade resting on only one corner, and that corner is crumbling. The question that faces the parties to the Non-Proliferation Treaty is whether they want to strengthen the edifice – and the cornerstone – or whether they are prepared to see the Non-Proliferation Treaty go the way of the New Strategic Arms Reduction Treaty – extinction.

Either way, there is much at stake. Reinvigorating the Non-Proliferation Treaty will take enormous diplomatic effort on the part of the non-nuclear-weapon states, and significant concessions (and diplomatic sensibility) on the part of the nuclear-weapon states. Extinction, on the other hand, is the easy way out, where blame can be allocated, the finger pointed at disarmament idealists and so-called nuclear weapons realists alike, and the global community left captive to a dangerous stalemate. The parallels with the UN Climate Change Commission's Conference of the Parties (COP) are uncanny.

How should Australia respond?

At this point in its political evolution, Australia appears to have little confidence that it could contribute to effective global action on any of these major threats to global security, and even less agency. That has not always been the case. In the early post–World War II years, Australia was unashamedly internationalist, and while its enthusiasm waned during the Vietnam War years, the Whitlam, Fraser, Hawke and Keating governments were internationally active in addressing nuclear disarmament and establishing effective aid programs to alleviate hunger and improve health standards, particularly in the Asia-Pacific region. The Rudd and Gillard governments took the dangers of climate change seriously.

In each of the domains represented by the four horsemen, Australia has become disengaged: it has cut its aid program, which tackled famine and pandemics, and has stepped back from its earlier disarmament efforts, which might prevent nuclear annihilation. And with respect to War, the red horseman, Australia has been a keen contributor to failed US adventurism in Iraq and Afghanistan. The Australian government currently shows no interest in preventing war between China and the United States over the status of Taiwan.

This is the result of a combination of complacency, national introspection and self-absorption, lethargy, a lack of national self-confidence, an absence of national ambition, and deep anxiety and insecurity. We are paralysed. We are in a state of crisis, overwhelmed by the problems facing us, reacting to them haphazardly, without any sense of what a better world might look like. We have no plan, and we have no vision. We resemble Nietzsche's 'last man': anaesthetised and inert, risk-averse, inward-looking and constantly seeking comfort and security.

But there is no reason for us to remain like that: we can reinvigorate ourselves by working out who we are, what we stand for, our values, and our interests. That is what we will turn to now.

8
Identity, Interests and Values

The only true and lasting meaning of the struggle for life lies in the individual, in his modest peculiarities and in his right to these peculiarities.

Vasily Grossman, *Life and Fate*

Australia is not confident of its place in the world. Our bluster and our reliance on the megaphone in the way we tend to conduct ourselves internationally is as much a reflection of the mindset that shapes our international and security policy as it is an admission that we do not cope well with complexity. This has become even clearer during the past three years or so, as we have turned our relationship with China into a theatre of the absurd played on the domestic political stage. The colour and movement of chest-thumping and catcalling may play well to those parts of the electorate that enjoy the image of the little Aussie battler socking it to the neighbourhood bully, thereby satisfying two stereotypes simultaneously. And misrepresenting the problem as being a challenge to national sovereignty, an assault on the national interest (whatever that might be) and an affront to our national values (whatever they might be) does little more than highlight our reliance on braggadocio instead of brains.

Like the dish that ran away with the spoon, our mouth often runs away with our mind. We are reluctant to apply sustained intelligence and tact – the hallmarks of diplomacy[1] – to the management of the many complicated issues we face nationally. Instead, we quickly turn to point scoring, or indulge in the sullen intransigence that a former senior public servant, the late John Enfield, was wont to call 'dumb insolence'.[2]

The various pathologies that have combined to form our security mindset, identified in the first chapter of this book, underpin our lacklustre and often ham-fisted performance on the international stage. And it has been this way for most of the past century or so. Yes, Australia has notched up diplomatic successes internationally. But we have not come near to achieving our ambition or fulfilling our potential. We are constrained by our self-imposed limitations. It need not, however, be that way. If we, as a nation, have the character to look at ourselves in the mirror, see ourselves as we are and recognise our various limitations and constricted behaviours, and then, having identified the problem, set about addressing them, we will be able to transform our diplomacy and reposition ourselves internationally. That is by no means easy, since, as Benjamin Franklin is reputed to have said, old habits die hard. But once the habits have been identified, they can at least be addressed.

At this point in our national evolution, the core problem is that we do not know who we are as a nation, we do not know what we stand for as a nation, and we do not know how to articulate a set of interests that gives us purpose as a nation. This manifests itself in a variety of ways: the never-ending discussion about whether Australia should preserve its links to the British monarchy or become a republic; the unwillingness (or is it inability?) of the post-1788 immigrant community to establish an accord with Australia's First Peoples; the pre-eminence and privilege accorded to the Christian denominations in what is increasingly a secular and pluralist society; our habit of always identifying with 'the West'; our inability to self-validate, hankering instead for external validation (the cultural cringe); and the exclusionary nature of the myths by which the most powerful elites in Australia define themselves. Concerns such as these, and broader international concerns relating to the decline in public support for democratic values in many democratic societies, led the national parliament to undertake a Senate inquiry into nationhood, national identity and democracy.[3] It is curious that, in what is an important report of great contemporary relevance, none of these terms were defined. Many of the submissions to the inquiry simply talked past each other. Consequently, the report makes well-intentioned recommendations which, if implemented, would go some way to addressing the symptoms of the problem the Senate committee sought to address. But it shied away from tackling the causes of those problems.

Some might argue that diffidence and uncertainty about identity goes with being a 'middle power', neither big nor small, always betwixt and between. Yet the Scandinavian countries do not appear to have that problem, nor the Baltic countries, nor the nations of Central Europe. New Zealand certainly has a sharper sense of its identity.

Public discourse on the fundamental traits that define a nation will always be contested. Communities and nations change and evolve. They are dynamic in every sense – culturally, economically, politically and socially. Mores change, as do perceptions of what is ethical and moral. Often, however, public discourse on these matters is symptomatic of deeper societal concerns about equality, equity, justice and the distribution of wealth and power. It is not uncommon for elites to exploit such public discourse to consolidate and enhance their power and privilege, at the same time marginalising or even excluding other groups. The so-called culture wars that have been the leitmotif of Australia's political contests over the past quarter-century have lent an ideological character to what might otherwise have been a serious and respectful national conversation. And in no small part, the culture wars have centred on identity – to the extent that the culture wars and identity politics have become the same thing.

Identity

Australians have a lot of trouble with identity. While for some it is the holy grail that might join the citizens into a homogeneous, unified nation, for others it is the distinguishing feature of their difference, their 'non-belonging' to a particular group within the broader community. Terms like 'unity', 'inclusion', 'difference' and 'diversity' become highly charged, jostling with each other in various forms of confected binary that confuse the arguments and polarise their proponents, rather than clarify the arguments and bring their proponents together. The word 'identity' itself is not particularly helpful. It derives from the late silver-age Latin word *idem*, which means 'the same'. So 'identity' is the quality that makes a group or a community all the same, 'identical'. How boring. Who'd really want 'sameness' as the key to identity? In that sense, 'identity' is tantamount to 'brand', the indicator that discrete things are grouped together.

The creation of a national identity has been a work in progress for conservative politicians from Deakin to Morrison. The most epigrammatic expression of this enterprise was John Howard's remark to *The Australian*'s Paul Kelly in 2009 that he was 'an ANZAC Bradman Australian'.[4] This is emblematic of two main features of the conservative side of the culture wars: a distinctly WASP (white Anglo-Saxon Protestant) ethnicity and a reverence for historical cultural symbolism. The Ramsay Foundation's pursuit of Western canonical symbols, along with its determination to establish them as normative expressions of Australian intellectual culture, is further evidence of that. One wonders, however, how much resonance an identity formed around what are essentially exclusive symbols – the Anzac myth and a cricketer – might have with Indigenous Australians, whose cultural symbols stretch back over 60,000 years, or non-European immigrant Australians, whose cultural symbols represent an astonishing array of communal histories from all parts of the world. Indeed, what might be called the 'mainstream' search for a national identity seems incapable of accommodating Australia's First Peoples as the historical wellspring of a putative national identity.

ABC journalist and Griffith University professor Stan Grant, for instance, calls out this problem with his lyrical and declamatory turn of phrase: 'I want to tell you how you [and he could be talking to John Howard] have always sought to define us. You called us Aborigines: a word that meant nothing to my people. And in that one word you erased our true identities.'[5] (Note his use of the plural.) The poignancy of his critique of an imposed identity is amplified when he writes:

> I was raised to know that I was the son of a Wiradjuri man and a Kamilaroi woman – this is my family, my heritage – yet in the eyes of the state my identity remains in flux. To proclaim myself an indigenous person is a political act, something to be negotiated between our bloodline and the law imposed on us. So, my country, these things are important. Faces and names and language and land are important. Without land we have no inheritance.[6]

These, along with shared beliefs – or values, perhaps – are the markers of identity. They are not mythic, or symbolic, or imposed. They are, to use the constitutional term, autochthonous – they arise from the earth.

Grant has offered a profound insight into the fault line that separates the First Peoples and the post-1788 immigrant arrivals to Australia: the difference between belonging and ownership. This difference must be appreciated and understood if it is to be reconciled. The First Peoples and their descendants, in both a physical and a metaphysical sense, belong to the continent of Australia in a symbiosis that has the continent belonging to them. It is not a question of ownership, in the sense of holding legal title. It is an ontological question that centres on a deeper spiritual union between people and land than any sense of ownership could bring.

The Uluru Statement from the Heart captures this ontological relationship:

> Our Aboriginal and Torres Strait Islander tribes were the first sovereign Nations of the Australian continent and its adjacent islands, and possessed it under our own laws and customs. This our ancestors did, according to the reckoning of our culture, from the Creation, according to the common law from 'time immemorial', and according to science more than 60,000 years ago.
>
> This sovereignty is a spiritual notion: the ancestral tie between the land, or 'mother nature', and the Aboriginal and Torres Strait Islander peoples who were born therefrom, remain attached thereto, and must one day return thither to be united with our

> ancestors. This link is the basis of the ownership of the soil, or better, of sovereignty. It has never been ceded or extinguished, and co-exists with the sovereignty of the Crown.
>
> How could it be otherwise? That peoples possessed a land for sixty millennia and this sacred link disappears from world history in merely the last two hundred years?[7]

Until this attitudinal difference is resolved, the quest for an agreed Australian identity will remain fruitless.

For its part, the progressive side of politics is also struggling to hold any coherent idea of national identity. Progressives are fond of 'mateship' – until they find that Indigenous Australians see mateship as an Anglo thing, an in-group endearment that excludes the out-group. It is no wonder that Indigenous people assiduously avoid the term. And the progressive approach to identity favours the idea of a republic as a way of casting off the remnants of colonial shackledom, until it discovers that Indigenous Australians see constitutional recognition as a necessary precursor to a republic. It is little wonder that Malcolm Turnbull was so quick to dismiss the Uluru Statement from the Heart: Indigenous recognition *and* a republic were, in the conservative view, two steps too far.

A search for national identity that privileges those who arrived after 1788, reflecting the belief that Australia would not be Australia without its Western civilisation,[8] is ultimately exclusionary, for it omits the fundamental unity that defines Indigenous identity, for instance – the 'at-one-ness' between Indigenous people and the land that so distinguishes them from the immigrants who arrived in 1788 and thereafter. This exclusionary approach to 'national identity' reflects the arrogant, defiantly monolingual Anglophone character of an immigrant elite that seeks to imprint its cultural dominance on the nation, forcing other groups either to assimilate or annihilate. 'Identity', it seems, is the branding iron of the spirit.

There are two core problems here.

First, 'identity' is not defined by values, important though they are, and certainly not by citizenship. If it were, Australians would fail on all counts. As Ian Cunliffe has pointed out, 'Patting ourselves on the back about egalitarianism, fair play and compassion for those in need is so much hypocritical poppycock while we turn a blind eye to ... iniquities and inequities, and fail to tackle tax dodging head on.'[9]

And second, 'identity' is not an expression of nationalism or of belonging to a nation-state. Rather, it is a much more local phenomenon, defined more by family, kinship, language, culture, belief, social mores, gender roles and place. This is not to dismiss the importance of a sense of nationhood: it is to recognise that a sense of nationhood and citizenship is not coterminous with 'identity'.

Stan Grant captures the dichotomy between identity and national citizenship. This is how he ends *Talking to my Country*:

> My father has always told me: 'You will come home.' To a young boy with a head full of dreams of the world that seemed foolish. Why would I come back, when all I wanted was to get away? But I know what he means now. He wasn't talking about a place – he was talking about my spirit. My spirit is home.
>
> When I was back in Australia one summer after years overseas, I took one of my sons to the local swimming pool near my parents' house. I was reliving the great ritual of my childhood. As we walked down the burning concrete steps, another Aboriginal boy walked towards us. For a moment he locked eyes with my son – they stood just staring at each other. As we walked on my boy turned to me and asked: 'Why does he look like me?'
>
> Why? Because this is where we are from.
>
> My country: Australia.

For many minorities, language and religious practice are distinguishing features of identity. For many people of Greek heritage in Australia, for instance, practice of the Greek Orthodox faith and, for the older generation, speaking Greek are determinants of identity, even if they are proud of their Australian citizenship. The same is true for Sikhs, who practise a distinct non-caste-based faith, attend the Gurdwara (where people of all faiths and none are equally welcome) and speak Punjabi. Lebanese Christians identify themselves as Arab speakers who practise the Maronite rite with a Syriac liturgy, maintaining their identity in the same way as Lebanese Muslims maintain theirs.

Language may also generate a meta-identity: the French, Germans, Spanish, Italians, Danes, Swedes, Norwegians – all have thriving print and film industries that preserve and promote their national culture. Yet many Europeans identify themselves by their locality, as much as they might by a common language. Germans from Brandenburg (who are mainly Lutheran) see themselves as quite different from Bavarians (who are mainly Catholic), just as French people from Brittany see themselves as quite different from people from Lorraine or Vosges. Finns, for example, may identify themselves as speakers of a unique language, but within Finland identity is much more ethnic and local, given the nation's history of Swedish and Russian occupation. And the nomadic peoples of northern Europe, the Sámi (Laplanders) identify as indigenous peoples, speaking the various national languages of the countries in which they mainly live – Norwegian, Swedish, Finnish and Russian – with identity determinants that are significantly more ethnic, cultural, linguistic and local than they are national. The same applies to the Romani, wherever in Europe they may be found.

The search for, or imposition of, a national identity tends to suppress indigenous peoples everywhere. It happened in Great Britain with the attempts to stamp out Welsh and the Gaelic dialects of Ireland and Scotland, and the Celtic language of Cornwall. It happened in North America, with the forced suppression of 'native' languages, and it certainly happened in Australia. One doubts that Stan Grant would see any part of his or his family's identity in terms of the Anzac myth or Don Bradman.

In her excoriating but ultimately optimistic book *Caste*, Isabel Wilkerson examines the destructive economic, political and social impacts of racism in America. While her book touches upon identity in many ways, she does not address identity specifically. But she does touch on some of the elements of identity as they are manifest in the Indian caste system. Writing about the Dalits – the 'untouchables' – she paints a picture of what creates an identity as 'other':

> Dalit names are generally 'contemptible' in meaning, referring to the humble or dirty work they were relegated to, while the Brahmins carry the names of the gods. Generally, you must know the significance of the name, learn the occupation of their forefathers, and perhaps know their village or their place in the village to ascertain their caste. But after centuries of forced submission and in-group marriage, they may also be identified by their bearing, accents, and clothing, all of which, over the centuries, were required to be lowly and menial, as well as a tendency to be darker than upper-caste people, though not always.[10]

The identity fracture lines in the United States militate against social cohesion. A society that reflects such a deep-set sense of 'the other' is a divided society, not simply an ethnically distributed one. Some white Americans from Washington State or Oregon may feel themselves to be as 'American' as white Americans from New Hampshire or Vermont. But saluting the flag and singing 'The Star-Spangled Banner' are symbols of nationalism, not identity or social cohesion. The sinews of social cohesion – health and employment safety nets, social security and racial harmony – are absent.

In the United States, as in Australia, 'national identity' is a pious but largely irrelevant aspiration at best, and a cynical and manipulative confidence trick at worst. It transforms identity from being the source of self-actualisation and belonging into a brand, a label that paints citizens with a veneer of sameness that disguises the difference and variation that generate vibrant, robust and socially creative societies. Far from building social cohesion, an imposed national identity papers over differences by promoting a stultifying conformity. Resilient societies are those where individuals and groups bring their identity with them. Resilient societies are inclusive societies, as distinct from simply cohesive ones.

The US academic and political economist Francis Fukuyama accords identity a central place in contemporary domestic and international politics:

> Identity grows … out of a distinction between one's true inner self and an outer world of social rules and norms that does not adequately recognize the inner self's worth or dignity. Individuals throughout human history have found themselves at odds with their societies. But only in modern times has the view taken hold that the authentic inner self is intrinsically valuable, and the outer society systematically wrong and unfair in its evaluation of the former. It is not the inner self that has to be made to conform to society's rules but society itself that needs to change.[11]

He also makes the acute observation that identity drives the pursuit of recognition. When that pursuit of recognition leads to the glorification of one set of group identity factors through the demonisation and exclusion of the identity factors of other groups, identity is weaponised. But when recognition affords status to identity across the board, the result is the growth in community wellbeing and the creation of human capital.

A society that is inclusive as well as cohesive respects and values difference. In Australia, social cohesion is more an artefact of sound economic and social policy than it is of some form of confected 'national identity'. To the extent that social cohesion is a characteristic of the Australian polity, it is a product of the inclusionary tendencies that ensured that the suffrage was extended to all citizens, irrespective of gender or race (except for those who were refused electoral rights until 1962, the First Peoples, for whom, even then, voting was optional), and that led to Mr Justice Higgins' Sunshine Harvester Decision in 1907. That, of course, did not extend to equal pay for women.

For most of the twentieth century, social cohesion in Australia was a work in progress.

While there have been important steps in creating social cohesion in Australia that is both broader and deeper – the passage of amendments to *The Marriage Act 1961* to extend marriage rights to same-sex couples is one clear example – social cohesion remains more a hope than a fact in Australia. While Indigenous Australians, women, migrants from non-English-speaking backgrounds, people with physical and mental disabilities, children and the aged, refugees and people whose circumstances consign them to marginalisation and poverty remain 'other' or 'outsiders', social cohesion will remain a work in progress and 'identity' a catchcry for privilege, entitlement and cultural elitism.

Yet there are signs of improvement. Bushfire catastrophes and the COVID-19 pandemic have brought together many more Australians in common endeavour, strengthening social inclusion and building resilience, especially at the local level. And where social inclusion accepts the many identities that constitute a multicultural society, none of them being normative or imposed, social cohesion is an inevitable result.

Despite these advances, the search for identity is constant and ongoing. As Australians, we know neither who we are nor what we stand for, hence we engage in a largely superficial discussion about 'values', talking past each other and hoping that agreement on social behavioural principles will tell us who we are. It will not, because it cannot.

Values

Most of the time, we are not even sure what 'values' are. So where do we go to discover them? The Department of Home Affairs website, of course, where the following turgid expression signals a lack of clarity at the political and bureaucratic levels:

Australian society values respect for the freedom and dignity of the individual, freedom of religion, commitment to the rule of law, Parliamentary democracy, equality of men and women and a spirit of egalitarianism that embraces mutual respect, tolerance, fair play and compassion for those in need and pursuit of the public good.

Australian society values equality of opportunity for individuals, regardless of their race, religion or ethnic background.

The English language, as the national language, is an important unifying element of Australian society …

Australian citizenship is a shared identity, a common bond which unites all Australians while respecting their diversity.[12]

This confused and confusing gobbledegook – a perfect example of what happens when sloppy thinking, bureaucratic sludge and political spin merge – conflates things that some Australians might 'value', like parliamentary democracy (in fact a political practice), the English language or even citizenship with 'values' – the behavioural principles that give expression to some of the 'things that bind'. By preferencing the English language, it excludes Indigenous Australians who have occupied and cared for this continent for over 60,000 years, and whatever their forms of governance might have been, they did not prefigure parliamentary democracy. Yet is their 'identity' un-Australian? Are their values un-Australian? The preferencing of English also excludes other minorities, more recent immigrants, whose mother tongue is other than English. Such confusion of citizenship with identity provides a partial explanation for the difficulty that some Australian politicians have in addressing questions of identity, belonging and reconciliation.

Australia seems to regard its defiant monolingualism as a badge of honour. The English language is not, however, a 'value'. Other nations are not so limited. In Belgium, both French and Flemish are recognised as national languages. Canada is bilingual. Switzerland has four national languages: French, German, Italian and Romansh.

Not to be outdone, Spain boasts Castilian (standard Spanish), Catalan, Aranese (a dialect of the French Occitan dialect spoken in Catalonia), Basque, Valencian and Galician as official languages. South Africa has eleven official languages, along with some twenty other spoken languages. For language diversity, Papua New Guinea is the standout, with over 800 languages spoken across the nation, with three spoken languages – Tok Pisin, Hiri Motu and English – along with Papua New Guinea sign language, officially recognised. With over 700 local languages, Indonesia is not far behind, but has identified Bahasa Indonesia as the official language. Most Indonesians have a strong local identity defined largely by language, but this stands alongside an equally strong sense of nationality.

It is important to recognise the polysemous nature of the word 'value'. Like 'man', 'bank', 'book', 'work' and many other words, 'value' has several meanings. We describe things as valuable because they can be given a value – be it monetary worth or historical significance. We can value things because they have meaning and worth – democracy, for instance, or education. But neither democracy nor education are 'values'. 'Values' are those abstract forces that drive action and behaviours. They are not necessarily ethical or good: greed is as much a value as generosity, cruelty as much a value as kindness. In this sense, values are tantamount to the principles that inspire people to do things.

In Australia's political discourse, the term 'values' lumps together mismatched ideas that might include motives, principles, practices that are valued and things that have worth attributed to them. It is rare for those who employ the term 'shared values', for example, to identify exactly what values are shared. Prime Minister Morrison, for instance, has claimed that Australia's relationship with India is:

> a very natural relationship, so much in common, so much shared, if not in language always certainly in the things that matter and the values that we hold and we both seek to champion those values together in our region and independently as very proud sovereign

> nations and very vibrant liberal democracies as well and I think we hold that flag up very proudly, each of us.[13]

But exactly what those values might be is generally left unsaid. As Jocelyn Chey has pointed out, many countries maintain lists of national values, many of which overlap:

> When Australian leaders refer to our values, they imply they are uniquely Australian, but this is not the case. Canada, Argentina, Singapore, for instance, all have lists of national values. 'Democratic values' do not belong exclusively to the European or Judaeo-Christian tradition. Australia has a history of using value talk to marginalise others. At the time of Federation, white Australians claimed that ethnic Chinese did not belong in the country because they lacked democratic values. This was demonstrably untrue, as John Fitzgerald showed in *The Big White Lie* (UNSW Press 2007).
>
> The People's Republic of China has its own set of official values, expressed in 24 characters that translate as prosperity, democracy, civility, harmony, freedom, equality, justice, the rule of law, patriotism, dedication, integrity and friendship. The Communist Party of China, this year celebrating its hundredth anniversary, officially upholds these values, although President Xi Jinping admits that it still falls short and 'the situation remains challenging and complex.' Corruption is a core concern for the Party, human rights abuses of Uighurs and Muslim minorities in China's western Xinjiang Region are alarming, and the judicial system lacks independence and transparency.[14]

Weaponising values is a constant ploy on the part of dominant elites to maintain their control over the body politic while marginalising those who do not belong, the 'other'. In this sense, 'values' become part of an elaborate confidence trick intended to constrain diversity rather than build cohesion.

One Australian politician who has addressed the question of national values in an authoritative, cogent and inclusive way is Senator Penny

Wong. In her Griffith Asia Institute's 'Perspectives: Asia' lecture in 2017, Senator Wong drew the link between identity and values. Her comments are to the point:

> [O]ur national identity is principally defined by the values that unite us as a nation. Values define who we are. Values guide our behaviour as individuals and as nations, determining the moral compass that is as necessary for national leaders as it is for the individual. When I use the term values, I mean the ideas be they ethical or not that motivate our action: ideas such as fairness and equality, or injustice and exclusion. Values are what drive action. Values motivate the pursuit of interests. If interests describe the reasons for action, values describe the motives for action. Hence values inform our interests and how we seek to advance and secure them. So it is important that we talk about those values, explore them and consider their contemporary relevance to how we think and what we do. Equally, it is critical that we recognise that the contest between values is the pivot on which public policy finds its balance.[15]

In her no-frills way, she identified the values that unite the Australian community:

> In my experience of the Australian community, I have found that the vast majority of our fellow citizens are good and decent people who have a pretty sound idea of the things that make us what we are: a strong adherence to a fair go for everyone, a live and let live approach to the beliefs and views that people might hold dear, a wish to help people who are doing it tough and pride in the fact that we are a tolerant and inclusive community.[16]

The values that unite communities change over time. The values that might have tolerated public executions at Tyburn or the sardonically named Place de la Concorde have given way to a more general aversion to capital punishment and public humiliation. India and the United States, two countries with which we supposedly 'share values', retain the death penalty, as do China, Indonesia, Malaysia,

Singapore, Thailand and Vietnam. Russia has declared a moratorium. In Australia's case, values have certainly evolved over time, the abolition of the White Australia policy being a clear example. As the Australian community thinks more deeply about the central place that the First Peoples should occupy in the national construct, Senator Wong's values list of 'equity', 'tolerance', 'compassion' and 'inclusion' might expand to include 'belonging'.

It is curious that values, which constitute the critical glue that holds a community together, can so easily be weaponised and used as an instrument of division. Members of any given national community might tolerate substantial political and religious differences between them, but when it comes to similar differences between nations, down come the shutters. So, for instance, Foreign Minister Marise Payne positioned the defence of values as the main battleground on which Australia chooses to conduct its relationship with China. 'There are [*sic*] a set of basic principles and democratic values that underpin our responses in our national interests which this government will never trade away,' she told *The Sydney Morning Herald* in March 2021.[17] Unfortunately, these principles, values and interests are nowhere identified or explained.

If the weaponisation of values increasingly distinguishes the conduct of bilateral relationships, as it has in Australia's case with the United States and India (the mantra of 'shared values') and with China (the defence of values), it has also become a stock-in-trade in multilateral organisations. The opening salvo of the G7 communique, released after the Cornwall meeting of 11 to 13 June 2021, proclaims:

> United as open societies and economies and guided by our shared values of democracy, freedom, equality, the rule of law and respect for human rights ... we are firmly convinced that these values remain the best foundation for the social and economic advancement of all humanity. We affirm that by investing in our people, tackling inequalities, including gender inequality, promoting dignity and championing freedoms, we will release innovation capable of tackling the great challenges of our time.[18]

This sets the scene for the subsequent paragraphs (49 and 60), which single out China for admonition relating to human rights in Xinjiang, political rights in Hong Kong and the extension of Chinese strategic positioning in the South China Sea.

Ultimately, the weaponisation of values, along with their selective application, is a self-defeating strategy. It only invites tit-for-tat responses that set standoffs in concrete and prevent dialogue and discourse. It is a signal failure of diplomacy. If, as many Australian foreign ministers have proclaimed, values and rights have universal application, why do they not prosecute them equally and defend them wherever they are decried or denied? The mistreatment of the Rohingya community in Myanmar, the discrimination and violence meted out to Muslims in India and the occupation of the West Bank do not attract the condemnation that China's treatment of its minorities receives.

Consistency and constancy in the protection and promotion of values is evidently difficult. It becomes even more difficult when values are seen as separate from interests, and placed in a competitive binary where they can be traded off against interests. The creation of an interests/values binary misunderstands the fact that interests must be founded upon values if they are to enjoy the support of the citizens, and if they are to have any chance of being realised in the wider international community. And to conduct the inevitable contests between states on the battlefield of values is a capitulation to naivety and sentimentality in the conduct of international relations. The real battleground is power. And power is the wellspring of the national interest.

The national interest

Perhaps it is just laziness and a lack of curiosity that leads so many politicians and public commentators to use the terms 'national interest' and 'national interests' interchangeably. Yet they could not be more different. It is another case of polysemy.

Senator Penny Wong is neither lazy nor lacking in curiosity. She is one of the few Australian politicians who have explained the difference between 'interest' (singular) and 'interests' plural. Speaking at the Lowy Institute in 2017, she deconflicted the two expressions:

> The national interest is about identity and power, giving foreign policy both legitimacy and authority. National interests are what Australia seeks to protect and promote through its foreign policy, giving foreign policy its purpose and energy. The national interest is substantive. National interests are purposive. Without a clear sense of identity and power, we run the risk of allowing others to determine our future for us.[19]

In some measure, this distinction borrows from both Jeremy Bentham and Hans Morgenthau. Setting out to identify the principles that should underpin political reform, Bentham explored the idea of 'interest', declaring that 'the interest of the community is one of the most general expressions that can occur in the phraseology of morals: no wonder that the meaning of it is often lost',[20] then noting that 'interest is one of those words which … cannot in the ordinary way be defined'.[21] But to the extent that Bentham's utilitarianism had a singular focus, it was 'the happiness of the party whose interest is in question', not just the private individual but 'every measure of government'.[22] In contemporary parlance, this equates to 'wellbeing'.

Hans Morgenthau began his career as a legal theorist whose work on international jurisprudence eventually led him to become one of the founders of the realist school of international relations. Realists see nation-states as the principal actors in international affairs, each seeking to maximise its possession and use of power. Morgenthau put it succinctly: 'The main signpost that helps political realism to find its way through the landscape of international politics is the concept of interest defined in terms of power.'[23] As Morgenthau analyses the elements of national power, it becomes clear that power is not univocal: the different components of national power and the differing ways in which they combine lend quite distinctive forms to national power. No two nation-states have the same power, and as they set about the global competition for influence, they play to their relative strengths. The raw contest for economic and military supremacy, for instance, tends to distinguish the competition between great powers and superpowers. Indeed, as the former Soviet Union discovered, the competition can exhaust them, essentially because they rely on only two of the elements of national power. The Nordic nations, on the other hand, are extremely skilful in their exercise of 'soft power', employing an effective diplomacy to their own advantage, and to the advantage generally of the countries with which they deal. They create value rather than expend energy and resources.

Morgenthau identifies eight principal elements of national power, four of them quantitative and four of them qualitative: the size of the landmass; natural resource wealth; industrial capacity; military strength; population; national character (things like endurance and resilience); national morale (a nation's determination to support its government in peace and war); and the quality of a nation's diplomacy. Morgenthau's comments on diplomacy are particularly pertinent:

> Of all the factors which make for the power of a nation, the most important, and of the more unstable, is the quality of diplomacy. All the other factors which determine national power are, as it were, the raw material out of which the power of a nation is fashioned. The quality of a nation's diplomacy combines those different factors into an integrated whole, gives them direction and weight, and awakens their slumbering potentialities by giving them the breath of actual power ... Diplomacy, one might say, is the brains of national power, as national morale is its soul.[24]

The implications of Morgenthau's observations for Australia are profound. By any measure, excepting the size of its population and the quality of its diplomacy (more about that below), Australia has considerable power. But as a nation, we do not understand that, and are diffident about such understanding of our national power as we do have. The indicators of Australia's national power are many: it boasts the twelfth-largest economy;[25] seven of its universities rank in the world's top 100;[26] four of its cities rank in the top ten of the Economist

Intelligence Unit's Global Liveability Index;[27] and, for a nation of sport lovers, Australia averages eighth position on the Olympic medals tally. Our vulnerabilities are clear, however. With a population of 25 million, Australia is comparatively underpopulated, lacking the population mass for a fully self-sustaining economy, large industrial workforce or large military forces. This is, as Michael Fullilove pointed out in his 2015 Boyer Lectures, a strategic vulnerability.[28] This 'little country mentality' is reflected in our national diplomacy, which has suffered significant underinvestment for at least the past quarter-century.

Australia's diplomatic ineptitude is a consequence of several interrelated factors. The most startling is the recent tendency to politicise virtually every significant foreign policy issue, usually for domestic political purposes, or to support personal political alignments at the international level – conversation between celebrities rather than convergence of policy interests. Instead of careful deliberation and consideration of all aspects of a matter, the contemporary practice is to elevate issues to the political level quickly, most often to provide a TV and photo opportunity for a minister. And as politicians seek the limelight, the corresponding action is to demean traditional diplomatic practice as bureaucratic, formal, inflexible and far too slow.

Politicians, at least in the Australian context, survive and progress on the back of their ability to cut and thrust, rather than to parry and deflect. For those who live in the world of boisterous chest-thumping, diplomacy is seen as too conciliatory, effete and wimpish, requiring the more 'feminine' skills of listening, collaboration and respect. Diplomacy demands a deep understanding of the importance of long-term public goods, the attainment of which is careful, deliberate and iterative. The 'riding to hounds and over the jumps' that distinguishes Australia's short electoral cycle is poor training for sustained diplomatic practice.

Fundamentally, the immediacy of politics trumps the importance of diplomacy as the key tool for generating international influence. The politician is portrayed as 'the fixer', while the professional diplomat is regarded as the cautious and risk-averse plodder whose task it is to set the stage for the arrival of the celebrity. Our diplomats have become courtiers, dancing attendance on their virtuosic ministers.

For over two decades, Australia's diplomatic capacity and capabilities have eroded. This has been the direct result of government funding decisions. In a landmark study published in March 2009, the Lowy Institute reported that Australia's network of overseas diplomatic missions was overstretched and hollowed out. Our public diplomacy was lacklustre, and the aid program faced significant challenges.[29] The Lowy study noted that Australia ranked twenty-sixth out of the thirty OECD nations by number of diplomatic missions.[30] It made a raft of recommendations, very few of which were implemented by the Rudd/Gillard governments or their successors.

In the intervening decade, things have worsened. The DFAT operating budget has continued to flatline, marking a continuing decline in resources in real terms.[31] AsiaLink research published in late 2019 reveals that Australia's spending on foreign affairs has fallen to just 1.3 per cent of the total federal budget.[32]

While Australia's diplomatic network continues to suffer funding cuts, and remains seriously under-resourced in language proficiency and subject matter expertise, it is required to meet ever higher performance targets and shoulder a growing consular load as more Australians travel (and get themselves into trouble with the local law-enforcement agencies).

The diplomatic profession has been amateurised. Successive governments have continued to appoint former politicians, generally with no language skills, no international negotiating experience and no subject matter expertise, to diplomatic posts. Those who seek preferment and sinecures never bid for the truly demanding posts, like Jakarta and Port Moresby, or any of the posts in Africa or South America. Rather, they seek comfort and what might appear to be status. But while the Holy See, Rome, The Hague, Brussels, New York (consul-general), Chicago and Houston may not rank as top-tier posts, they are nonetheless useful training grounds for diplomats on the way up. Tokyo, Washington DC, London, New Delhi, New York (United Nations), Wellington and Auckland do count as top-tier posts where our national interests are deeply engaged. These are posts for professionals rather than political 'mates' who are either owed something or are better kept out of the way.

Caricature is a favourite Australian pastime, applying the scalpel of ridicule to any tall poppy that might be at hand. So Barry Humphries created the grotesque Sir Les Patterson as a commentary on diplomatic pretension.[33] Whether Humphries was channelling Vince Gair[34] (ambassador to Ireland 1974–76), John Armstrong[35] (high commissioner to the United Kingdom 1972–75) or Sir John Kerr[36] (who resided in London for some years following his resignation as governor-general) is unclear. But any young diplomat who has assisted visiting ministers or politicians in their cups regards the prospect of a diplomatic appointment for any of them with concern.

The simple fact is that the 'spoils of office' and 'gravy train' approach to diplomacy does not provide Australia with the professional and leadership qualities that are necessary if it is to play an international role commensurate with its national power.[37] Political skills, such as they may be, are no substitute for the subject matter expertise and the skills in international advocacy and negotiation (where our representatives come up against some of the best in the world) that are prerequisites if complexity is to be managed and opportunity realised.[38]

The long-term professional networks and relationships that are the essential operating environment in which the conduct of diplomacy takes place are fundamentally different from the short-term and generally superficial relationships typically established at the international political level. Relationships built around political convenience may be nice to have, but they are no substitute for the painstaking investment that goes into diplomatic relationships.

'The national interest' may be a subtle concept. It is certainly an important one, because it offers a shorthand way of capturing what the nation is all about – its identity and its power.

Australia's national interests

If our national values – to the extent that Australia has formulated or agreed them – express what Australia stands for, our national interests give expression to the overarching goals of national public policy. And if the nation can be no more secure than its citizens, in that critical sense of national security that has the individual happiness and wellbeing of the citizens as its wellspring, it is essential that we agree, promote and protect our national interests. Yet we struggle to find an authoritative or coherent set of national interests in the national political conversation. It is as though Humpty Dumpty prevails once more, words meaning what their users choose them to mean, 'neither more nor less'. A notable exception is the extended reflection on national interests by Senator Penny Wong, to which we shall return below.

Like values, interests are often described in linear and serial terms when, more accurately, they are intersecting domains that constitute the purposes of public policy. They are analytically distinguishable, but functionally inseparable. Because the world of public policy is dynamic, interests do change over time, if not as ultimate goals of public policy then at least in the balances that must be struck between them from time to time. The global experience of the coronavirus pandemic put a renewed emphasis on human wellbeing and economic security, for instance, with relatively less emphasis on investing in military force as a guarantor of national security.

In her 2017 Lowy address, Senator Wong proposed four principal national interests:

- the security of the nation and its people;

- the economic prosperity of the nation and its people;
- a stable, cooperative strategic system in our region (a cohesive neighbourhood); and
- constructive internationalism supporting the continued development of an international rules-based order (a cohesive world).[39]

Senator Wong established a compelling argument for these elements as the basis of a foreign policy that was both transactional and transformational. In a world that is adapting itself to the continuing transmutations of the coronavirus and their economic and social consequences, it would be interesting to know whether she would include, as a core national interest, the maintenance of the sinews and tissues of the nation. Clearly, the ability of the nation to build a body politic that incorporates all the strengths that derive from its diversity and to act to its own benefit, as distinct from having government implement threat-based policies, offers a comprehensive approach to nation-building. It certainly merits deeper consideration as one of the key 'national interests'.

Acceptance and inclusion

The core national interest is building and strengthening the acceptance and inclusion that are the sine qua non of personal wellbeing, contentment and happiness – the necessary underpinnings of community and state security. The coronavirus pandemic has brought additional salience to this core national interest, which goes to the heart of Australia's success in managing the various local outbreaks of COVID-19. The success of the Commonwealth and state/territory governments has depended on the willingness of the citizens to work together to the benefit of the broader community. In societies that are significantly more stratified than is Australia's, and where the pursuit of individual preferences comes at the expense of the broader community, infection and death rates have been significantly higher. It is important to reflect that in a federation such as Australia, the constitutional allocation of powers means that the state and territory governments are necessarily closer to the community than is the Commonwealth government. In consequence, the state and territory governments enjoyed both the authority and trust to impose lockdowns, isolate people in their homes, mandate social controls such as mask-wearing and social distancing. This was due in no small measure to the relatively high levels of acceptance, inclusion and tolerance in the broader Australian community – the key elements of the 'morale' that Morgenthau saw as a dimension of national power.

Acceptance and inclusion are evident in the Australian community, but they are elusive and fragile. Demagoguery and populism can quickly marginalise individuals and divide communities, especially when racism and religious intolerance are the instruments of choice. Ideology is the enemy of inclusion, because it feeds into alienation, marginalisation and sectarianism. And these in turn feed the cancer of internal dissension, which can ultimately precipitate internal collapse, even to the point of civil war. Without acceptance and inclusion as a core national interest, the spectre of social upheaval is ever present. What is more, when acceptance and inclusion collapse, they are difficult to re-establish, because trust and respect go with them.

Security

Chapter 2 established that, in the twenty-first century, 'security' comprehends very much more than the ability of the government to provide the military capabilities to defend against armed attack. As the COVID-19 pandemic has underscored, human security is front and centre in the multitude of contemporary global strategic concerns.

The global strategic environment is unlike anything that the international community has faced before. In previous decades and centuries, economic and military power have been fairly coterminous: the military power of empires (including the post–World War II US empire) was based on and reflected their economic mass. The strategic disruption of the twenty-first century is a consequence of the divergence between economic and military power, allowing and encouraging powerful states to build their access and influence through geo-economic interventions rather than through geostrategic ambition supported by military deployments. While the United States, for instance, has continued its preference for military expeditions to secure its strategic interests, especially in the Middle East, China has chosen a massive economic program to realise its strategic interests. It has, of course, significantly expanded its military capabilities at the same time, but with a clear focus on the direct defence of China rather than the development of expeditionary forces to achieve its international strategic goals. This disruption and divergence have set the scene for a substantially different set of strategic issues for Australia to deal with, though our default position is to carry on regardless, offering conventional solutions to unconventional problems.

The starting point for the security of the nation is the security of each citizen: their personal, family and community security, based on their emotional, financial and physical wellbeing. Australia is finding it difficult to accommodate itself to the new security paradigm, where the consequences of climate change and pandemics are at least as significant a threat to the wellbeing of the citizens as the threat of armed conflict. Australia is finding it even more difficult to postulate policy settings that address these contemporary security issues, preferring to re-prescribe old nostrums. For as long as Australia views its security principally through the lens of defence capability, military systems and an approach to law enforcement that promotes the rights of the state over the rights of the individual, engineering a new security paradigm and developing appropriate security policies will remain a dream – or a nightmare.

The ongoing elaboration of national security policy demands more sophisticated analytical and policy formulation skills than the current practice of binary reductionism permits. Australia's security future will not be determined by a choice between the United States, as perpetual protector, and China, as emergent threat. While they both tower over our strategic future, it would be a signal failure of strategic imagination to assume that they can never be reconciled, and a failure of diplomatic capability to deliver that reconciliation. For the strategic, as well as political, fact is that Australia is in a region where interests are more often shared than separate. The art is to develop a diplomacy that delivers our security interests by strengthening the resilience of the smaller powers in a way that attracts the constructive engagement of the two great powers. Very few nations, even great ones, will chose isolation over participation. Senator Wong captured this challenge well:

> We need simultaneously to broaden, deepen and strengthen our historic links with allies while we develop new ways of managing relationships with new powers, China and India among them. If our core policy focus is on ensuring that the benefits of economic prosperity, productivity growth and international trade are equitably distributed, nationally and internationally, then our security policy interests become more manageable. In short, beggar thy neighbour is no more a recipe for security and stability than is threaten thy neighbour.[40]

The great lesson of history is that security is an artefact of the brain, not brawn.

Prosperity

Historically, Australia has enjoyed remarkable prosperity. It is not a given, however. As the years immediately following the arrival of Europeans in 1788 and the years of the Great Depression amply illustrate, economic deprivation imperils social cohesion. Regardless of their political persuasion, Australian governments have addressed their responsibilities for national prosperity with determination and success. On any measure, Australia is a prosperous country. Among the OECD countries, Australia ranks tenth in GDP per capita,[41] and according to the International Monetary Fund, Australia ranks twelfth in nominal GDP.[42] Despite the COVID-19 global pandemic, Australia's GDP continued to grow on the back of China's demand for iron ore, pushing the size of the Australian economy beyond that of Brazil for the first time in twenty-five years, and close to equalling that of Russia.[43]

But, as the *Inequality in Australia 2020* report noted, economic inequality in Australia has been growing steadily over the two decades from 1999 to 2020.[44] The average wealth of the top 20 per cent of Australians grew ten times faster than that of the bottom 20 per cent. In household wealth, the gap is even greater: those in the highest 20 per cent enjoy an average wealth of $3.3 million, ninety times the average of those in the lowest 20 per cent ($36,000).

The paradox is clear: while the nation is prosperous, many of its citizens are not. Decades of middle-class welfare, preferential property taxation arrangements that have enriched the older generation at the expense of their children and tax cuts for the wealthy have substantially redistributed Australia's prosperity to those who are least in need.

When prosperity is measured simply by the dollar value of the economy, it is easy for governments to fall victim to the Panglossian conceit that 'everything is for the best in this best of possible worlds'. The self-satisfaction that accompanies 'a beautiful set of numbers' – about which federal treasurers love to crow – conceals the fact that national prosperity is not shared by the millions of citizens whose financial security is parlous. The wellbeing of the citizens – their ability to have a happy personal life, a rewarding working life and a dignified retirement – is as much an indicator of national prosperity as the national bank balance. So prosperity, as a key national interest, is not an unqualified good. It comprehends much more than national wealth. It also comprehends much more than the extraction of minerals and hydrocarbon energy resources, or the export of agricultural products: it also comprehends the development of the nation's human and social capital to deliver income streams at the national and personal levels that represent a fair return on both investment and labour. Prosperity must engage the imagination of the citizens if it is to survive fluctuations in economic fortunes, economic downturns and events such as global financial crises and pandemics. And, of course, the continued delivery of national prosperity must address the consequences of global warming.

To maintain national prosperity, the Australian government must also invest strenuously in the creation and maintenance of an equitable international rules-based order. To its credit, Australia has been a long-term contributor to building an open international trading system and the rules that underpin it. From the creation of the Cairns Group in 1984 to the formation of the G20 in the aftermath of the 2007 global financial crisis, Australia played an active role in the world's economic and financial councils. In a global economy that wants to take refuge behind tariffs and other trade barriers in the wake of the coronavirus pandemic, Australia needs to step up its efforts to repair the authority and credibility of the WTO. The painstaking work of trade diplomacy is always preferable to vociferous slanging matches. Our diplomatic history suggests that Australia's diplomats have both the skill and the application to deliver the long-term international institutional arrangements on which our prosperity ultimately rests.

A cohesive neighbourhood

Geographically, Australia is fortunate enough to border on the engine room of the global economy. Security, stability and prosperity to our north is central to our security, stability and prosperity. So we need to invest in the Asian region at all levels – socially, politically, economically, diplomatically and culturally. The nations of Asia share long histories of mutual accommodation and engagement, their ethnic and cultural differences notwithstanding. Australia has much to learn from them. Australia also has much to offer them, particularly in being able to demonstrate that adherence to the rule of law, respect for the basic freedoms and investing in an open, inclusive and tolerant society contribute as much to economic prosperity as to social harmony. Talking up the positives is much more effective in the world of diplomacy than talking down the negatives: promoting our national strengths is always preferable to criticising what we might regard as our neighbours' deficiencies.

While the early postcolonial histories of the South-East Asian countries led to troubled cross-border relationships in the quarter-century following the end of World War II, the statesmanship of the prime ministers/presidents of Indonesia, Malaysia, Singapore, Thailand and the Philippines saw the creation of ASEAN and its subsequent expansion to include Brunei, Cambodia, Laos, Myanmar and Vietnam. And although it is fashionable for some Western commentators to deride ASEAN as a grouping that talks a lot and does very little, the fact that it has been able to maintain a strategically stable region for nearly five decades is a political triumph. While in present circumstances Myanmar is a troubled and troublesome member of ASEAN, its members would prefer to keep Myanmar inside the tent than outside, principally because its membership affords the other nine nations the opportunity to maintain subtle pressure on Myanmar and to preserve avenues for consultation and discussion.

The ASEAN members have also been able to maintain professional working relationships with China, even though they have similar problems to Australia's in their dealings with it. Vietnam, Thailand and Singapore are particularly adroit in keeping a measure of equilibrium in their relationships with the region's dominant power. Of course, they have in some instances over a millennium's worth of experience on which they can build. In this, too, Australia can learn from them.

A cohesive regional neighbourhood does not just happen: it must be worked at and tended. It demands considerable diplomatic investment, something that Australia has simply not been prepared to make in recent years. Sometimes fraught and sometimes surprisingly close, our relationship with Indonesia has been allowed to atrophy. We cannot blame the COVID-19 pandemic. Indeed, Australia should have initiated immediate consultations with its neighbours, including China, when the coronavirus struck, looking for common approaches to managing the virus and to protecting populations against its virulence. Prime Minister Howard demonstrated remarkable statesmanship when he provided $1 billion to Indonesia in the immediate aftermath of the tsunami that hit in 2004. He turned a catastrophe into a diplomatic and human security opportunity. Prime Minister Morrison would have done well to follow his example.

A cohesive world: Constructive internationalism

In many respects, achieving a cohesive neighbourhood is the necessary but not sufficient step towards helping to construct a cooperative global community – a goal that helped materialise the establishment of the United Nations in the immediate aftermath of World War II. The Australian foreign minister, Dr Evatt, was an enthusiastic supporter of the United Nations, and demonstrated that Australia could play a truly constructive role in healing the wounds of war and in creating international institutions to manage the world's affairs peacefully and avoid the catastrophe of war.

'Constructive internationalism' is Senator Penny Wong's more pragmatic re-expression of former foreign minister Gareth Evans's more values-laden 'good international citizenship'. Basically, they mean the same thing: a secure and prosperous future for Australia, as for other 'second XI' powers (to channel a cricketing analogy), depends on our success in maintaining the international institutional system in good order, adapting it when it becomes obsolete and creating new institutions better able to deal with emergent problems. Gareth Evans was, and remains, a strong advocate for strong international institutions and Australia's active role in their operation. He was, and remains, an advocate for their continuous reform as new circumstances demand adaptation. Yet many of the global institutions need serious repair, as a combination of obsolescence, funding cuts, leadership failure, technical capacity decline and, most significantly, lack of support and sponsorship on the part of world leaders, have left them moribund. This is nowhere clearer than in the continuing decline of the authority, credibility and legitimacy of the United Nations and its agencies – the World Health Organization, for example.

The UN Security Council, for instance, has fallen victim to its unrepresentative structure and to the ability of any single permanent member, of which there are five, to derail the consensus that the council needs to resolve problems and effect outcomes that benefit the victims of armed conflict, usually non-combatant civilians. The UN Security Council is an artefact of World War II, where the spoils of international leadership went to the victors. Britain, China, France, Russia and the United States remain important countries, but they are not representative. They are all nuclear weapons states, yet there are at least four such states and a couple of aspirants that are outside the fold: Brazil, Germany, India, Japan and Nigeria all have sustainable claims to permanent membership. The veto power is not only anti-democratic but also anti-humanistic in that it puts the narrow interests of a particular state above the needs of people who are caught up as victims of war. The humanism of idealistic leaders in the immediate post–World War II years, reflected in the preambular paragraphs of the UN Charter, has given way to the cynicism of political automatons.

This really matters. Nations like Australia and other countries that value order and transparency in international affairs (not all of them democracies, by the way) have a long-term interest in ensuring that the UN system works. The fiasco attending the WHO's investigation of the origins of the COVID-19 pandemic is emblematic of a failing international institutional system. It needs fixing, and Australia needs to play its part. That is what constructive internationalism is all about.

Far too often, Australia's international interests are sacrificed on the altar of domestic political bickering. Statesmanship falls victim to political pettiness. Gareth Evans, for instance, helped to set up the UN Transitional Authority in Cambodia (UNTAC), established the Canberra Commission to Eliminate Nuclear Weapons, drove Australia's activism in the UN Human Rights Commission and promoted the early work done to establish the UN Framework Convention on Climate Change. His legacy was effectively trashed by the change of government in 1996. In a quarter of a century, Australia has failed to realise the enormous potential with which its place in the world has endowed it. This is an abject failure of diplomacy, which, as noted earlier, is the touchstone of national power. The Nordics and New Zealand actively prosecute their demands for an effective and strong international institutional system. Australia stands by sullenly on the sidelines.

So, where to?

The manifest policy failures that continue to dog us both illustrate and reinforce the comorbidities that have eroded Australia's role in the global community. Our relationship with the United States has become increasingly abject as our focus on the military relationship has become increasingly obsessive. Our relationship with China is at once hysterical and unconfident. Our relationships in Asia are disengaged and supercilious. Our relationships in the Pacific, including with New Zealand, are condescending and high-handed. We are heading towards pariah status in the world's climate change forums. Our once proud record on human rights is in tatters due to the billions spent to dishonour our obligations under the United Nations' 1951 Refugee Convention. And our fists have become ever tighter as our investment in international development assistance continues to fall. At the same time, we have become more introspective, our waning self-confidence ever more on display as government ministers trumpet a fictitious 'world's best practice' benchmark for almost everything they do. And a largely compliant media feeds the vanity of our political leaders.

We are a lonely nation. Whether it is tampering with cricket balls, fiddling our carbon emissions data or revoking major defence contracts, we have self-identified as a nation of cheats and deceivers.

It does not have to be this way, however. To the extent that we recognise that we have a problem, to that extent we are on the way to solving it. That demands imagination and leadership. What would a more confident world view look like?

9
Imagining a New International Game Plan

Imagination is not a gift usually associated with bureaucracies.

The 9/11 Commission Report[1]

Most disasters begin with a failure of imagination. The comfort and complacency that result from conventional thinking about unconventional problems, especially when such thinking happens in the echo chamber of convergent mindsets, often precipitates a failure to 'join the dots'. The loss of life and destruction at Pearl Harbor was such a failure. So, too, was the fall of Singapore, where the Royal Navy and seaward-facing defences were no match for the Imperial Japanese Army as it raced down the Malayan Peninsula. The Vietnam War was a failure of imagination at every level. On a much smaller scale, the near-success of Sandline in imposing a mercenary military solution to the political problems of Bougainville in 1998, and potentially bringing down Sir Julius Chan's government in Port Moresby, was a failure of imagination as much on Australia's part as it was on the part of Papua New Guinea.[2] The National Commission on Terrorist Attacks Upon the United States (known generally as the 9/11 Commission) judged the destruction of the World Trade Center in New York on 11 September 2001 to be a failure of imagination.[3] And perhaps the biggest failures of imagination to affect the global community in its entirety are the accelerating impacts of global warming and the continuing reliance on nuclear weapons by the great powers; these are failures of both imagination and leadership.

It is no surprise that these two qualities, imagination and leadership, go together.

Preoccupied as it is with threats (currently the fear of China) and its constant insecurity (of which bellicosity and belligerence are commonly symptomatic), Australia has, in recent decades, preferred to hunker down in the hesitant and unconfident role of bit player than to galvanise itself in the vigorous pursuit of opportunities. It is easy to barrack from the sidelines. It is hard to maintain the energy and enthusiasm to sustain the activity levels that a constant and long-term role demands. While Australia's macho political leaders regularly trumpet how the nation 'punches above its weight', Australia is largely invisible as an international actor. We prefer to bob along in the wake of our great and powerful friend, the United States, happy in the role of dependable acolyte and ally. But our inertia and insouciance come at a cost, not only in the reputational damage we inflict on ourselves but also, and more significantly, in opportunities foregone.

As we saw in Chapter 8, Australia enjoys considerable national power, infrequently recognised and rarely put to work in our national interest. And the quality of our diplomacy, which brings all the elements of national power together, has continued to decline for almost three decades. This is not simply a result of mindless efficiency dividends, the relentless pursuit of 'doing more with less' (which inevitably becomes 'doing less with even less'), the dissipation of our diplomatic capacity and presence, and the growing practice of appointing failed politicians to plum diplomatic postings. It is more a result of a lack of diplomatic ambition and leadership on the part of successive governments, political introspection that reduces everything (including international relations) to domestic political barneying, and pedestrian performance by a succession of prime ministers and foreign ministers. The partnership that once distinguished the relationship between diplomatic professionals and the political leadership, delivering sound foreign policy as the basis for government decisions, has given way to an amalgam of jingoism, naivety, self-indulgence and whimsy. Instead of respected confidants, our diplomats are expected to be obsequious courtiers. This is not to suggest that the professionals always get it right – compliance with Indonesia's incorporation of East Timor (or was it appeasement?) was not the brightest of Australia's diplomatic moments. But disdain for professional policy advice on the part of senior ministers and their evident preference for intelligence-based 'assessments' do not generate enduring outcomes. The reason for this is clear: threat-based advice is necessarily reactive, short-term and transactional; interests-based advice – that is, advice framed around Australia's national interests – is strategic, long-term and transformational. It is here that imagination reveals itself.

Contentment with the mundane, together with aversion to risk, militate against imagination. So too does a fixation on 'the world as it is' undermine any creative effort to give shape to 'the world as we would like it to be'. These are not binary states, locked into a kind of eternal antinomy. It is by dealing with the world as it is that we create the world as we would like it to be. But we must imagine that world and design a game plan to achieve it. To do so, we must transform dependence into partnership, apprehension into confidence, arrogant disdain into the pursuit of common goals, and lecturing into listening.

Dependence into partnership: Imagining a new Australia–US relationship

Chapter 2 examined Australia's relationship with the United States through the lens of the ANZUS Treaty. There is nothing wrong with the ANZUS Treaty per se. It is an artefact of its times, narrow in its scope and limited in its requirements of both parties. It is a symbol of Australia's immediate post–World War II insecurity, its fear of a resurgent and rearmed Japan. And while we might like to think that the treaty assuages our more contemporary fear of China and its geostrategic rise, the history of the treaty suggests that US presidents will not put their country or its interests at risk on Australia's behalf. Yes, there would be consultation. But recourse to armed force to defeat China on Australia's behalf is beyond any US imagining. President Kennedy demonstrated that in the much less complicated circumstances of 1963. The United States, and Australia for that matter, might hope that the threat of armed force would deter a military threat against Australia. Ultimately, however, the Guam

Doctrine, so artlessly but effectively enunciated by President Nixon, would apply. Australia would need to stand on its own feet.

But the ANZUS Treaty, which is narrowly constrained to military and defence relations, has been promoted into a talisman of the entire bilateral relationship and accorded an iconic status that obscures the complexity and depth of Australia–United States relations.[4] It is a relationship that is crying out for a more contemporary and mature reconfiguration, one that is based not on marine-grey or khaki-tinted sentimentality betokening dependence, but on shared interests that will only be achieved through partnership. Emma Shortis has called for a radical rethink of Australia's 'exceptional friendship' with the United States, addressing more than what a palatable or more independent foreign policy might look like. In her view, 'the starting point for [a] radical reshaping needs to be a genuine, historically informed understanding of why Australia behaves as it does in the world, and how deeply that is connected to both our relationship with the United States and the broader histories we share'.[5]

In a momentous few days for Australia and its government, between 16 and 24 September 2021 Prime Minister Morrison announced the AUKUS partnership, created to deliver nuclear-propelled submarines (so that Australia can take armed conflict up to China's front door) and attended the inaugural meeting of the Quad heads of government (to impose further constraints on China's ambitions in Asia). The three members of AUKUS are each looking for quite different things: the United States is looking to enhance its pre-eminence in Asia as part of its 'pivot'; the United Kingdom is looking to award itself a global role as it moves further away from Europe and indulges in imperial reminiscence; and Australia is looking to return to the bosom of its two 'great and powerful friends'. To say the least, AUKUS offers a constrained view of the future.

The Quad, comprising Australia, India, Japan and the United States, is a curious creature that resembles the former Southeast Asia Treaty Organization – and will possibly have about the same lifespan, as the divergences in the members' national security culture and strategic mindset do not augur well for the grouping's longevity. Australia is searching for security reassurance and China's containment; India is happy to join a multiplicity of associations so long as it retains its strategic autonomy; Japan wants to send a low-cost signal to China, while remaining in the same strategic camp as the United States and its allies; and the United States seeks to realise its geopolitical pivot to Asia at the lowest possible cost.

The position and long-term status of the United States as the leader of the free world is not in question. But its position as the global superpower is under serious challenge by China, and has been even more seriously jeopardised by the missteps of President Trump, who in a single term managed to trash the authority, credibility and legitimacy of his nation. The prospect of a decline in the status and authority of the United States has been a matter of keen debate for three decades. The debate on whether it can return to its former pre-eminence is only intensifying, and the prospects of such a return are doubtful at best and dismal at worst. The debate really matters for Australia, however, and Australia needs to participate in it.

Paul Kennedy's 1988 book *The Rise and Fall of the Great Powers* created a mini-storm in the United States, with Kennedy accused of all sorts of academic solecisms – particularly that of denigrating the power and authority of the United States. He and Joseph Nye conducted an amusing and respectful debate in the letters pages of *The New York Review of Books*.[6] The pundits of the Kennedy School of Government at Harvard took umbrage at the fact that a British historian appeared to be wishing imperial decline upon the leader of the West. In a retreat into confirmation bias, they dubbed him a 'declinist'. The defenders of US exceptionalism and singularity might have been just a little thin-skinned. As Patrick Porter, another British academic, commented, more in explanation of Kennedy than in his defence:

> Underpinning Kennedy's argument was an astute observation that America's global position arose in atypical, indeed extraordinary historical conditions, whereby the Old World of Europe

> shattered itself in World War Two, a war which strengthened America's economic base and military power, making its relative position artificially strong, a state of affairs that could not go on indefinitely. Decline, in this context, meant not the melodrama of the Occident at sunset, falling into the sea, but a shift from a position of unipolar dominance to becoming a heavyweight in a more polycentric world.[7]

In some measure, though differently from the way he imagined it, Kennedy's prognoses have proved to be more correct than his critics wanted to believe. At the heart of his thesis was the view that a decline in a great power's economic strength inevitably caused a decline in its strategic power and standing:

> [There is a] conundrum which has exercised strategists and economists and political leaders from classical times onward. To be a Great Power – by definition, a state capable of holding its own against any other nation – demands a flourishing economic base ... [B]y going to war, or by devoting a large share of the nation's 'manufacturing power' to expenditures upon 'unproductive' armaments, one runs the risk of eroding the national economic base, especially vis-à-vis states which are concentrating a greater share of their income upon productive investment for long-term growth.[8]

But in charting a course to a somewhat different place in a more polycentric world, Kennedy was not alone. The acerbic Gore Vidal, in his collection of lectures published in 1992 as *The Decline and Fall of the American Empire*, identified moral ambiguity and political overreach as the key to the erosion of US power. Vidal went so far as to identify a precise date for the death of the US empire: 16 September 1985, the day that 'the Commerce Department announced that the United States had become a debtor nation'.[9]

In a 2003 speech delivered at Yale University, former President Clinton imagined the United States was no longer the military, political and economic superpower in the world, and the constraints on US choices and behaviours that such a change might entail.[10] Nearly two decades later, that scenario is slowly materialising. American power is contested as China emerges as the dominant power in Asia and as a clear global strategic competitor to the United States. Yet the latter remains in pursuit of pre-eminence – the top dog in a world that is not quintessentially canine.

In his Tanner Lectures, delivered at Princeton University in 2010, Bruce Ackerman argued that the end point of US triumphalism was the rogue president representing an ideological extreme.[11] Ackerman tracked two phenomena that have combined to transform the nature of the US presidency and, in consequence, the republic: a communications strategy that emphasises soundbite appeals, and a super-politicised White House staff that would override the bureaucracy, ordering them to implement the popular mandate. While Ackerman did not predict Donald Trump's ascension to the presidency, he did forecast the inevitability of an extremist president. He further argued that an extremist president was even more dangerous when supported by an increasingly politicised military. Ackerman provoked considerable criticism, bordering on derision, for his 'eccentric jumble of proposals', as one reviewer put it.[12] In important respects, however, Ackerman's spectre materialised: Trump.

> By constructing a new form of presidential administration, centrists like Clinton and Obama are preparing the way for a tragic future in which extremist presidencies take the center of the bureaucratic stage. Their steady stream of presidential directives will override expert assessments of the facts, or traditional understandings of the law, provided by the agencies. They will call upon the entire executive branch to join the exciting enterprise of executing the president's mandate from the people. And these instructions will receive an enthusiastic reception – since the bureaucracy will be under the command of presidential appointees, who gained their deputy assistant secretaryships on the basis of their partisan loyalties.[13]

The Trump presidency both revealed and exploited fundamental fault lines in the American polity. It fed on the sense of betrayal expressed by industrial and agricultural workers and the middle class as real income levels have declined and economic marginalisation increased. Social inequality and the palpable sense of grievance that accompanies it, especially among poor white youths, was exploited mercilessly by Trump, culminating in the 6 January 2021 assault on the Capitol in Washington DC. While the internal collapse of the United States is not in prospect, its political institutions are as fragile as its social infrastructure. This is of much greater importance to Australia and our long-term relationship with the United States than is China's management of the politics of Hong Kong or the treatment of the Uighurs in Xinjiang Province, brutal as both have been.

Prior to his election, President Biden announced a foreign policy 'for the middle class' that would 'unite the economic might of democracies around the world to counter abusive economic practices and reduce inequality'. Marking a return to its traditional ambition, the president said that 'the Biden foreign policy agenda will place the United States back at the head of the table', resorting to the traditional (but not conclusive) binary to represent the cost of failure:

> If we continue [Trump's] abdication of that responsibility [to be at the head of the table], then one of two things will happen: either someone else will take the United States' place, but not in a way that advances our interests and values, or no one will, and chaos will ensue. Either way, that's not good for America.[14]

But the emergence of yet another 'Biden Doctrine'[15] suggests that old habits die hard, and that the exceptionalists who continue to staff the Pentagon retain their influence over US foreign and security policy, advocating retention of or a return to US global pre-eminence. In a thoughtful essay in *Foreign Affairs*, Hal Brands characterises the Biden Doctrine as encapsulating an existential clash between democracy and autocracy. It comprises three elements:

> First, the United States must strengthen the cohesion and resilience of the democratic community against its autocratic rivals and make such democratic solidarity truly global, since so

> many aspects of the threat require a global response. Second, it must lead the world's democracies in addressing transnational problems that no nation can solve on its own. And [third] it must build a 'position of strength' for global rivalry by reinvesting in its own competitiveness and demonstrating that democracies can still deliver for their citizens.[16]

This represents a decidedly Manichaean view of the world, and whether it will survive as a 'doctrine' is moot, not least of all because neither democracy nor autocracy is univocal. They take many forms. Are Hungary, Poland, Singapore or Turkey democracies? Are China, Russia, Saudi Arabia, Vietnam and Zimbabwe autocracies? As John Keane has argued, the fact that commentators randomly describe countries such as China as 'autocratic', 'despotic', 'totalitarian' or 'tyrannical' does not make them so.[17] Indeed, Keane identifies many features of the 'phantom democracy' operating in China,[18] as they do to some extent in Indonesia, Singapore and Malaysia. Is the United States a democracy, given the wholesale gerrymandering and restriction on suffrage practised in many of the Republican-dominated states? James Traub suggests that US democracy is in real trouble: '[T]he United States may soon become the world's only established democracy where members of one party have managed to make it much harder for members of the other party to cast a ballot.'[19] To be sustainable, any US claim to be the world's leading democracy and head of the democratic nations must reflect sound electoral practice and an equitable contest of policies and views. Otherwise, it risks accusations of hypocrisy and hubris.

This matters much more to Australia and the other democratic allies of the United States than talking up security threats, conducting military exercises that are little more than sabre-rattling, establishing military bases across the globe and indulging in military adventurism that seems always to end in disaster. A United States where democracy is purchased, gerrymandered or constrained, where capital punishment continues to be on the statute books of more than half the states (as well as the federal government, the US military and American Samoa), where there are more handguns and personal weapons than there are citizens and where racial inequality remains endemic does not look like the leader of the free world. The security of Australia and its citizens – and that of the United States and its citizens, for that matter – is much more a product of the protection and promotion of personal and democratic rights than it is of extended nuclear deterrence and bristling military capabilities. President Biden is right to imagine building a coalition of like-minded nations that respect the rule of law and the rights of their citizens as the engine room of an effective global rules-based order. But to deliver that coalition demands that the United States addresses its domestic issues. Instead of talking up 'the China threat', Australia and the United States would do much better to establish a real democratic partnership that delivers greater prosperity and wellbeing to our citizens than unitary governments running command economies are able to do. If the United States (and Australia) fails that challenge, then US claims to global leadership are nothing more than 'The Emperor's New Clothes' acted out on the global stage.

There are some early indications that the cause may already have been lost. As Howard French, in his perceptive review of three strikingly different books on the topic published in 2021, puts the issue:

> [The] question … is … whether the US, instead of turning inward, can once again summon the wherewithal to help 'solve common problems that face all states.' The answer is uncertain. What is clear, though, is that an international transition of some ill-defined sort is well underway. [W]ill the US, at the very least one of 'a small handful of first-tier great powers,' continue to cling to 'a mystical American exceptionalism' or instead devise a 'pragmatic, responsible, and publicly articulated strategy' for dealing with the profound changes that are already afoot?[20]

In other words, is the United States ready for a change of gear from 'pre-eminence' to 'eminence'? This is of fundamental strategic significance for Australia, and the answer matters.

President Clinton's 2003 rumination has come to pass. Whether the world is described as multi-polar or polycentric, there are now multiple centres of power, power which is itself differentiated. Military and economic power, which have traditionally gone hand-in-glove, have now begun to diverge. Nine states, including one of the world's most impoverished countries, have nuclear arsenals. At least nine states enjoy very substantial natural resource wealth (Australia, Brazil, Canada, China, Iran, Russia, Saudi Arabia, the United States and Venezuela). While China and the United States will continue to dominate world economic rankings, Japan, Germany, India, the United Kingdom and France remain significant, with Nigeria, Brazil and Indonesia emerging as significant economic centres. Managing in a world where power is significantly diversified demands new ways of thinking. The old binary paradigms no longer serve any useful purpose, if they ever did. So Australia needs to re-imagine its relationship with the United States, transforming its traditional dependence into a partnership as it does so.

Australia is quite accustomed to and comfortable with receiving the odd bit of advice and direction from the United States. Anyone familiar with the US reaction to the 1986 Dibb Review will recall Washington's consternation with what some in the Pentagon regarded as an uppity Australian push for an independent defence policy. By advocating national self-reliance in the management of credible defence contingencies within the framework of the alliance with the United States, Dibb nonetheless managed to excite some American defence planners more accustomed to seeing Australia as the ever-faithful epigone. Yet the status of perpetual acolyte is demeaning and undermines our national interest – identified in Chapter 8 as the combination of national power and identity. It certainly diminishes our reputation in Asia, where much smaller countries than Australia maintain their independent identities and a strong relationship with the United States.

Australia needs to emulate the practice of the United States' NATO partners, which are much more adept at dealing with it on a basis of equality rather than deference, their defence links notwithstanding. Canada, which shares an almost 9000-kilometre border with the United States and a significantly more integrated economy, engages with its neighbour through many formal and informal arrangements at the political and economic levels. And while United States–Canada defence cooperation is evidently close, it does not dominate their mutual perceptions. Of course, Canada and Australia have quite different histories in their dealings with the United States: Canada had two wars with the United States in the eighteenth and early nineteenth centuries, winning both with British help. Australia, for its part, has taken on the role of willing accomplice, as distinct from trusted adviser. That needs to change.

To restore its credibility internationally, the United States needs to restore its credibility at home. It needs to restore equity and harmony to its domestic political practice, just as it needs to put equality at the centre of domestic race relations. That, and meaningful recognition of First Peoples – their rights and their connection with the land – are issues that Australia and the United States share, and may lend themselves to serious discussion to the advantage of all parties. Australia and the United States need desperately to develop common cause on climate change, both to work together to establish ever more stringent carbon-reduction targets and to undo the serious reputational damage Australia has inflicted upon itself. Similarly, Australia and the United States should work together in developing and marketing renewable energy systems especially suited to Asia. As wealthy nations, they need also to collaborate across a broad range of public policy domains, including public health, education, urban design, housing affordability and, perhaps most difficult of all, taxation policy.

Fundamentally, Australia needs to speak truth to power, working with the United States to address the constraints on its leadership of the free world and its credibility as a protector and promoter of democratic principles and practice. This means working with the United States to encourage its full participation in the United Nations and its agencies, as well as reviving US interest in the Trans-Pacific Partnership (and its accession to the Comprehensive and Progressive Agreement for the Tans-Pacific Partnership) as a strategic instrument.

To achieve this, Australia needs to do two things. First, it needs to build its self-confidence, eschewing the cultural cringe and advocating policies and activities that build global resilience. Political reform, promotion of the rule of law, accountability of government, transparency in public decision-making, and curbs on corruption all play into President Biden's goal of strengthening international support for democracy. Second, Australia needs to rebuild its diplomacy and expand its diplomatic footprint across the United States. This is not a prescription for even more sinecures for failed politicians. It is a recognition of the fact that to recalibrate, strengthen and deepen our relationship with the United States, we need diplomatic and public policy professionals. We need partnerships at all levels, including but not restricted to defence. And we need sustained advocacy.

Apprehension into confidence: Imagining a new Australia–China relationship

If recalibrating the Australia–United States relationship is about capitalising on convergence of interests, recalibrating the Australia–China relationship is about limiting the effects of divergence and creating common interests where we can. It is a much more difficult task, not only because it is as hard to steer around the issues that cause mistrust as it is to build on those that create trust, but also because China's place in the world, and consequently its foreign policy, is changing fast. Yan Xuetong expresses this well:

> China's post-pandemic foreign policy is just beginning to take shape. Beijing has always adjusted its policies to shifting domestic and foreign circumstances, following Deng Xiaoping's approach of 'crossing the river by feeling the stones.' The coming era will be no different: achievements and failures will inform China's path and choices. The backdrop to these adjustments, however, will be a radically altered global landscape, in which unilateral decisions by Washington and the various alliances and issue-specific coalitions it leads will no longer be as viable as they once were. As many

> states prepare for a return to life after the pandemic, they should come to terms with this new reality.[21]

Given its preoccupation with fear and threat, Australia's approach to China is currently one of apprehension. But as President Roosevelt said in the equally (if differently) confronting circumstances of the Great Depression, 'the only thing we have to fear is fear itself – nameless, unreasoning, unjustified terror which paralyzes needed efforts to convert retreat into advance'.[22] Fear clouds policy judgement, essentially because fear is itself a reaction to events that drives further reaction and, as such, severely constrains creativity and imagination.

But if fear is difficult to shift, conventional mindsets are even more stubborn. For the reasons spelled out earlier in this book, we are habituated in our approaches to dealing with complex problems. We tend to evaluate everything in terms of our collective experience and 'received wisdom', constructing a platform of assumptions on which we then seek to develop policy. But it is like trying to drive forward by looking through the rear-view mirror – very tricky. Very often our assumptions are incomplete where they are not tendentious. We easily fall victim to 'confirmation bias', which gives authority to precedent and the 'tried and true' approaches of earlier times. This is compounded by the conservative and hierarchical nature of decision-making within government in Australia, where new ideas are so easily dismissed as evidence of poor judgement – failure to adhere to 'the line' and support the views of 'the boss'. This is nowhere truer than in our current China policy settings, where panic, as David Brophy has termed it, has spawned paranoia and pandering.[23] This, as Brophy charts, is less due to ressentiment coming from the traditional sources of advice to government – the Department of Foreign Affairs and Trade, and its experienced China hands – than from a powerful and persuasive ideological convergence of opinion across a relatively small group of China critics. While there are certainly grounds for some of their concerns, it is simply not a policy option for Australia to adopt the approach of King Canute. The tide of China's rise is not reversible. We need to learn to live with it. And we need an approach to China that best delivers on our national interests without unnecessary provocation – without 'poking the panda'.

The task for Australian policymakers is to transform apprehension into confidence. This is not easy to achieve because it requires us to confront and dismiss the phobias that so constrain the self-assurance on which confidence fundamentally rests. While, in the international and security policy domain, it is important to be able to keep conflicting ideas in play as a policy solution is constructed, apprehension and confidence cannot coexist. Confidence is the product of analysis, planning, prudent implementation, careful evaluation and the ability to change course if the evidence so demands. Fear prevents all that from happening.

To imagine a new relationship with China and chart a course that will deliver a confident and constructive bilateral relationship, Australia needs to transcend the narrow defensive thinking that underpins the AUKUS partnership and the establishment of the Quad. Australia must be able to integrate its policy settings across five different but intersecting dimensions of international and security policy.

- We must identify the interests and values that inform our international and security policy with the greatest *clarity* possible.

- We must defend our interests and values, both in how we realise them domestically and in how we promote human rights internationally, with the greatest *consistency* possible.

- We must advocate our values by emphasising how they support and improve the lives of our citizens, rather than simply criticise China for what it might or might not do; we must be explanatory rather than declaratory.

- We must identify where Australia's interests converge with China's to afford us the greatest chance of leveraging common enterprise: climate change, energy efficiency, agronomy and agricultural research, medical science, academic partnerships and improvements to human security in the Pacific all offer prospects for cooperation.

- And we must appreciate that we are at best a bit player for China, remote, endowed, marginal and, because of our dependence on the United States for our ultimate security, painted in the colours of the Stars and Stripes. But we must not allow ourselves to become a bitter player.

Apart from skill, the integration of these approaches demands consistency and patience – qualities that we can learn from our Asian neighbours.

So, what are these interests and values that we need to identify with the greatest possible clarity? As Chapter 8 pointed out, our interests are not defined by what we might be interested in, just as our values are not defined by what we might value. The national interest is the substantive character of Australia – our national power and our identity. Our national interests consist of the factors that give purpose and direction to our foreign policy. While political freedoms in Hong Kong, Tibet and Xinjiang might be indicators of the sort of China we might prefer to deal with, desiderata in a best of all possible worlds, they are not national interests, any more than a return to the status quo ante in the South China Sea is a national interest. As Senator Penny Wong has argued, our national interests are much more immediate: the security of the nation and its citizens; the prosperity of the nation and its citizens; the harmony, stability and security of our neighbourhood; and constructive internationalism whereby we are able to contribute to an orderly and peaceful world.[24]

Our national interests are informed by our values. They are not locked into some form of binary, where interests and values are traded off against each other. As Isaiah Berlin argued in his magisterial essay 'The Originality of Machiavelli', if there is any trade-off to be done, it is between interests as a set and between values as a set.[25] And, like our national interests, our national values are straightforward: a 'fair go' for all; respect and tolerance for the views of others; compassion towards those who are doing it tough; inclusion and the acceptance of diversity.

In advocating our values and defending our interests, it is important that we articulate how they work for us, and how they make us a better and happier society in which individual wellbeing and community wellbeing afford protection against living in fear or being savaged by the consequences of inequality, poverty and want. Clarity about interests and values is not an invitation to catcalling and criticism of those whom we might wish to criticise for not sharing our values. In the international policy domain, pluralism with respect to interests and values is a necessary precondition of harmony and stability. Instead of accusing China of lacking appropriate human values (which is untrue) or pursuing interests that are inimical to global peace and stability (which is equally untrue), we would do much better to engage with China to establish common ground wherever we can. And that will inevitably mean that we can explain how the national political and social operating rules by which we live best serve us, offering them as a model for others to follow if they wish, rather than trying to impose them as a straitjacket to force conformity to some normative standard. An explanatory approach to the advocacy of values and interests is more likely to succeed than a declaratory assertion of 'norms' and accusations of failure to meet such norms.

In dealing with Chinese diplomatic and military representatives for almost fifty years, I have found none of them reluctant to engage in discussion about where Confucian and Western values align and differ. With the justification of history at least, Chinese people are proud of their cultural and social values, curious about the emphasis on individualism that distinguishes Western liberalism and puzzled by the stridency with which some Westerners proclaim their values as normative. Values are not universal. Nor are they absolute. Rather, they differ as widely as human social behaviours differ.

China's political and social roller-coaster has shaped both the experiences and the expectations of three generations of Chinese citizens. They are proud of what they have achieved at the personal and community levels. They are equally proud of the prospects they have created for themselves. But in my experience at least, they are reluctant to proselytise, no more wishing to impose on others what might work for them than to have others impose their operating systems on China. In a perceptive essay, Wang Jisi, president of the Institute of International and Strategic Studies at Peking University, has commented that 'in China, the country's growing status is a source of confidence and pride'.[26] As the citizens of China, especially the younger generation, observe the political dysfunction, socioeconomic inequality, ethnic and racial divisions, and economic stagnation that has plagued the United States and other Western democracies, a sense of defiant triumphalism has emerged.[27] So it should come as no surprise that China is in no mood to be lectured by the West, and certainly not by Australia, about the inadequacies, real or imagined, of its political behaviours or of the values on which they are based. Nor is it in any mood to accept that the values of the West should initiate political reforms in China.

Nonetheless, China has real problems with its credibility and trustworthiness. As with all great powers, impetuosity and overreach often triumph over deliberation and good sense. China is the new kid on the great power block, but often behaves less like a great power and more like a nuisance, putting both its naivety and pettiness on display. The theft of New Zealand's Zespri golden kiwifruit clone by a Chinese national and its propagation in Sichuan Province is just a small example of China's cut-throat approach to other countries' intellectual property laws and the enforcement of commercial licence agreements.[28] By failing to recognise and enforce a New Zealand company's right to its intellectual property, China is implicitly condoning its theft. The net result is the bull-in-the-china-shop (pardon the pun) syndrome. Sometimes, this is just irritating. But at other times, it is dangerous for both China and the wider international community. A case in point is its constant probing of global IT systems and the cyber-attacks that have become ever more sophisticated.[29]

While Russia has simply created a permissive environment in which criminal gangs can launch cyber-attacks against whatever attractive targets they can find – usually for industrial-scale theft – China's Ministry of State Security appears to run a system of hacking franchises that encourage IT nerds to access international patents, intellectual property and industrial secrets for commercial gain and exploitation. A free-wheeling approach to cyber espionage may, at one level, appear to support China's commercial interests by supplying valuable intellectual property to Chinese industrial enterprises, in much the same way as US industry profited from the wholesale misappropriation of British and European intellectual property and patents in the nineteenth century.[30]

As its precipitate actions in Hong Kong have reminded everyone, China maintains a clear separation between the conduct of its international economic relationships and its international political and strategic relationships. Its security and legislative actions in Hong Kong, the political and strategic pressure it exerts in the South China Sea and in the Taiwan Strait, and its political, social and cultural domination of Tibet and Xinjiang are premeditated and calculated. This is less an exercise in dualism than it is a willingness to exploit the fact that, at this stage in China's global strategic positioning, its power derives from its commanding economic position. Its geo-economic strength is the precursor to its geostrategic positioning as not just a competitor to the United States, but its equal. The international business community has already adjusted to this fact. As Kurt Tong points out:

> The contradiction in Hong Kong's political and economic circumstances reflects the fact that politics only narrowly affects the core incentives that guide financial and business decisions. The gravitational pull of large economies is a powerful force – maybe even strong enough to resist the growing antagonism between China and the West ... Washington and its partners should lower their expectations and abandon the illusion that the right mixture of punishments will prompt a reversal in Chinese policy.[31]

In current and prospective circumstances, fear of China will not provide the agility and flexibility required if Australia is to reimagine its China relationship. There are important areas in which Australia's and China's interests converge, even if the underlying values differ. We have deeply shared interests in addressing the causes and consequences of global warming – mitigation and adaptation. Similarly, we have deeply shared interests in managing the COVID-19 pandemic and preventing a recurrence. China's expansion into the South China Sea notwithstanding, we have deeply shared interests in the maintenance of peace and stability in Asia. We also share interests in moving towards a nuclear-weapons-free world. We share interests in negotiating an international agreement on cybersecurity standards to protect the integrity of global communications, the global finance and banking system, the integrity of university databases and the intellectual property of commercial enterprises.

To reimagine fully a recalibrated Australia–China relationship, we also need to appreciate the fundamental change in balance between Australia and China that has occurred over the past half-century. Back then, our population size notwithstanding, Australia and China were economic equals. That has long since dissipated. China's economy is now ten times bigger than Australia's, and growing. While our landmasses are comparable, and Australians enjoy both a higher standard of living and appreciably greater social amenity, the fact is that China has come to dominate the geopolitics of Asia, in which we are simply one nation, albeit not insignificant. In the economic domain, we have a few things that China needs (high-grade iron ore and wool being two of them), and more things that China wants but does not need, and can get elsewhere (coal, wheat, barley, wine and crayfish, for example). We might like to imagine that China is not indispensable to us. But we are certainly not indispensable to China. In the political domain, there is one thing above all that China wants, and that we can easily give to China: respect. China's contribution to Australia's security during World War II was significant, and we should respect that. China's achievements since World War II are prodigious, and we should respect that. China's potential is equally enormous, and we should respect that. Moreover, China is the custodian of an intellectual, political and social culture of some antiquity, one that has exerted immense influence over its neighbours to the east and south. We should respect that, too. Interestingly, while China's influence on the cultures of its neighbours has been great, it has not swamped them, any more than Greece or Rome swamped the cultures of Central and Northern Europe. By any measure, China is a great power and deserves respect.

Yet fear is evidently the main motivation behind Australia's decision to acquire nuclear-powered submarines in partnership with the United Kingdom and the United States under the awkward AUKUS acronym. For the United States, the ability to operate (if not own) hunter-killer submarines may give its 'pal down under' a cameo role in the conduct of maritime warfare, including nuclear warfare, in the North Pacific. But for China the decision is emblematic of Australia's retreat into belligerent irrelevance.

While there may be some who think that to respect a country for its achievement and its potential is tantamount to appeasement, nothing can be further from the truth – unless fear, rather than the possibility of cooperation, is the dominant element in the relationship. But where cooperation is the focus of the relationship, accommodation tends to define the modus vivendi. In Australia's case, as with the rest of China's Asian neighbours, accommodation is a sensible basis for a constructive bilateral and multilateral diplomacy.

Arrogance into common purpose: Imagining a new relationship with Indonesia and South-East Asia

At the political level, Australia maintains an entirely superficial relationship with Indonesia, as it does with the remaining nations of South-East Asia. When President Joko Widodo last visited Australia, in February 2020, Prime Minister Morrison greeted him with a fulsome and totally phoney expression of 'trust that underpins only the truest of friendships',[32] to which the president replied with a more ambiguous description of Australia as Indonesia's *'sahabat paling dekat* (closest friend)'.[33] '*Dekat*' is more about proximity than it is about affection, where 'closest' (meaning 'dearest') might be translated as '*tersayang*'. In a single phrase, President Widodo captured the ambiguity and ambivalence that distinguishes Australia's diplomatic conduct across Asia: we are physically close and emotionally/culturally distant.

Australia's prime ministers and foreign ministers like to boast about their close links with Indonesia. Arrogance and braggadocio generally substitute for truth, and nowhere more than in the case of the Australia–Indonesia political relationship. Its enduring feature is its hollowness, best exemplified in the gruesome attempts by political leaders to insert mangled Indonesian phrases into their speeches. The Indonesian audience was amused and appalled when the Australian governor-general, intending to say '*bapak*' (meaning 'sir') referred to President Widodo as '*bapok*' (variously translated as 'gay' or 'transvestite'). The character of our political relationship with Indonesia and the other South-East Asian nations is largely a product of our politicians' inability to come to grips with their cultures. Fawning condescension and cultural imperialism, so often manifest in gratuitous lecturing and talking down to Asia's leaders, serve only to reinforce our reputation for arrogance. And that, in turn, is a product of the racism and fear of 'the other' that has underpinned Australia's general approach to its place in the world since 1788.

If our political relationship with Indonesia and the rest of Asia is bumbling, condescending and inept, our diplomatic relationship has a rather different texture. Generally, the quality of Australia's day-to-day diplomacy in Indonesia and South-East Asia remains high: our diplomats are professional, focused and hardworking. Most of Australia's diplomats in Asia speak the language of their host country, some to an exceptional standard. But their professional skills are often practised in a policy vacuum, where the political leadership has failed to deliver coherent and enduring policies. The result is that much of our relationship management is ad hoc, lacking strategic direction and a sense of convergence in the articulation of shared national, regional and global objectives. This unfortunate situation is almost entirely due to the domestic focus of Australia's political leaders, who constantly play to the parochial sensitivities of the electorate. While most Australians appreciate that their livelihoods, security and wellbeing are directly dependent on Australia's place in the global economy, they generally lack any sense of connection to the global community. In large measure, this reflects the inability of the nation's political leaders to provide a compelling narrative that establishes Australia's place in the world. And on the rare occasions that Australian prime ministers do pronounce on foreign policy, they get very little domestic traction and are ignored in Asia.

Except, of course, when they make a gaffe, or overreach.

Two decades after the event, Australia continues to wear the consequences of the 'deputy sheriff to the US' title attributed to Prime Minister John Howard. There is no evidence that Howard ever uttered the phrase in his unscripted *The Bulletin* interview with Fred Brenchley, published on 29 September 1999, or that he articulated anything like 'the Howard Doctrine'. That appears to have been editorial licence on *The Bulletin*'s part.[34] The sobriquet aside, the tenor of Howard's remarks offended the Indonesians. Our image as the loyal acolyte to the United States does not go down well in Asia, particularly Indonesia. Coming as they did in the early days after Australia had led the UN peacekeeping force into East Timor, suggestions that Australia would contemplate pre-emptive military action in Indonesia angered the Indonesian government, and continue to reverberate today in the Indonesian armed forces. Trust is a fragile thing, and the painstaking efforts during the Keating and early Howard governments to establish respect and trust were shattered in a moment.[35] They have never returned. Indonesians continue to take umbrage at the monitoring of President Yudhoyono's mobile phone, the alleged bugging of Timor Leste's cabinet room, the declaration of the seabed boundary (seen by many in Indonesia as unfairly favouring Australia) and ongoing suspicion of covert Australian support for the independence movement in West Papua. As a *Jakarta Post* editorial put it, '*makin kenal makin tak sayang*' – the more you know, the less you love.

Australia's self-image as a substantial Asian power (the proverbial middle power forever punching above its weight) is not reflected in Asian attitudes. In the authoritative ASEAN survey *The State of Southeast Asia: 2021*, Australia's economic, political and strategic influence registered as negligible across most countries, and as zero in Indonesia. There was little confidence in Australia's ability to provide leadership in championing a global free trade agenda (again, zero in Indonesia), and even our ability to provide leadership in maintaining the rules-based order and upholding international law, Australia ranked after New Zealand (in Indonesia, we ranked equal with New Zealand). In the business of strategic hedging with 'third parties' (excluding China and the United States), the survey reports: 'The EU and Japan remain the clear front-runners for ASEAN in this strategic hedging game. 40.8% of the respondents choose the EU, followed closely by Japan (39.3%). Australia remains a distant third option for ASEAN at 7.5%, similar to last year's result (8.8%).'[36]

Australia did, however, outrank India, South Korea and the United Kingdom. As a provider of tertiary education for ASEAN's youth, Australia ranks fifth after the United States, the United Kingdom, an EU member and Japan, while in Indonesia Australia ranks equal second (with an EU member) after the United States. And even as a holiday destination, Australia comes fifth after Japan, an EU member, any other ASEAN member (Thailand in particular) and New Zealand, though ahead of the United States and the United Kingdom. As much as we might think that we cut a figure in Asia, the fact remains that we are an outlier that continues to pay a price for our Europhilia, our domination by US interests and our defiant monolingualism.

The ambivalence of Indonesia and other ASEAN members towards Australia in many ways reflects Australian attitudes. Nearly 60 per cent of Australians think that Indonesia is not a democracy, while 45 per cent do not have much confidence in President Widodo and lukewarm feelings towards Indonesia generally. Just over 50 per cent of Australians do not trust Indonesia to act responsibly in the world (which compares with about 40 per cent who do not trust the United States to act responsibly, and over 80 per cent who do not trust China to act responsibly).[37]

Attitudinal surveys conducted over several decades simply do not reflect or substantiate the strategic importance of Indonesia and South-East Asia to Australia – or Australia's importance to them, for that matter. This is a significant failure in both foreign and defence policy, reflecting the absence of leadership and vision on the part of successive Australian prime ministers. It is also a reflection of our overreliance on the United States to do the heavy lifting in the defence of Australia and our incapacity to invest in building the coalitions necessary for regional stability and security. We talk big and act small.

Indonesia is the key to a reimagined relationship with South-East Asia for reasons of both its proximity and its potential as one of Asia's economic powerhouses. We need to reinvest resources and diplomatic capacity into the relationship, though the highest priority is to transform and reconfigure our relationship management paradigm. There are six steps that we need to take if we are both to lift our game and to realise the opportunities that are on offer in Asia.

First, we need to recognise that far too many people in Asia see us as arrogant, insensitive buffoons. *The Ugly American* of the late 1950s has become *The Ugly Australian* of the 2020s.[38] We talk too much, and too loudly, confirming our reputation as know-alls. When we do not disparage the cultural mores of Asia, we ignore them or, even worse, trivialise them in our inept attempts to imitate them. Our senior politicians insist on mangling Asian languages in their vertiginous condescension. One has only to see the boorish beer-swilling behaviour of Australian tourists in Bali, the Philippines and Thailand to understand how destructive the Australian stereotype can be. We come across as white supremacists and pay a heavy price for our inability to forge a meaningful rapprochement between the First Peoples of Australia and the later immigrant communities.

If we are to avoid being described as '*kurang ajar*' (rude, literally 'uneducated') by Indonesians, we must learn to carry ourselves with dignity and pay attention to decorum, speak softly and deliberately, refrain from the uproarious laughter that is a sure sign of insecurity and nerves, and encourage our Asian hosts to open the conversation rather than ourselves dominating discussion from the outset. We certainly need to ensure gender balance in our official and commercial delegations, and ensure that women have talking roles besides simply attending. Some of our most successful diplomats in Asia have been women, not only because they are skilled and professional but also because they tend to be modest and respectful. They know how to charm their interlocutors without resorting to fawning deference.

Second, having learned how to carry ourselves properly in Asia, we need to work with our Asian colleagues to identify common goals and develop the institutional structures necessary for their realisation. This is of critical importance if we are to reimagine our key relationships. Australia has already developed effective relationships in the security arena, though the defence relationships tend to wax and wane as the political relationship goes through its ups and downs. But the defence relationship should not be the defining element in the bilateral package. The more important relationships are in the broad field of human security: food and energy production and availability; clean water, including recycling; the availability of effective medical support; good tertiary education, particularly in the STEM disciplines; and managing the consequences of climate change. And there are massive commercial opportunities in all these facets of human security: while development assistance programs will continue to have a place, it is important that we work with regional governments to invest in the human security of their citizens. In Indonesia, it is called '*gotong rojong*' – mutual help.

Australia could achieve much in strengthening democratic institutions in Asia, especially in Indonesia, Malaysia, Singapore, Thailand and the Philippines, where formal relationships between the presiding officers of the Commonwealth parliament and the parliaments of the region, marked by official visits at least once in each electoral cycle, would substantiate Australia's support for and investment in their parliamentary democracy. In the same vein, Australia could signal its support for the rule of law in Asia by instituting regular exchanges between Australian courts and their Asian counterparts. To build coalitions between like-minded nations, parliaments and courts offer both symbolic and practical avenues for strengthening key democratic institutions, while at the same time building confidence in their effective operation.

Third, we need to invest seriously in our knowledge of the languages and cultures of Asia. It is completely counterintuitive that training in Asian languages is declining in Australia at exactly the time that Asia is playing an ever-stronger role in the global economy. In 2021 alone, four university-level Asian languages were dropped from curricula: Chinese and Japanese at Swinburne, and Indonesian at the University of Western Sydney and La Trobe. Murdoch University also announced that it was abandoning Indonesian, though later postponed the change.[39] These decisions compound the problem, placing the uptake of Asian languages in primary and secondary schools in a cycle of accelerating decline as the availability of teachers dries up. If the teaching of Bahasa Indonesia is waning, the teaching of Mandarin is in freefall. The Asian Studies Association of Australia has charted the mounting problems facing the teaching of Mandarin in Australia, and the declining uptake among students. And the blame is laid implicitly with the federal government as the hostility between Canberra and Beijing has intensified, with media reports suggesting China poses a threat to the Australian education system.[40]

This is a strategic issue: if we fail to equip ourselves with the critical tools of relationship management – language and cultural understanding – we will remain the 'odd man out' in Asia, languishing at the bottom of the region, friendless and irrelevant. Notwithstanding the efforts of the Keating and Rudd governments to expand the availability of language teaching at the secondary and tertiary levels, funding was withdrawn by the Howard, Gillard and Abbott governments, and has not been restored. Too many Australians are happy to rely on the English-language proficiency of our Asian neighbours without realising that economic and political partnership, especially where there is joint investment, demands Asian-language proficiency. This is a fact that the Department of Defence has long recognised, with a sizeable pool of language-proficient attachés managing defence relationships of increasing complexity. But in the commercial, medical and scientific communities, much more needs to be done. To maintain the status quo is tantamount to a refusal to materialise the opportunities that await Australia in Asia, and will only serve to maintain a significant barrier to effective engagement.

Fourth, we need to expand our footprint in Asia, not only in the government and official domain but, more importantly, in the domains of commerce, education, investment and scientific collaboration, especially in climate change mitigation and adaptation. That may mean that governments need to identify incentives for commercial collaboration and investment in Asia. Australia needs to extend its range of relationship with South-East Asian industry bodies. Peak industry groups across the Australian economy are happy to collaborate with their British and American counterparts. They should continue to do so. But equally they should broaden their focus – and their commercial opportunities – by establishing long-term relationships with their Asian counterparts, especially in Indonesia, Malaysia and Vietnam.

Fifth, we need to identify the symbols of collaboration and participation, and to exploit them assiduously. Senior politicians and business leaders are only too willing to traipse off to the United States or the United Kingdom when our strategic future lies much closer to home. For Australia, a serious diplomatic investment in ASEAN and its institutions is a no-brainer, yet we potter around the edges of the association, substituting action with soothing words. This is not to suggest that Australia should aspire to membership of ASEAN, though were it offered (as President Widodo seemed to suggest in what looked like an exercise in off-the-cuff kite-flying in 2018[41]), Australia should give serious consideration to joining. The real question is how Australia might establish the grounds for an invitation, an outcome more likely to attain the necessary consensus within ASEAN were Australia to begin working with ASEAN on an extended range of programs delivered by an extended range of ASEAN institutions. Building up extended institutional relationships, whether or not

Australia is invited to join, is a necessary precursor to a deeper and more effective Australian engagement in South-East Asia.

And sixth, we need to reinvest substantial financial resources in building up both our presence and our activity levels across Asia. Successive governments have nickel-and-dimed the Department of Foreign Affairs and Trade for over fifty years.[42] Spending on diplomacy has reduced in real terms, while defence spending will rise by over $270 billion during the coming decade.[43] By 2020, DFAT's total budget, which includes development assistance funding, has dropped to 1.3 per cent of GDP, a decrease of more than $1.5 billion at a time when the world is increasingly disrupted and difficult. As Melissa Conley Tyler has pointed out:

> Scaling back has a real effect on Australia's influence. If Australia reduces the scholarships to bring future regional leaders to study in Australia, for instance, they'll likely study and form bonds elsewhere. If Australia reduces its investment in Indonesia's education system, it will be dominated by the country's other major funder, Saudi Arabia. When Australia pulls back on its diplomacy, other countries take up the slack.[44]

But a reverse nickel-and-diming will not restore real capacity or credibility to Australia's diplomatic effort. It needs serious reinvestment in skills (especially language skills), people and real estate, and the resources to fund a serious expansion of activities. As was noted in the previous chapter, diplomacy is what integrates the nation's power, affording it applicability and focus. It cannot be done on a shoestring. Governments must reprioritise: if it was deemed necessary to expand the national intelligence agencies fivefold, but simultaneously pare back our national diplomatic effort, it is little wonder that Australia has transformed itself from being a constructive and confident voice in Asia to adopting the role of bystander. It was not always thus. As one of Asia's wisest scholars, and an eminent Australian citizen, Wang Gungwu, has written, '[W]hat Australians value about their culture: the law, the respect for human rights, the parliamentary system, which are not features of Asian societies, are what attract Asians.'[45]

In little over a quarter of a century, we have gone from being the kind of country that many in Asia would have liked to model themselves on to one that is seen as a largely irrelevant remnant of white colonialism.

Lecturing into listening: Imagining a new Australian role in the Pacific

Talking too much often indicates a lack of confidence. Talking down to interlocutors usually indicates bumptious condescension. And descriptors such as 'wolverines' (in the case of some members of the Australian parliament) or 'wolf warriors' (in the case of some Chinese diplomats) evoke images of blowhards who prefer chest-thumping to dialogue. It is also an extraordinarily 'blokey' sort of thing to do. Gender diversity would certainly help fix this problem.

Chapter 5 argued that Australia has much to be humble and modest about in the Pacific. Exploitation of Pacific islanders and high-handedness towards their leaders have been standing characteristics of Australian approaches to the countries of the region. And to that the Morrison government and its ministers have added a boisterous calling-out of China's alleged strategic intentions in the region, as though we could single-handedly push China back to the Sea of Japan. The decision of Prime Minister Morrison to deliver a major Pacific policy pronouncement at a military establishment in Queensland, rather than in a Pacific capital, to announce a 'step-up' as a kind of atonement for past omissions, and to describe 'our Pacific family' as the lucky recipients of our tough love all suggest that our habits are ingrained. It is one thing for Australia to proclaim its membership of the Pacific family, to the extent that such a claim might be true. It is altogether another to talk about the Pacific family as though Australia owns it and is its natural paterfamilias.

We should observe closely how the various Pacific communities conduct themselves if we are to acquire the cultural skills that might permit us to play a more constructive role in the Pacific, even (to the extent that it is either possible or acceptable) a leadership role. Pacific leaders are not given to boasting. They are not given to 'shirtfronting' other leaders, as Prime Minister Abbott suggested he might like to do to the Russian president.[46] Rather, Pacific leaders deal with each other on the basis of mutual respect and deference. Indeed, Pacific people in general observe traditional social conventions in their dealings with each other. The Samoan language, for example, has a polite form that is used in formal communication, as distinct from the colloquial form that is used in day-to-day communication. Samoan culture more generally is governed by a complex of social protocols that govern behaviour and interpersonal dealings to maintain social cohesion.[47] While there is a significant level of congruence across the cultures and languages of Polynesia, there is extraordinary linguistic and cultural diversity throughout Melanesia, with more than a thousand distinct linguistic-cultural groups across Papua New Guinea, the Solomons and Vanuatu. The distinctions of language and culture go to the heart of identity in Melanesia. Similarly, Micronesia exhibits wide cultural and linguistic diversity that also establishes identity at both the individual and community levels. Consequently, cultural practices across Melanesia and Micronesia at once protect the individuality and identity of communities, while respecting the individuality and identity of other communities. Intra- and inter-communal relationships across the Pacific are characterised more by respectful reticence than by the boisterous bonhomie more familiar to Australian politicians.

To reimagine a relationship that is at once affective and effective, there are three steps that Australia needs to take.

First, we need first to recognise our relentless imperiousness in the Pacific. To get out of the hole into which we have fallen, we must stop digging. We must resist arrogance, bluster and condescension, and eschew anything that smacks of racism or misogyny. We must also learn how to display the quiet confidence that comes with a mature appreciation of the political and economic issues that face the Pacific, and refrain from evaluating those issues simply as facets of a strategic competition between two dominant powers. And that means that we should represent our relationship with the United States quite differently. We can no longer afford to be seen in the Pacific as a US dependant, a faithful follower in a relationship shaped by the experiences of World War II in Micronesia. Rather, we need to represent ourselves as the partner of choice for all the Pacific nations, rather than as some kind of strategic representative of the United States.

Second, having recognised that lecturing the Pacific is our default position, we must start listening. To their credit, Australia's diplomats in the Pacific are, for the most part, skilled both in representing Australia and in listening to their host governments. They enjoy good access to the leaders of the Pacific, even if that is not as valued within DFAT as diplomatic postings to the United States, North Asia or Europe. The government needs diplomatic expertise in the Pacific at the most senior levels of the department. But the political leaders who do business in the Pacific need to learn much more about the art of diplomacy, and practise it. Just as Australia's relationship with India is about much more than cricket and curry, so Australia's relationships in the Pacific are about much more than beer and rugby.

And third, we must change our operating paradigm in the Pacific from one of head-to-head competition with China to one that begins with collaboration and cooperation with the nations of the Pacific, and then extends to those countries, including China, that provide development assistance. Our focus must be on the human security of the peoples of the Pacific, rather than the strategic contest between China and the United States. The best way to achieve some measure of control over the strategic contest between China and the United States is to encourage them to sit at the same table as every country that has an interest in a peaceful and prosperous Pacific. It is to encourage a constructive diplomacy rather than military dispositions that are simply designed to contain China, as if that were possible.

Imagining new relationships in a time of significant global disruption is a necessary beginning to a fundamental diplomatic repositioning of Australia – so important if we are to avoid being left behind as the continent in the Southern Hemisphere that has neither enemies nor friends. But while it is necessary, imagination is not sufficient. To build an effective regional coalition, we must engage.

10
Engagement: The Antidote to Isolation

Duty is what no one else will do at the moment.

Penelope Fitzgerald, *Offshore*

Australia's journey from convict colony to globally connected nation-state has never been particularly surefooted. For much of our history, we sheltered under the protection of 'the mother country', indulging in a dependent Anglophilia that we found so comforting that we preferred to march to the sound of the British drum than to one that we beat. At certain times, however, our insecurities become latent, so we build up our confidence and gain a measure of agency, charting our own course and realising the opportunities that confidence often brings.

For instance, the early political and social exuberance that followed Federation encouraged a remarkable group of women to push for equal suffrage in all the democracies. The newly minted confidence that came with Federation saw the enshrinement of gender equality in the voting franchise (though not racial equality, it should be noted) and economic equity in the workforce conciliation and arbitration system. Australia had transformed itself into a social laboratory.[1] This might have been expected to flow into a more assertive role in international affairs, though the White Australia policy, advocated by Prime Minister Deakin as the foundation of Australia's security policy, might have narrowed an independent diplomacy to the British, European and North American countries. World War I put an end to all that, as Australia rushed to Britain's aid in support of what was already a fading imperial grandeur. It also put an end to the hope of the Australian-supported suffragette movement in Great Britain. And the Australia that emerged from the catastrophe of World War

I was more sober and introspective, grieving for the 'lost generation' – the 60,000 who were killed and the 156,000 who were wounded. Australia's insecurity came to the fore once more as Prime Minister Hughes argued for harsh reparations to be imposed on Germany and had Japan's proposals for the abolition of racial discrimination excluded from the Treaty of Versailles. And, once again, we were happy to hide behind the skirts of 'the mother country'.

Australia had a brief flirtation with a more independent foreign policy in the early days of World War II when it established missions in Chongqing (Chungking), Tokyo and Washington. The bombing of Pearl Harbor in December 1941 and the fall of Singapore in February 1942 saw Australia exchange Britain's skirts for those of the United States. As World War II progressed, and as the tide in the Pacific turned in favour of the Allied forces, the Curtin government began to plan for post-war reconstruction.

Three remarkable things then occurred that combined to transform Australia. First, the government provided serious reinforcement to the public service by appointing a group of outstanding university graduates to redesign the nation's economic and social policy – a group that included Henry Bland, Allen Brown, H.C. 'Nugget' Coombs, Douglas Copland, John Crawford, Fin Crisp, Richard Randall and Roland Wilson. Consequently, and perhaps more importantly, the Chifley government established the remarkable professional partnership between the federal government and its public-service professionals that would endure for a quarter of a century.[2] Australia's post-war governments accepted that they needed to build the institutions necessary for modern government – the departments and agencies that provide the capability and capacity without which the dreams and hopes of ministers cannot be delivered. They were, moreover, prepared to invest in the institutions of government, building up the analytical, conceptual and delivery tools of modern public administration (capability) and the practical skills (capacity) that are critical if a government is to be soundly advised and its decisions effectively executed. Second, the government recognised that Australia's economic growth depended on a progressive population policy supported by an ambitious immigration program, where immigration was seen as an exercise in applied economics rather than a means of controlling access to Australia. And third, it established an external affairs department that brought together some of the best diplomatic professionals Australia has ever seen. John Burton, Paul Hasluck, James Plimsoll, Arthur Tange and Keith Waller provided the intellectual depth and experience that was crucial to the groundbreaking international work of H.V. Evatt and Percy Spender. Although they were political opponents, they put Australia on the international stage in a way that it had not been since Billy Hughes at the post–World War I Paris peace talks.

Instinctively, Prime Ministers Curtin, Chifley and Menzies appreciated that leadership and vision were essential if Australia was to exercise an activist and constructive diplomacy. They also appreciated their need for the resources and talent to deliver their policies and realise the opportunities that the post–World War II world offered. The seamless relationship between clear-eyed and strong political leadership and the advisory and executive functions of the public service was critical to the success of Australia's early post-war positioning as a new and influential power in Asia and the Pacific.

Enterprise partnership

Australians are good at coming together in mutual support, especially in the face of economic hardship and natural disaster. It is the key to the nation's resilience. It was one of the three fundamental drivers of Australia's emergence from penal colony to the robust and confident communities that eventually came together as the Federation, the other two being good government and abundant natural resources that gave substance to the national economy. The rugged individualism that is a distinguishing feature of US society, for instance, is less commonly observed in Australia, just as 'mateship' is not central to the American self-image, though perhaps the misogyny that is implicit in 'mateship' is. The impulse towards sharing burdens is less a consequence of any ingrained sense of obligation than it is a consequence of a tendency towards mutuality – burden sharing on the one hand, and enjoying the social benefits of cooperation on the other. One of the sure signs of social mutuality is the very evident amenity of so many of Australia's cities and towns: the parks and gardens, community halls, community swimming pools, public sporting facilities and the war memorials that are such a focal point in towns and villages across Australia (and New Zealand, for that matter). Even the cemeteries are manicured and mown. If racism, misogyny, insecurity, separation and the cultural cringe are in our DNA, so too is social mutuality, inclusion and (although it is a work in progress) acceptance of and respect for diversity.

Australians are also good at building teams. We have a dedication to team sports that borders on the religious. While we are not particularly good at working within hierarchies (the 'tall poppy syndrome', combined with a natural tendency towards insubordination and larrikinism that does not fit well with the stratification of responsibility), we do well in more organic management systems. Women's teams, in particular, tend to display the highly flexible forms of leadership where the person in charge at any one moment is the person at the centre of the action rather than the captain. And teams work best where the emphasis is on trust, where mistakes are learned from rather than penalised, and where communication is open and direct. On deployment, for example, the Australian Defence Force models the effectiveness of teams, not just in the tightly knit world of the special forces but also in the highly skilled teams that keep submarines operational and jet fighters and surveillance aircraft in the air and on target. Function outperforms rank every time.

The government and administrative teams formed in the aftermath of World War II were novel and imaginative. They were also very much an artefact of the Australian experience – mutual help during the Depression and survival in war – and as such are emblematic of how Australia can approach problems holistically. The advisory and delivery functions housed in the main departments of state were nonpartisan and apolitical. But the key to their success was the close professional relationship between the decision-makers (the cabinet and ministers) and their departmental heads and senior executives. This is not a form of symbiosis, where two entities coexist but perform separate functions. Nor is it a form of politicisation of the public sector, where political alignment is the measure of survival and success. It is purposive and outcome-focused, reliant essentially on trust, mutual respect and communication.

While the conduct of Australia's foreign and defence policy had its ups and downs in the five decades following World War II – the establishment of the Southeast Asia Treaty Organization, the Suez Canal fiasco, the commitment of an Army brigade to Vietnam (requiring conscription for its sustainment) and the tacit agreement to Indonesia's incorporation of East Timor were not our most successful ventures – Australia was outward-looking and engaged, and, importantly, the government and the public service worked together. Australia was able, for instance, to conduct military operations against Indonesian armed forces in Borneo during Indonesia's armed confrontation with the newly formed Malaysia and simultaneously run an effective diplomatic mission in Jakarta.

Prime Minister Menzies largely dominated Australia's conduct of foreign affairs between 1949 and 1966, affording his foreign ministers little scope for independent action. His successors were so caught up in the Vietnam War that they had little opportunity to chart a more expansive foreign policy. And in the heady years of the Whitlam governments, the prime minister tended to dominate the international stage, as he did the domestic one. Throughout this period, however, the Department of Foreign Affairs remained a trusted adviser both to its minister and to the cabinet, with Australia expanding its footprint, and more importantly the quality of its relationships, across Asia and the Pacific. This alignment continued through the Fraser, Hawke and Keating governments, with two foreign ministers, Andrew Peacock and Gareth Evans, providing leadership to the department and harnessing its considerable intellectual resources.

Defence and foreign policy have frequently followed parallel but unconnected paths. With its focus on defending the nation against armed attack, defence policy generally tackles international problems from a narrower perspective. Unusually, at least in my experience, Gareth Evans and Kim Beazley recognised that, to be effective, defence and foreign policy needed to work not just in parallel but to common purposes: the maintenance of strategic stability and military cooperation in our immediate region. To that end, as ministers for foreign affairs and trade and defence respectively, they led their departments in a cooperative endeavour to present two major submissions on foreign and defence policy for cabinet's consideration in late November 1989. Beazley's submission, *Australia's Strategic Planning in the 1990s*,[3] and Evans' submission, later delivered as a ministerial statement, *Australia's Regional Security*, on 6 December 1989,[4] showed what could be done to deliver a unified and forward-looking approach to Australia's broader security interests.

In his ministerial statement, Evans established 'comprehensive engagement' and 'constructive commitment' as the driving themes of Australia's policy approach both to Asia and to the Pacific. In important respects, this represented the high-water mark of Australia's policy approach to South-East Asia and the Pacific. Together with Beazley's cabinet submission, Evans' statement established the policy foundations for Australia's successful leadership of the United Nations Transitional Authority in Cambodia (UNTAC), which brought peace to a country that had been almost destroyed by the genocide committed by Pol Pot's Khmer Rouge between 1975 and 1979. Vietnam's invasion in 1979 ended the genocide, but introduced a decade of political instability that found resolution in the Paris Agreement of 1991. As an example of what coordinated policy settings can achieve, Lieutenant General John Sanderson's impeccable delivery of a UN-mandated operation established a high bar.

Estrangement

Through the late 1980s and early 1990s, Gareth Evans sustained a remarkably energetic diplomacy in pursuit of his 'good international citizenship' policy, which he also articulated as one of Australia's principal national interests. His achievements in bringing Australia into a significantly broader and deeper relationship with the nations of Asia, particularly China and Indonesia, and in making his nation a more confident contributor to global diplomacy were significant. He provided the leadership that enabled his team of talented officials to deliver transformational international policy outcomes. Australian efforts were central to the establishment of the Asia-Pacific Economic Cooperation (APEC) forum in 1989, to the successful conclusion of the Chemical Weapons Convention in 1992, and to the ASEAN Regional Forum (ARF) in 1994. In some respects, the establishment of the Canberra Commission on the Elimination of Nuclear Weapons was the boldest of Evans' initiatives, addressing as it did an existential threat to humanity by arguing compellingly for the complete elimination of nuclear weapons.

Amazingly, and shockingly, the Howard government, immediately upon its election in 1996, moved to terminate the Canberra Commission. This began a process of regional and global estrangement on Australia's part that saw good international citizenship transacted through an active multilateral diplomacy replaced by a renewed emphasis on the ANZUS Treaty and Australia's security reliance on the United States. The election of the Howard government also began a series of 'efficiency dividends' and budget cuts in DFAT that reduced both its diplomatic efficacy and the impact of the Official Development Assistance program.

This was not simply a change in style. The shift away from multilateral diplomacy to a concentration on bilateral diplomacy was a shift in substance. It rejected the idea that activism in multilateral fora could effect transformational change in global political and security behaviours, promoting instead the view that national economic and security interests were better safeguarded through bilateral efforts, especially through a deep economic and military relationship with the United States. This was delivered in the form of a revamped ANZUS engagement at the ministerial level – the annual AUSMIN meeting between the US secretaries and State and Defense and their Australian counterparts – and, in 2005, the Australia–US Free Trade Agreement.

The estrangement from Asia and multilateralism and the retreat into the narrower world of bilateralism was an exercise in political product differentiation. Evans was derided for his overweening diplomatic ambition as the Howard government reverted to a dependency syndrome that had not been seen since the early 1950s, when Australia cemented its dependency in the ANZUS Treaty. It established a playbook that was maintained by the opposition after the 2007 election. When Prime Minister Rudd embarked on a more activist multilateral diplomacy, including his bid for a seat on the UN Security Council, he was accused of 'stunts and slogans',[5] essentially to damage him politically, thereby establishing the practice of conducting critical foreign policy debates on the stage of domestic political invective rather than pursing the national interest for its own sake. This is largely where Australia finds itself in contemporary circumstances. Australia's relationship with China is an artefact of how successful the government can be in generating fear in the community rather than managing the impacts of China's ascension to a position of regional dominance and global eminence.

The estrangement from Asia was accompanied by an equally serious domestic estrangement: that of government from its public-service advisers. The introduction of partisanship into the conduct of foreign and security policy was also a consequence of the growing political sectarianism in Australia, where the conduct of politics was increasingly based on sharp differences in political ideology rather than differences of view on values and interests.

The pursuit of political ideology is inimical to trust and respect: if the ideology is not shared, how can advisers be trusted? This loss of personal and institutional trust was evident in one of the first decisions of the Howard government: the sacking of six secretaries who had been close to the Hawke and Keating governments – ostensibly to rid the government of any vestiges of the Hawke/Keating legacy in the higher echelons of the public service.[6] It was no accident that one of those dismissed was the secretary of DFAT, Michael Costello. It quickly became clear to the public service that its function was to carry out the bidding of the government, not to advise it. This message was driven home with the dismissal of Paul Barratt as secretary of the Department of Defence in 1999.[7] Barratt and his minister, John Moore, did not enjoy a particularly constructive professional or personal relationship.[8] Barratt's sin was to provide written advice to the minister defending the operational and strategic effectiveness of the Collins-class submarine, and advising on the pathway to rectifying noise and combat-system problems. At the time of his dismissal, Barratt's advice to the minister remained unread. An irony was apparent in the rejection of John Moore at the by-election that followed shortly after in the division of Ryan, where, for the first (and last) time, a Labor candidate was elected in a traditionally conservative seat.

In his address to the Institute of Public Administration in August 2019, Prime Minister Morrison made emphatic his view that the role of public servants was to implement their ministers' policies:

> [T]he public service is at its best when it is getting on with the job of delivering the services Australians rely on and ensuring Governments can implement the policies they have been elected to deliver for the Australian people ... It's about the implementation ... I don't know how many beautiful strategy documents I've seen over my course of life, in public service and in other fields, people can celebrate these strategy documents, they can be incredibly impressive, but I tell you what, the only strategies that are any good are the ones that are implemented and work.[9]

This goes some way towards explaining the Morrison government's transactional approach to public policy, including its foreign and defence policy. Interestingly, it offers an entirely different take on the relationship between ministers and their policy advisers from that of the experienced ministers of the 1980s and 1990s, who saw partnership with their advisers as the key to both good policy design and good policy delivery.[10] In previous decades, senior politicians of both major political stripes had a deep sense of duty. They saw themselves as sharing an obligation to build community, to establish equity, to foster inclusion and to value diversity. That is not a singular pursuit.

Unadvised government

The past twenty-five years have witnessed a progressive decline in confidence and trust between government and the public service. While some agencies appear to retain effective working relationships with their ministers, Senate Estimates hearings reveal multiple instances where government decisions appear not to have been based on advice, and where political involvement in program design and delivery is opaque. In such circumstances, accountability is impossible and the exercise of ministerial responsibility completely avoidable. Pork-barrelling is an established political pastime in Australia, though in recent years it has become more brazen.[11] Even senior government ministers with good reputations seem compelled to duck and weave as they attempt to 'spin' what the editorialist in *The Australian Financial Review* described as 'hyper-politicised rationalisations of indefensible rorts'.[12] And the idea that decisions taken by any government without analysis and advice – a practice beloved of despots – is necessarily in the public interest, and therefore defensible, is a nonsense in a democracy. Or it should be. Simon Longstaff has summed up the issue brilliantly:

> It is entirely unacceptable that self-serving political considerations take priority – with improvements in the public interest being relegated to a 'lucky accident'. Moreover, if ministers decide … then how come they are never responsible for anything that happens? Short of being found guilty, by a court, of committing a crime, it appears that ministers are responsible for everything good that happens and nothing bad … The process has a name – the 'normalisation of deviance' – by which the unthinkable becomes practically inevitable.[13]

The 'normalisation of deviance' brings with it several suspect and ultimately dangerous practices. First, political staff increasingly trump the advice of the public-service departments. For example, the practice within ministers' offices of approving 'draft' ministerial submissions before they are presented to ministers as 'finals' is pernicious, dangerous for both the minister and the government. Second, the growing reliance of ministers on sources of information that they find acceptable, or convergent with their own personal and political predilections, is also pernicious. The practice of purchasing access to ministers through fundraisers, of grooming 'trusted' journalists to report favourably and to advise obsequiously, and of granting preferred access to favoured think tanks and public commentators all combine to reinforce a critical lack of contestability in arriving at crucial decisions. Third, the opaqueness of contemporary government decision-making and the invisibility of political advisers has led to what Jonathan Daley has described as the 'black hole of accountability': 'advisers can provide plausible deniability for ministers while by convention they cannot be called to appear before parliamentary committees'.[14] And fourth, cabinets have long held 'political discussions' in the cabinet room, without officials in attendance. The usual reason for 'political discussions' is the unwillingness of ministers to air their own or the governing party's dirty linen in front of officials, or to facilitate the resolution of a political dispute between two or more members of the cabinet. That is reasonable enough. What is not reasonable is decision-making and the consequent expenditure of public monies without due process, consideration and accountability.

Anecdotally, however, the frequency of cabinet meetings without officials in attendance – 'political discussions' where there are no cabinet minutes or records other than ministers' diaries – has increased in recent years. So have apparently off-the-cuff prime ministerial and ministerial pronouncements without proper consultation and advice. At a basic level, this robs the government of the day, and its ministers, of the protection of considered advice. But it can also lead the government and the nation into a policy black hole. The announcement on Sunday-morning television in March 2021 by the minister for foreign affairs of Australia's demand for an independent international inquiry into the origins of the coronavirus pandemic looked nothing like a considered and measured policy. Any collegiate cabinet consideration of the consequences would not have delivered so crass an announcement in so apparently unpremeditated a manner.

Unadvised government is undisciplined government. Yet discipline in government is essential if decision-making is to be sound, equitable and in the interests of the nation and the community. What is at stake here is not a return to past practices for their own sake. Rather, it is recognition that ramshackle decision-making leads to fecklessness, inconsistency and unintended consequences. Australia's current relationship with China may be an unintended consequence of poor and unadvised decision-making. Just as poor and unadvised decision-making are avoidable, so too are the unintended consequences.

To re-engage with China and with the entire South-East Asian region should be among Australia's highest foreign policy objectives. With an unimpeded line of sight between the government and its advisers, and with discipline in government decision-making, that becomes more achievable. But there are a couple of other obstacles that need to be overcome.

Overcoming the 'three deficits'

Australia is not the only Western country that continues to suffer the consequences of the three deficits: in confidence, leadership and trust.

Citizens cannot be confident when their leaders are not. Modern political leaders are confronted by a chaotic world where plans are discarded before they are even initiated. Determination and focus are under constant stress from randomness and chance. So it is little wonder that government action increasingly resembles 'whack-a-mole', with ad hoc decision-making and temporary fixes standing in for strategy and long-term solutions. And when leaders are constantly looking over their shoulders for signs of political treachery – the proverbial 'stab in the back' which now seems to be the inevitable fate of Australian prime ministers – personal and political insecurity erode whatever confidence there might have been.

Chapter 1 described how insecurity has been deep in the Australian psyche since 1788. With insecurity goes lack of confidence, so it is no simple matter to build confidence at either the community or political levels. There is no quick fix. Rather, we need a deliberate and managed rediscovery of those values that sustain both a sense of purpose in the political leadership and a measure of consensus across the community. This would certainly be supported by a return to a truly collegiate form of cabinet government that would engender the team spirit that is a key indicator of a thriving democracy. Confidence lies deep in the subconscious of an inclusive and resilient nation. We often see confidence as a personal attribute, and of course it is. But the sure knowledge that 'we are all in it together' is one of the most significant factors in sustaining confidence over the long haul. The confidence deficit, however, can only be eliminated if the leadership deficit is eliminated first.

One of the surest signs of the leadership deficit at the national and global levels is the rise of populism. Populists like Donald Trump, Viktor Orbán, Recep Tayyip Erdoğan and Jair Bolsonaro hold the reins of power, but they are not leaders. They do not bring their electorates with them as much as control the national institutions that would otherwise constrain their government. So they control their electorates, not serve them. In Australia's case, we are not led so much by populists as by people who want to be popular. They take their direction from focus groups and polls rather than setting an agenda that wins the confidence, support and trust of the voting public. The fractured nature of Australian politics over the past couple of decades has constrained would-be leaders from displaying the boldness and single-mindedness that are necessary attributes of leaders. A leader can tell the story and paint the picture that builds engagement and support at the community and political levels. Leaders are not just visionary: they can communicate their vision, argue for it, deliver a compelling advocacy for change and reform, and by so doing generate the political authority without which vision cannot be realised. Leaders build trust.

But the trust deficit is measured by the cynicism of modern governments, which is in turn matched only by the cynicism of their electorates. The Pew Research Center has tracked the decline in public trust in the US government for over sixty years. In President Eisenhower's day, three-quarters of the US population trusted their government. Today, barely a quarter of the same community trusts its government.[15] This decline is replicated around the world, where democratic governments are distrusted by about 80 per cent of their citizens. A contributing factor to Great Britain's exit from Europe was the trust deficit affecting the European Union. Commenting on the EU Summit in 2020, for example, *The Guardian* wrote that 'this bitter summit has exposed poisonous mistrust between some leaders, as well as the EU's struggle to deal with nationalists in central Europe, who are feared to be trampling on Europe's basic values'.[16] While the conduct of this summit was exacerbated by the rampant COVID-19 pandemic in Europe at the time, it was clear that central to the tensions was an erosion of core values and the feelings of betrayal by both the poorer new EU members (such as Hungary and Poland) and the established members seeking to protect the rule of law.

Australia has not escaped this decline in trust: its leading institutions, including government, business, NGOs and the media, are among the least trusted in the world – and this at a time when Australia has experienced over a quarter of a century of economic growth.[17] In politics and international relations, trust is hard to build and easy to lose. It is even harder to build it back again once lost. It is a product of integrity, intelligence, modesty and tact at the personal level, and of constancy, consistency, deliberateness and measure at the governmental and official levels. But trust and cynicism simply do not go together. Nor do brashness, hubris and overreach generate trust.

Confidence, leadership and trust are essentially artefacts of character at the personal level, and of consistency and even-handedness at the governmental level.

Reconfigured engagement

So, what would an engagement strategy look like?

The starting point, perhaps, would be to determine who we are and what we stand for. As our lack of assuredness and confidence have continued to mark the way we carry ourselves internationally, we have become increasingly ambiguous in the way we talk about our interests, and increasingly ambivalent about our values. Our prime ministers like nothing more than to mix with the great and powerful – to cut a figure, so to speak – but it's always for domestic consumption. We leave neither footprints nor fingerprints on any of the major issues confronting the regional or global communities. As Richard Denniss and I have pointed out, our international performance on climate change has been abysmal.[18] If the long-term health of our continent and its peoples depends on reducing carbon emissions, not to mention the health of our neighbours in South-East Asia and the Pacific, our dogged pursuit of coal and gas exports is simply unconscionable. We are not just an outlier, affording a measure of doubtful respectability to Russia and Saudi Arabia as global polluters, but increasingly a pariah, as the countries we usually identify with as 'like-minded' pursue real targets and real emissions cuts. Our governments like to posture on apparently constructive and collaborative interests and high-minded values. But our real interests are wanton exploitation of fossil fuel resources as quickly as we can, and greed without any consideration of the downstream costs to ourselves or our neighbours.

Once we have settled on a clear set of interests and values – clarifying who we are and what we stand for – we need to address the four principal pathologies that affect our strategic mindset: racism, misogyny, isolation and insecurity (the principal indicator of which is the cultural cringe).

Across Asia and the Pacific, Australia is seen as a deeply racist country. And for most Asian and Pacific communities, the main indicator of Australia's ingrained racial bias is the inability of the post-1788 community to come to an understanding with Australia's First Peoples. This stigma must be remedied if Australia is to embark upon a meaningful reengagement with the region in which we live. Here, Australia could take a cue from New Zealand. While there remains inequality and social tension between Māori and pākehā in New Zealand, the fact of the Waitangi Treaty and the steps the New Zealand government has taken in recent years – under both major parties, it should be noted – has enhanced its image and its effectiveness in the Pacific. And the formal apology made by Prime Minister Jacinda Ardern to the Samoan community in Auckland on 1 August 2021 offers a concrete demonstration that reconciliation empowers nations.[19]

It may take some by surprise that a recalibration of our international standing should include a serious attack on what is often seen as simply a domestic issue: endemic racism. But it is all about authenticity. By addressing the recommendations of the Uluru Statement from the Heart,[20] by dealing with the unacceptably high rate of First Peoples incarceration, by making substantial progress on the issues raised by the annual *Closing the Gap* report[21] and by facing up to the history and the consequences of the Stolen Generations,[22] Australia will restore its international reputation.

Similarly, Australia must 'walk the talk' on gender issues. The gender imbalance that distinguishes most of the nation's leading institutions, starting with the national parliaments and courts, and the constant recurrence of inappropriate behaviour and sexual harassment in Australian workplaces are symptomatic of the structural misogyny that affects Australia. The remedy lies not just in the introduction of quotas to ensure that women are fully represented in the national institutions, professions, business enterprises and workplaces, important though that is. It lies in ensuring that women are fully and proportionately involved in all aspects of national decision-making and policy advising. It means more women politicians, more women ministers and more women diplomats.

Australian governments use the nation's isolation as an excuse for non-involvement and inaction. Although we are one of the wealthiest nations in the world in per capita terms, we impose artificial limits on officials' travel, preferring instead to have the bells and whistles of ministerial visits. We need both. But we not only act isolated: we think isolated. And, as the establishment of the AUKUS partnership so amply demonstrates, old habits die hard, especially when fear and uncertainty are on the rise. For this reason, we need serious investment at all levels in effective cultural awareness training and, more importantly, the restoration of broad-scope Asian-language training in primary and secondary schools, and the re-establishment of advanced language courses in the universities. The wider availability of Asian-language training, and the consequent increase in the number of Australians who can speak an Asian language with reasonable fluency, will also expand Australia's commercial links into Asia. Australian tourism into Asia is important, as is Asian tourism into Australia. People-to-people links are critical.

And we must address the latent insecurity that is the cause of our brashness and overreach, particularly in Asia. As Chapter 8 detailed, Australia has considerable national power. It has little enough, apart from population numbers perhaps, to be insecure about. But we continue to apologise for ourselves, hanging on to the United States, and to a declining extent the United Kingdom, as a means of self-validation. The cultural cringe is demeaning, both to ourselves and to those to whom we cringe. As we re-engineer our relationships with Asia, we will find that we have as much to offer Asia as Asia has to offer us, and for that reason there is no cringing in either direction. Comfortable, low-key, professional relationships in Asia will become the default position as we inject confidence into our national posture, and will, by the same token, reinforce that confidence.

And if we can align our interests and values, build the sense of equality that eliminates racism, cure our misogyny, deal with our isolation and treat our insecurity, we will be in a perfect position to build the coalitions that are essential if our interests are to be realised and our values modelled.

No enemies, no friends

Australia is not aggressive enough to have enemies, nor attractive enough to have friends. But it does not have to be that way. While fomenting aggression would be a loser's recipe for disaster, and something that no serious Australian government would contemplate, especially towards China or any of our other neighbours, making Australia an attractive economic and political partner is well within our gift. It does require a lot of self-knowledge, however, and a lot of determination. It requires leaders with vision and courage, not just the survival instinct that allows them to maintain a tenuous grip on power. Yet our self-interest should drive us that way, since prosperity, security and relevance to our neighbourhood are what our international and security policies basically comprehend. The task for Australia – its citizens and its leaders – is to recognise our potential and to realise it.

Notes

Preface

1 In a conversation that took place in Geneva in early 1980, Sir James Plimsoll, Australia's High Commissioner to India from 1963 to 1965, told me that Prime Minister Jawaharlal Nehru had mentioned to him that, during their meetings in Beijing in 1954, Mao Zedong told Nehru that the People's Republic of China could contemplate 100 million deaths were it to fight a war. 'That's reasonably impressive,' Plimsoll commented wryly.

2 Lieutenant Colonel Duncan Foster, *The Australian Army Reading List 2019* (Canberra: Australian Army Research Centre, 2018).

3 Hugh White, *How to Defend Australia* (Melbourne: La Trobe University Press, 2019).

4 Rory Medcalf, *Contest for the Indo-Pacific: Why China won't map the future* (Melbourne: La Trobe University Press, 2020).

5 APLN, 'Implications of the AUKUS deal', *The Pulse*, 22 September 2021.

Chapter 1. An Insecure Mindset: Our Strategic Paradigm

1 W.J.L. Wharton (ed.), *Captain Cook's Journal During His First Voyage Round the World Made in H.M. Bark Endeavour 1768–71* (London, 1893).

2 Wharton (ed.), *Captain Cook's Journal*, journal entry for Monday, 9 October 1769.

3 John A. Powell, 'Us vs them: The sinister techniques of "othering" – and how to avoid them', *Guardian Australia*, 8 November 2017. So deep is this latent racism that its very existence is hotly contested by those who most practise it. 'Why, some of my best friends are ...'

4 R.G. Menzies, 'West New Guinea – Statement by the Prime Minister', 12 January 1962, https://pmtranscripts.pmc.gov.au/sites/default/files/original/00000431.pdf.

5 Allan Gyngell, *Fear of Abandonment: Australia in the World since 1942* (Melbourne: La Trobe University Press, 2017). It can equally well be argued that Australia's fear of abandonment stretches back to 1788.

6 Isabella Higgins & Sarah Collard, 'Captain James Cook's landing and the Indigenous first words contested by Aboriginal leaders', *ABC News*, 29 April 2020, www.abc.net.au/news/2020-04-29/captain-cook-landing-indigenous-people-first-words-contested/12195148.

7 C.M.H. Clark, *A History of Australia* (Melbourne: Melbourne University Press, 1977), vol. 1, p. 49. See also p. 110, where Clark reverts to the implicit racism directed towards Aboriginal people by the early colonial immigrants.

8 Robert Hughes, *The Fatal Shore* (London: Vintage Books, 2003), p. 18.

9 François Bernier's *Nouvelle division de la terre par les différentes espèces ou races qui l'habitent* was published anonymously in Paris in 1684.

10 Theresa Richardson, 'John Locke and the Myth of Race in America: Demythologizing the Paradoxes of the Enlightenment as Visited in the Present', *Philosophical Studies in Education*, 2011, pp. 101–12.

11 Elizabeth Kolbert, 'There's No Scientific Basis for Race – It's a Made-Up Label', *National Geographic*, 12 March 2018.

12 Edward Said, *Orientalism* (New York: Vintage Books, 1979), p. 232.

13 Hughes, *The Fatal Shore*, p. 277.

14 Lauren Harris, 'The riots history erased: Reckoning with the racism of Lambing Flat', *Guardian Australia*, 7 August 2018.

15 The nature of constitutional discrimination against Australia's First Peoples is well dealt with by Elisa Arcioni, 'Excluding Indigenous Australians from "the People": A reconsideration of sections 25 and 127 of the Constitution', *Federal Law Review*, vol. 40, no. 3, 3 September 2012, pp. 287–315.

16 Alfred Deakin, 'Speech to the electors of Ballarat', 29 October 1903, see https://electionspeeches.moadoph.gov.au/speeches/1903-alfred-deakin.

17 Hugh White, *How to Defend Australia* (Melbourne: La Trobe University Press, 2019), p. 287.

18 White, *How to Defend Australia*, p. 44.

19 Cathy Park Hong, *Minor Feelings* (London: Profile Books, 2021), p. 86.

20 Hughes, *The Fatal Shore*, p. 89. Manning Clark describes the scene 'which beggared description' in less elevated terms; see Clark, *A History of Australia*, vol. 1, p. 88.

21 Anne Summers, *Damned Whores and God's Police* (Sydney: University of New South Wales Press, 2016 [1975]), p. 404.

22 Nick Dyrenfurth's exploration of this cultural trope is as depressing as it is enlightening. See his 'John Howard's Hegemony of Values: The politics of "mateship" in the Howard decade', *Australian Journal of Political Science*, vol. 42, no. 2, June 2007, pp. 211–30, and 'Mateship: Secular Australia's religion and how John Howard hijacked it', *Sydney Morning Herald*, 25 December 2014.

23 Geoffrey Blainey, *The Tyranny of Distance* (Sydney: Pan Macmillan Australia, rev. ed. 2001), p. 174, reflecting on Russel Ward's use of the term in *The Australian Legend*. Robert Hughes offers a more bitter definition of mateship: loyalty forged by repression (*The Fatal Shore*, p. 353).

24 Julie Arostegui, 'Gender and the Security Sector: Towards a more secure future', *Connections*, vol. 14, no. 3, Summer 2015, p. 8.
25 Blainey, *The Tyranny of Distance*, p. 365.
26 Blainey, *The Tyranny of Distance*, p. 373.
27 Cheryl Saunders, Adrienne Stone & Joshua Quinn-Watson, 'A constitution shaped by distance', *Pursuit* (University of Melbourne), 24 May 2018, https://pursuit.unimelb.edu.au/articles/a-constitution-shaped-by-distance.
28 Deborah Kikkawa, 'Turning back the tide of Indigenous language loss: Children to the rescue?', Department of Social Security, undated, see www.dss.gov.au/sites/default/files/documents/02_2015/indigenous_language_loss.pdf.
29 'Australian values', webpage, Department of Home Affairs, https://immi.homeaffairs.gov.au/help-support/meeting-our-requirements/australian-values.
30 Blainey, *The Tyranny of Distance*, p. 371.
31 Blainey, *The Tyranny of Distance*, p. 152.
32 Blainey, *The Tyranny of Distance*, p. 154.
33 Alfred Deakin, 'Election Speech', 29 October 1903, see https://electionspeeches.moadoph.gov.au/speeches/1903-alfred-deakin.
34 Field Marshal Viscount Kitchener of Khartoum, 'Memorandum on the Defence of Australia', Melbourne, 12 February 1910, p. 5.
35 R.G. Menzies, 'Speech: Declaration of war', 3 September 1939, *Australian Screen* (National Film and Sound Archive website), https://aso.gov.au/titles/radio/menzies-speech-declaration-war/clip1.
36 John Curtin, 'The task ahead', *The Herald* (Melbourne), 27 December 1941.
37 John Curtin, 'Speech to America', 14 March 1942, http://john.curtin.edu.au/audio/00434.html.
38 Harold Holt made this declaration in Washington on 30 June 1966. See Paul Rodan, 'Harold Holt and the art of personal diplomacy', *Inside Story*, 1 July 2016, https://insidestory.org.au/harold-holt-and-the-art-of-personal-diplomacy.
39 John Howard, Speech in the House of Representatives, 17 September 2001.
40 Malcolm Fraser, 'Australia's dependence on a major power lies deep in our national psyche', *Guardian Australia*, 29 April 2014.
41 Michael Shoebridge, 'It's time for Australia to invoke ANZUS', *The Strategist*, 14 April 2020, www.aspistrategist.org.au/its-time-for-australia-to-invoke-anzus.
42 Gyngell, *Fear of Abandonment*, p. 5.
43 Hugh White, 'Standing alone: Why Australia can't rely on America', *The Strategist*, 24 December 2019, www.aspistrategist.org.au/standing-alone-why-australia-cant-rely-on-america.

44 See Rollo Hesketh's excellent essay 'A.A. Phillips and the "cultural cringe": Creating an "Australian tradition"', *Meanjin*, vol. 72, no. 3, 2013, https://meanjin.com.au/essays/a-a-phillips-and-the-icultural-cringei-creating-an-iaustralian-traditioni.

45 Hilary McPhee, 'A culture of conformity', 7 August 2015, https://hilarymcphee.com/a-culture-of-conformity.

46 Keith Johnson & Robbie Gramer, 'The great decoupling', *Foreign Policy*, 14 May 2020.

47 See, for example, Linda Robinson et al., *Modern Political Warfare* (Santa Monica: RAND, 2018), www.rand.org/content/dam/rand/pubs/research_reports/RR1700/RR1772/RAND_RR1772.pdf.

48 See, for example, Thomas Mahnken, Ross Babbage & Toshi Yoshihara, *Countering Comprehensive Coercion* (Washington: Center for Strategic and Budgetary Assessments, 2018), https://csbaonline.org/uploads/documents/Countering_Comprehensive_Coercion,_May_2018.pdf.

Chapter 2. What Is 'Security' Anyway?

1 Cicero, *De Officiis* (Concerning Responsibilities, often translated as 'On Duties'), Book 1, sections 69 and 72. On both occasions that Cicero uses the term 'security', he does so with the sense 'tranquillity of mind' rather than 'freedom from fear or threat'. That is not how the modern security warriors use the term. For an excellent modern edition, see M. Winterbottom (ed.), *De Officiis* (Oxford: Oxford University Press, 1994), pp. 28–29.

2 Hans J. Morgenthau, *Politics Among Nations: The Struggle for Power and Peace* (New York: Alfred A. Knopf, 4th edition, 1967), p. 399.

3 Stratfor, 'In Washington, war fatigue is setting in', *Real Clear Defense*, 2 August 2017, www.realcleardefense.com/articles/2017/08/02/in_washington_war_fatigue_is_setting_in_111955.html.

4 The Ammerdown Group, *Rethinking Security: A Discussion Paper*, May 2016, https://rethinkingsecurityorguk.files.wordpress.com/2016/10/rethinking-security-a-discussion-paper.pdf.

5 Francis Fukuyama, *Identity* (London: Profile Books, 2019), p. 40.

6 *Q&A*, ABC TV, 9 December 2019.

7 Peter Fimrite & Chase DiFeliciantonio, 'As fires race out of control, Big Basin redwoods burn, giant trees at Armstrong under threat', *San Francisco Chronicle*, 23 August 2020.

8 The 'Spanish Flu', which is thought to have originated in pigs, infected up to 500 million people and killed between 50 million and 100 million.

9 United Nations Office on Drugs and Crime, *World Drug Report 2019* (Vienna: United Nations, 2019), booklet 2, p. 1.

10 Christine Clough, 'Transnational crime is a $1.6 trillion to $2.2 trillion annual "business", finds new GFI report', *Global Financial Integrity*,

27 March 2017, https://gfintegrity.org/press-release/transnational-crime-is-a-1-6-trillion-to-2-2-trillion-annual-business-finds-new-gfi-report.

11 For a short but comprehensive statement on drug law reform, albeit from an Australian perspective, see Mick Palmer, 'Drugs policy – there has to be a better way', *Pearls and Irritations*, 20 March 2018, https://johnmenadue.com/mick-palmer-drugs-policy-there-has-to-be-a-better-way.

12 Office of the Secretary of Defense, *Nuclear Posture Review* (Washington DC: Department of Defense, 2018).

13 Nicola McGarrity & Jessie Blackbourn, 'Australia has enacted 82 anti-terror laws since 2001. But tough laws alone can't eliminate terrorism', *The Conversation*, 30 September 2019.

14 George Williams, 'A decade of Australian anti-terror laws', *Melbourne University Law Review*, vol. 38, 2011).

15 Philip Bobbitt, *Terror and Consent: The Wars for the Twenty-First Century* (New York: Allen Lane, 2008), p. 182.

16 Bobbitt, *Terror and Consent*, p. 236.

17 The catastrophic bushfires that affected Australia between September 2019 and February 2020 are symptomatic of the lack of vision among international leaders – a lack of vision that causes people to perish.

18 Alex Reilly, 'Australian politics explainer: The MV Tampa and the transformation of asylum-seeker policy', *The Conversation*, 27 April 2017, https://theconversation.com/australian-politics-explainer-the-mv-tampa-and-the-transformation-of-asylum-seeker-policy-74078.

19 For a full account, see the report of the Senate Select Committee on a Certain Maritime Incident, 23 October 2002, www.aph.gov.au/Parliamentary_Business/Committees/Senate/Former_Committees/maritimeincident/report/index.

20 For an excellent analysis of the sovereignty issue, see Katherine Gelber & Matt McDonald, 'Ethics and Exclusion: Representations of sovereignty in Australia's approach to asylum-seekers', *Review of International Studies*, vol. 32, 2006, pp. 269–89. The securitisation aspects of refugee flows are well covered by Michael Pugh, 'Drowning not Waving: Boat people and humanitarianism at sea', *Journal of Refugee Studies*, vol. 17, no. 1, 2004, esp. pp. 55–56.

21 Geoffrey Lee Martin, 'Australia closes door on boat people', *The Telegraph* (UK), 24 September 2001.

22 'Controversial Australian Border Force visa checks, Operation Fortitude cancelled', *ABC News*, 28 August 2015, www.abc.net.au/news/2015-08-28/operation-fortitude-cancelled/6733008.

23 Stephanie Zillman, 'Don Dale CCTV footage of police aiming weapons at youth detainees draws mixed reaction', ABC News, 15 January 2019, www.abc.net.au/news/2019-01-15/don-dale-cctv-footage-leak-michael-gunner-says-police-doing-job/10714322.

24 Heather McNab, 'NSW Police chief defends strip searches', *The Canberra Times*, 18 November 2019.

25 'Melbourne police captured on video taking down disability pensioner', *ABC News*, 3 April 2018 www.abc.net.au/news/2018-04-03/melbourne-police-on-video-taking-down-disability-pensioner/9591006.

26 Isolde (Izzy) Raj-Seppings, 'I'm the 13-year-old police threatened to arrest at Kirribilli House protest. This is why I did it', *Guardian Australia*, 21 December 2019.

27 Lily Mayers, 'NSW Police asked 15yo to expose himself as part of festival strip search, inquiry hears', *ABC News*, 3 December 2019, www.abc.net.au/news/2019-12-02/nsw-police-strip-searched-25-children-at-festival-inquiry-hears/11756902.

28 Pallavi Singhal & Angus Thompson, '"Systemic unlawfulness": 88 per cent of NSW Police searches found nothing', *The Sydney Morning Herald*, 17 February 2020.

29 Stan Grant, 'A decade on from the NT intervention, the "torment of powerlessness" lives on', *ABC News*, 21 June 2017.

30 Linda Briskman, 'Australia's wake up call from the UN: Yes, we're a racist country', *The Conversation*, 31 May 2011, https://theconversation.com/australias-wake-up-call-from-the-un-yes-were-a-racist-country-1506.

31 Paddy Gibson, '10 impacts of the NT Intervention', *SBS NITV News*, 21 June 2017, www.sbs.com.au/nitv/article/2017/06/21/10-impacts-nt-intervention.

32 Department of the Prime Minister and Cabinet, *Closing the Gap: Report 2020*, Commonwealth of Australia, 2020, https://ctgreport.niaa.gov.au; Isabella Higgins, 'Closing the Gap report shows only two targets on track as PM pushes for Indigenous-led refresh', *ABC News*, 12 February 2020, www.abc.net.au/news/2020-02-12/closing-the-gap-report-2019-indigenous-outcomes-not-on-track/11949712.

33 Kent Roach, 'Australia Responds: Hyper-Legislation', in Kent Roach, *The 9/11 Effect: Comparative Counter-Terrorism* (Cambridge: Cambridge University Press, 2011), pp. 309–60.

34 Nicola McGarrity & Jessie Blackbourn, 'Australia has enacted 82 anti-terror laws since 2001. But tough laws alone can't eliminate terrorism', *The Conversation*, 30 September 2019, https://theconversation.com/australia-has-enacted-82-anti-terror-laws-since-2001-but-tough-laws-alone-cant-eliminate-terrorism-123521.

35 Paul Karp, 'Peter Dutton says Victorians scared to go out because of "African gang violence"', *Guardian Australia*, 3 January 2018.

36 Michael Pembroke, 'Increasing militarisation of police invites tragedy', *The Sydney Morning Herald*, 29 June 2018. See also Justice Pembroke's letter to the editor, 'The role and function of the ADF and civil police', *The Australian Defence Force Journal*, no. 203, 2018, p. 9.

37 Francisco Aravena, *Human Security: Emerging concept of security in the twenty-first century*, Disarmament Forum 2, UNIDIR, 2002, p. 8, www.peacepalacelibrary.nl/ebooks/files/UNIDIR_pdf-art1442.pdf.

38 Aravena, *Human Security*, p. 9.

Chapter 3. Dependence and Faith-Based Policy: ANZUS

1 Bertrand Russell, *Human Society in Ethics and Politics* (London: George Allen & Unwin, 1954), p. 217. A prolific writer, Russell published this somewhat rambling treatise when he was eighty-two, and followed it up with another twenty before his death at age ninety-eight. Like much of his writing, it is both illuminating and fun to read.

2 Scott Morrison, 'In our interest', The 2019 Lowy Lecture, 3 October 2019, www.lowyinstitute.org/publications/2019-lowy-lecture-prime-minister-scott-morrison.

3 Cameron Stewart, 'Joe's mates in the States', *The Weekend Australian Magazine*, 27 July 2019.

4 Russell Parkin & David Lee, *Great White Fleet to Coral Sea: Naval Strategy and the Development of Australia-United States relations, 1900–1945* (Canberra: DFAT, 2008), p. 10.

5 Alfred Deakin, 'Invitation to United States Fleet', 14 April 1908, part of Miscellaneous *Morning Post* letters, 1908, Papers of Alfred Deakin, https://nla.gov.au/nla.obj-226190359/view.

6 Alfred Deakin, 'American Fleet's Visit', 25 April 1908, part of Miscellaneous *Morning Post* letters, 1908, Papers of Alfred Deakin, https://nla.gov.au/nla.obj-226190595/view.

7 See also Gary Brown & Laura Rayner, 'Upside, downside: ANZUS: After fifty years', *Current Issues Brief 3 2001-02*, Parliamentary Library, www.aph.gov.au/About_Parliament/Parliamentary_Departments/Parliamentary_Library/Publications_Archive/CIB/cib0102/02CIB03.

8 For a comprehensive picture of the growth of anti-Chinese sentiment in the second half of the nineteenth century, see Ian Welch, *Alien Son* (PhD thesis, ANU, 2003, https://openresearch-repository.anu.edu.au/handle/1885/49261), especially Chapter 7, 'Demonising the Chinese: The pathology of cultural difference 1855–1906'.

9 See Curtin's famous newspaper article 'The task ahead', published in *The Herald* (Melbourne) on 27 December 1941.

10 See cablegram of 22 September 1950 from the Australian Mission to the UN to the Department of External Affairs, https://dfat.gov.au/about-us/publications/historical-documents/Pages/

volume-21/18-cablegram-from-australian-mission-at-the-united-nations-to-department-of-external-affairs.aspx.

11 In one of my early outings as a junior diplomat, I experienced the convergence of these pathologies when Australian ministers met with their Japanese counterparts at the first Australia–Japan Ministerial Committee, convened in Canberra in 1972. The eight Australian ministers were led by Foreign Minister Nigel Bowen with Deputy Prime Minister Doug Anthony. The five Japanese ministers were led by Foreign Minister Masayoshi Ohira with Yasuhiro Nakasone, the Japanese minister for international trade and industry. Each of them was subsequently prime minister of Japan. The two sides stared at each other across the boardroom table in the (now demolished) CSIRO headquarters – located next to the Australian War Memorial, where the remains of the Japanese midget submarine sunk in Sydney Harbour in 1942 could be seen through the boardroom windows. The atmosphere was icy. Nigel Bowen had served in the Australian Army in the Pacific theatre, while the Australian minister for national development, Reginald Swartz, had fought in the Malaya campaign, had been a prisoner of war in Changi and was subsequently sent to work on the Thailand–Burma railway. For his part, Minister Nakasone had served in the Imperial Japanese Navy, and was already known as an advocate of Japan's rearmament and the development of a substantial self-defence force. Notwithstanding Prime Minister McMahon's welcoming remarks about friendship and cooperation, cordiality was in short supply. (McMahon's opening address can be read at https://pmtranscripts.pmc.gov.au/release/transcript-2693.)

12 Department of Foreign Affairs and Trade, '13 Cablegram from Spender to Menzies and Australian Delegation, United Nations', NAA: A11537 [1], https://dfat.gov.au/about-us/publications/historical-documents/Pages/volume-21/13-cablegram-from-spender-to-menzies-and-australian-delegation-united-nations.aspx.

13 For an excellent and concise analysis of the negotiating history of the ANZUS Treaty, see Joseph M. Siracusa, 'The ANZUS Treaty Revisited', *Security Challenges*, vol. 1, no. 1, pp. 89–104.

14 See footnote 10.

15 Department of Foreign Affairs and Trade, '14 Cablegram from Menzies to Fadden', NAA: A11782, 1950/1, https://dfat.gov.au/about-us/publications/historical-documents/Pages/volume-21/14-cablegram-from-menzies-to-fadden.aspx.

16 Department of Foreign Affairs and Trade, '15 Cablegram from Embassy in Washington to Spender', NAA: A1838, 250/7/10, https://dfat.gov.au/about-us/publications/historical-documents/Pages/volume-21/15-cablegram-from-embassy-in-washington-to-spender.aspx.

17 John Williams, 'ANZUS: A blow to Britain's self-esteem', *Review of International Studies*, October 1987, p. 251.

18 Office of the Historian, '337. Memorandum of Conversation', *Foreign Relations of the United States, 1961–1963, Volume XXIII, Southeast Asia*, document 337, https://history.state.gov/historicaldocuments/frus1961-63v23/d337.

19 Office of the Historian, '337. Memorandum of Conversation'.

20 Office of the Historian, '337. Memorandum of Conversation'.

21 Office of the Historian, '338. Memorandum for the Australian Ambassador (Beale)', *Foreign Relations of the United States, 1961–1963, Volume XXIII, Southeast Asia*, document 338, https://history.state.gov/historicaldocuments/frus1961-63v23/d338.

22 See 'Paper presented to the Australian Ambassador (Beale)', in Office of the Historian, '343. Memorandum of Conversation', *Foreign Relations of the United States, 1961–1963, Volume XXIII, Southeast Asia*, document 343, https://history.state.gov/historicaldocuments/frus1961-63v23/d343.

23 R.A. Woolcott, 'The American alliance and Vice President Biden's recent visit', *Pearls and Irritations*, 23 July 2016, https://johnmenadue.com/richard-woolcott-the-american-alliance-and-vice-president-bidens-recent-visit.

24 David B. Larter, 'The US military ran the largest stress test of its sealift fleet in years. It's in big trouble', *Defense News*, 31 December 2019, www.defensenews.com/naval/2019/12/31/the-us-military-ran-the-largest-stress-test-of-its-sealift-fleet-in-years-its-in-big-trouble.

25 Office of the Historian, '29. Editorial Note', *Foreign Relations of the United States 1969–1976, vol. 1, Foundations of Foreign Policy, 1969–1972*, document 29, https://history.state.gov/historicaldocuments/frus1969-76v01/d29.

26 Hugh White, 'A very unreassuring bombshell: Richard Nixon and the Guam doctrine, July 1969', *The Strategist*, 25 July 2019, www.aspistrategist.org.au/a-very-unreassuring-bombshell-richard-nixon-and-the-guam-doctrine-july-1969.

27 President Donald Trump, Remarks at the unveiling of the 9/11 and Article 5 Memorial and Berlin Wall Memorial, 25 May 1017, https://nato.usmission.gov/may-25-2017-president-trumps-remarks-911-article-5-memorial-unveiling.

28 Allan Behm, 'The decline of US global leadership: Power without authority', *The Interpreter*, 7 October 2019, www.lowyinstitute.org/the-interpreter/decline-us-global-leadership-power-without-authority.

29 'A president on a mission', *The Economist*, 9 November 2019; 'Emmanuel Macron warns Europe: NATO is becoming brain-dead', *The Economist*, 7 November 2019.

30 Prime Minister Howard, Speech in the House of Representatives on the terrorist attacks in New York and Washington on 11 September 2001, *House of Representatives Hansard*, 17 September 2001, p. 30739, https://parlinfo.aph.gov.au/parlInfo/genpdf/chamber/hansardr/2001-09-17/0004/hansard_frag.pdf;fileType=application%2Fpdf.
31 Graeme Dobell, 'Great Australian foreign policy speeches: Howard on 9/11 and the US alliance', *The Interpreter*, 15 August 2014, www.lowyinstitute.org/the-interpreter/great-australian-foreign-policy-speeches-howard-911-and-us-alliance.
32 Kim Beazley, 'Why ANZUS does not automatically commit us to follow the US to war', *The Sydney Morning Herald*, 11 August 2017.
33 Kim Beazley, *House of Representatives Hansard*, 30 August 2001, p. 30706 https://parlinfo.aph.gov.au/parlInfo/genpdf/chamber/hansardr/2001-08-30/0125/hansard_frag.pdf;fileType=application%2Fpdf.
34 Kim Beazley, 'ANZUS Alliance', Joint Standing Committee on Foreign Affairs, Defence and Trade Seminar, 11 August 1997, https://parlinfo.aph.gov.au/parlInfo/search/display/display.w3p;db=COMMITTEES;id=committees%2Fcommjnt%2Frcomw970811a_jfa.out%2F0002;query=Id%3A%22committees%2Fcommjnt%2Frcomw970811a_jfa.out%2F0002%22.
35 Troy Bramston, 'Scott Morrison: ANZUS is Liberals' "greatest move"', *The Australian*, 9 October 2019.
36 RMIT/ABC Fact Check, 'Fact check: Does ANZUS commit the US to come to Australia's aid, as Foreign Minister Julie Bishop claims?', 23 July 2014, www.abc.net.au/news/2014-07-08/does-anzus-commit-us-to-come-to-australias-aid-fact-check/5559288.
37 'Downer flags China shift', *The Age*, 18 August 2004.
38 Senator David Johnson in conversation with Tony Jones, *Lateline*, ABC TV, 12 June 2014.
39 Stephen Kuper, 'Beyond consulting: Is it time to expand ANZUS for a new era?', *Defence Connect*, 22 October 2019, www.defenceconnect.com.au/key-enablers/4990-beyond-consulting-is-it-time-to-expand-anzus-for-a-new-era.
40 Geoffrey Barker, 'Has ANZUS passed its use-by date?', *Inside Story*, 13 June 2011, https://insidestory.org.au/has-anzus-passed-its-use-by-date.
41 Paul Barratt, 'Managing ANZUS in the age of Trump', *Pearls and Irritations*, 28 November 2016, https://johnmenadue.com/paul-barratt-managing-anzus-in-the-age-of-trump-quo-vadis-series.
42 Senator Penny Wong outlined a nuanced and sophisticated approach to the Australia–United States bilateral relationship in a speech titled 'Australia and the US in the Age of Disruption', Cranlana (Melbourne), 22 November 2017, www.pennywong.com.au/speeches/australia-and-the-us-in-the-age-of-disruption-cranlana-melbourne.

Chapter 4. China: Our Comprehensive Incomprehension

1 John Garnaut, '"Fear and greed" drive Australia's China policy, Tony Abbott tells Angela Merkel', *The Sydney Morning Herald*, 16 April 2016.

2 For a detailed analysis of the evolution of Australian parliamentary attitudes towards China, see the excellent monograph by Timothy Kendall, *Within China's Orbit? China through the eyes of the Australian parliament* (Canberra: Parliamentary Monographs and Research, 2008).

3 J.B. Ronald, a Labor member of the first parliament and a Presbyterian minister, speaking on the Immigration Restriction Bill, said: 'Let us keep before us the noble idea of a white Australia – snow-white Australia if you will. Let it be pure and spotless.' (*House of Representatives Hansard*, 6 September 1901, p. 4666, https://parlinfo.aph.gov.au/parlInfo/download/hansard80/hansardr80/1901-09-06/toc_pdf/19010906_reps_1_4.pdf;fileType=application/pdf#search=%221900s%201901%2009%2006%22).

4 John Budarick, 'Media outlets are racializing Melbourne's "African gang" problem', *The Conversation*, 1 August 2018, www.abc.net.au/news/2018-08-01/media-outlets-racialising-african-gang-problem-melbourne/10060834.

5 Natasha Guantai, 'Are there Black people in Australia?', *Overland*, 15 March 2015, https://overland.org.au/2015/03/are-there-black-people-in-australia.

6 See *House of Representatives Hansard*, 2 December 1947, p. 2948, https://parlinfo.aph.gov.au/parlInfo/download/hansard80/hansardr80/1947-12-02/toc_pdf/19471202_reps_18_195.pdf;fileType=application/pdf#search=%221940s%201947%22.

7 Donald Horne, 'Confrontation in Peking', *The Bulletin*, 17 July 1971.

8 David Barnett, 'Transcript of Discussions between Gough Whitlam and Zhou Enlai, 5 July 1971', in David Barnett, *For the Record: Gough Whitlam's Mission to China, 1971* (Western Sydney University: The Whitlam Institute, 2013), pp. 20–25.

9 E.G. Whitlam, 'Whitlam: Dateline Peking', *The Sunday Australian*, 11 July 1971.

10 Bill Hayton, *The Invention of China* (New Haven and London: Yale University Press, 2020), p. 246.

11 'Chinese consul-general welcomed to Melbourne', *The Argus*, 23 March 1909.

12 'About People', *The Age*, 24 September 1910, p. 13.

13 'About People', *The Age*, 24 September 1910, p. 13.

14 Tiger Zhifu Li, *Dancing with the Dragon: Australia's Diplomatic Relations with China (1901–1941)*, MA thesis, University of Sydney, 2018, p. 21.

15 It is important to note that the decision by the League of Nations (of which the United States never became a member) to mandate the administration

of the Pacific island chains to Japan was strongly opposed by the US Navy, advice that President Wilson chose to ignore. Many Americans consider that the United States paid a very high price for this concession in World War II, in both blood and treasure, particularly in Saipan, Tinian and Truk.

16 For a snapshot of the Treaty of Versailles and its consequences, see David Watt, 'The signing of the Treaty of Versailles', *Flagpost*, 4 July 2019, www.aph.gov.au/About_Parliament/Parliamentary_Departments/Parliamentary_Library/FlagPost/2019/July/Versailles.

17 Robert G. Kane, '"Evil customs of the past": The Japanese challenge to a segregated new world order at the Paris Peace Conference in 1919', World War 1 @ 100 – A Symposium on the Centennial of the Great War, 8 November 2014, Utica College, New York.

18 Max Suich, 'Diplomacy that led to human catastrophe', *The Australian*, 23 June 2012. Suich goes on to comment: 'Today the Hughes veto sounds presumptuous and rashly provocative. It was. But it is not unusual in the history of Australian foreign policy, which of course at this stage was at its earliest and most underdeveloped state.'

19 The expiry of the Anglo-Japanese alliance in 1923, and its non-renewal, set Japan onto a path to jingoistic nationalism and militarism that eventuated in its occupation of Manchuria, the occupation of China and the rape of Nanking and, eventually, the attack on Pearl Harbor. The consequences of Japan's exclusion from the global leadership group post–World War I were profound and offer important insights into the self-defeating strategy of estrangement rather than engagement.

20 See, for instance, E.T. Williams, 'Japan's Mandate in the Pacific', *American Journal of International Law*, vol. 27, no. 3, July 1933, pp. 428–39.

21 'Mr E.S. Little for China', *The Sydney Morning Herald*, 28 February 1921, p. 7.

22 Li, *Dancing with the Dragon*, p. 10.

23 James Cotton, 'Sheaf, Egbert Thomas (1869–1948)', *People Australia*, https://peopleaustralia.anu.edu.au/biography/sheaf-egbert-thomas-27626.

24 Li, *Dancing with the Dragon*, p. 10.

25 In September 1941, Bowden was appointed as Australia's official representative in Singapore. On the day before the Fall of Singapore, Bowden and his staff attempted to flee Singapore by motor launch but were apprehended by the Japanese and escorted to Bangka Island, already the scene of the rape and murder of twenty-two Australian Army nurses. Bowden was murdered by Japanese soldiers on 17 February 1942, the only Australian diplomat to have been executed in the line of duty. See Darryl Bennet, 'Bowden, Vivian Gordon (1884–1942)', *Australian Dictionary of Biography*, vol. 13, (Melbourne: Melbourne University Press, 1993).

26 The intelligence group comprising Australia, Canada, Great Britain, New Zealand and the United States.

27 Malcolm Turnbull, 'More than a mine, more than a market: History, empathy, economics in the China relationship', NAB Australia-China Business Week, Sydney, 5 September 2014, www.malcolmturnbull.com.au/media/speech-nab-australia-china-business-week.

28 Louisa Lim, 'Rewriting history in the People's Republic of Amnesia and beyond', *The Conversation*, 28 May 2018, https://theconversation.com/rewriting-history-in-the-peoples-republic-of-amnesia-and-beyond-90014.

29 J.B. Chifley, Speech, *House of Representatives Hansard*, 23 March 1950, p. 1176, https://parlinfo.aph.gov.au/parlInfo/download/hansard80/hansardr80/1950-03-23/toc_pdf/19500323_reps_19_206.pdf;fileType=application%2Fpdf#search=%22hansard80/hansardr80/1950-03-23/0000%22.

30 R.G. Menzies, Speech, *House of Representatives Hansard*, 24 September 1947, p. 179, https://parlinfo.aph.gov.au/parlInfo/download/hansard80/hansardr80/1947-09-24/toc_pdf/19470924_reps_18_193.pdf;fileType=application%2Fpdf#search=%22hansard80/hansardr80/1947-09-24/0000%22. Menzies' reference to 'the very ecstasy of suicide' – a reference he made in at least one subsequent speech (Annual Federal Council Meeting of the Liberal Party, Canberra, 25 September 1961, https://pmtranscripts.pmc.gov.au/release/transcript-372) – is a curious side-trip into political ideology for Menzies, ever the political pragmatist. It refers to a comment published in the UK *Sunday Observer* regarding the UK Labour leader George Lansbury's refusal to step back from his pacifist policies at the 1935 Labour Party Conference, a refusal that cost Lansbury his leadership of the party.

31 For a particularly insightful account of the complex relationships between the Nationalist, Communist and surrendered Japanese forces in the immediate post–World War II years, see Donald G. Gillin and Charles Etter, 'Staying On: Japanese Soldiers and Civilians in China, 1945–49', *The Journal of Asian Studies*, vol. 42, no. 3, May 1983, pp. 497–518.

32 Harry Truman, *Memoirs*, vol. II (New York: Doubleday & Company, 1955), p. 91.

33 For a succinct overview of US support for Chiang Kai-shek's Nationalists, see Xiao Lu, *American Policy and the Downfall of the [sic] Nationalist China: A Survey of Major American Historical Literature of China's Civil War*, MA thesis, ANU, 1987, p. 12.

34 Lu, *American Policy and the Downfall of the [sic] Nationalist China*, pp. 12, 23–24, 27–28, 41 *et passim*.

35 Department of Foreign Affairs and Trade, '31. Submission to Cabinet', *Volume 22: Australia and Recognition of the People's Republic of China, 1949–1972*, NAA: A4940, C230, www.dfat.gov.au/about-us/publications/historical-documents/volume-22/Pages/031-submission-to-cabinet.

36 Colin Mackerras, 'China and the Australia–U.S. Relationship: A historical perspective', *Asian Survey*, vol. 54, no. 2, March/April 2014, pp. 223–46.

37 See, for instance, Department of Foreign Affairs and Trade, '41. Submission to Cabinet', Volume 22: Australia and Recognition of the People's Republic of China, 1949–1972, NAA: A1838, 3107/3311, www.dfat.gov.au/about-us/publications/historical-documents/volume-22/Pages/041-submission-to-cabinet.

38 Hasluck's 'The Situation in East Asia – Formosa and the Recognition of Communist China' (cabinet submission, 16 June 1955), was a key opportunity lost. Hasluck argued cogently for recognition on the grounds that times had changed, and so had world opinion, but then manoeuvred himself into a position of supine acceptance of the position that 'Australia should not consider recognition by itself but only in coordination with recognition by a number of other countries'. See Department of Foreign Affairs and Trade, '58. Submission to Cabinet', *Volume 22: Australia and Recognition of the People's Republic of China, 1949–1972*, NAA: A4906, xvi, www.dfat.gov.au/about-us/publications/historical-documents/volume-22/Pages/058-submission-to-cabinet.

39 Gyngell, *Fear of Abandonment*, p. 41.

40 Department of Foreign Affairs and Trade, '108. Cablegram to Canberra', *Volume 22: Australia and Recognition of the People's Republic of China, 1949–1972*, NAA: A1838, 3107/33/1/1, xiii, www.dfat.gov.au/about-us/publications/historical-documents/volume-22/Pages/108-cablegram-to-canberra.

41 Wilson Au-Yeung, Alison Keys & Paul Fischer, 'Australia–China: Not just 40 years', *Economic Roundup*, no. 4, 2012, https://treasury.gov.au/publication/economic-roundup-issue-4-2012/australia-china-not-just-40-years.

42 William McMahon, Speech, Young Liberals' rally, Melbourne, 12 July 1971, https://pmtranscripts.pmc.gov.au/release/transcript-2444.

43 McMahon, Speech, Young Liberals' rally, Melbourne, 12 July 1971.

44 William McMahon, 'President Nixon's statement on China', Press statement 74/1971, https://pmtranscripts.pmc.gov.au/release/transcript-2446.

45 Department of Foreign Affairs and Trade, '157. Submission to Cabinet', *Volume 22: Australia and Recognition of the People's Republic of China, 1949–1972*, A1838, 625/10/6, www.dfat.gov.au/about-us/publications/historical-documents/volume-22/Pages/157-submission-to-cabinet.

46 Quoted in Stephen FitzGerald, 'Managing Australian foreign policy in a Chinese world', *The Conversation*, 17 March 2017, https://theconversation.com/stephen-fitzgerald-managing-australian-foreign-policy-in-a-chinese-world-74607.

47 S.A. FitzGerald, *China and the World* (Canberra: ANU Press, 1977), p. 89; see also Garry Woodard, 'Relations between Australia and the People's Republic of China: An individual perspective', *The Australian Journal of Chinese Affairs*, no. 17, January 1987, pp. 143–50. Woodard was FitzGerald's successor as ambassador. His somewhat idiosyncratic but sympathetic account offers some fascinating glimpses into the Fraser government's approach to relations with China.

48 This policy evolution and its aftermath is well covered by Andrew Clark in 'How a lone, young diplomat, Stephen FitzGerald, turned around policy on China', *The Australian Financial Review*, 29 December 2015.

49 'Children of the revolution', *Sydney Morning Herald*, 26 December 2003.

50 R.J.L. Hawke, Speech, 9 June 1989, https://pmtranscripts.pmc.gov.au/release/transcript-7633.

51 R.J.L. Hawke, Media statement, 16 June 1989, https://pmtranscripts.pmc.gov.au/release/transcript-7641.

52 Jason Feng & Alan Weedon, 'China's Tienanmen generation reflect on how Bob Hawke gave them a permanent Australian home', *ABC News*, 9 June 2020, www.abc.net.au/news/2020-06-09/china-tiananmen-square-massacre-bob-hawke-australian-asylum/12332084.

53 For a comprehensive analysis of the 1995–96 US–China Taiwan crisis, see Gary Klintworth, 'Crisis Management: China, Taiwan and the United States – the 1995–96 crisis and its aftermath', Research Paper 14 1996–97 (Canberra: Parliamentary Library, 1997) www.aph.gov.au/About_Parliament/Parliamentary_Departments/Parliamentary_Library/pubs/rp/RP9697/97rp14.

54 'Australia–United States Ministerial Consultations 1996 Sydney Statement', Joint Security Declaration, 27 July 1996, www.dfat.gov.au/geo/united-states-of-america/ausmin/Pages/australia-united-states-ministerial-consultations-1996-sydney-statement.

55 Stephen Sherlock, 'Australia's Relations with China: What's the problem?', *Current Issues Brief*, 23, 1996–97, www.aph.gov.au/sitecore/content/Home/About_Parliament/Parliamentary_Departments/Parliamentary_Library/Publications_Archive/CIB/CIB9697/97cib23.

56 For an extended and insightful analysis of Prime Minister Howard's China policy between 1996 and 2007, see R.C. McDowall, *Howard's Long March* (Canberra: ANU E Press, 2009).

57 *The Bulletin*, 29 September 1999.

58 Katharine Murphy, 'Donald Trump suggests China "a threat to the world" while praising Scott Morrison as a "man of titanium"', *Guardian Australia*, 21 September 2019.

59 Rafael Epstein, 'Downer prepared to stand against US over Taiwan', *The World Today*, ABC Radio, 18 August 2004, www.abc.net.au/worldtoday/

content/2004/s1179403.htm; 'Downer flags China shift', *The Age*, 18 August 2004.

60 A.J. Behm, 'Australian Strategic Policy and the Age of Uncertainty', *Security Challenges*, vol. 5, no. 2, 2009, p. 15.

61 Hugh White, 'Rudd's China Policy', *The Monthly*, December 2009–January 2010.

62 I was part of Malcolm Fraser's team that visited China in 1982, and assisted Premier Zhao Ziyang during his visit to Canberra, Sydney and Queensland in 1983. The reciprocal visits contributed handsomely to the relationship.

63 See, for instance, Tony Walker, 'Timeline of a broken relationship: How China and Australia went from chilly to barely speaking', *The Conversation*, 9 December 2020, https://theconversation.com/timeline-of-a-broken-relationship-how-china-and-australia-went-from-chilly-to-barely-speaking-151567.

64 See A.J. Behm, 'How Good Is the Australia–China Relationship', *The Australia Institute Report*, 26 June 2020, https://australiainstitute.org.au/wp-content/uploads/2020/12/200626-How-good-is-the-Australia-China-relationship.pdf.

65 Behm, 'How Good Is the Australia–China Relationship', p. 11.

66 Sir James Plimsoll, in conversation with the author, Geneva, March 1980.

67 Julie Bishop, 'Change and uncertainty in the Indo-Pacific: Strategic challenges and opportunities', 28th IISS Fullerton Lecture, Singapore, 13 March 2017, https://singapore.embassy.gov.au/sing/ForeginMinisterFullertonSpeech2017.html.

68 Graham Allison & Fred Hu, 'An unsentimental China policy', *Foreign Affairs*, 18 February 2021.

69 Hayton, *The Invention of China*, p. 249.

Chapter 5. Australia's Pacific Problem

1 Scott Morrison, 'Australia and the Pacific: A new chapter', Speech, 8 November 2018, Lavarack Barracks, Townsville, 8 November 2018, www.pm.gov.au/media/address-australia-and-pacific-new-chapter.

2 Scott Morrison, Interview with Ben Fordham, 2GB, 11 June 2020, www.pm.gov.au/media/interview-ben-fordham-2gb-4.

3 Chris Owen, 'How Western Australia's "unofficial" use of neck chains on Indigenous people lasted 80 years', *Guardian Australia*, 7 March 2021, www.theguardian.com/australia-news/2021/mar/07/how-western-australias-unofficial-use-of-neck-chains-on-indigenous-people-lasted-80-years.

4 Alex McKinnon, 'Blackbirds: Australia's hidden slave trade history', *The Monthly*, July 2019.

5 Richard Lovett, 'Fears of Queensland control', in B. Jinks, P. Biskup & H. Nelson (eds), *Readings in New Guinea History* (Sydney: Angus and Robertson, 1973), p. 32.
6 D. Shineberg, 'Town, Robert (1794–1873)', *Australian Dictionary of Biography* (Canberra: Australian National University, 1976), vol. 6, https://adb.anu.edu.au/biography/towns-robert-4741.
7 J.A. Nilsson, 'Mackay, John (1839–1914)', *Australian Dictionary of Biography* (Canberra: Australian National University, 1974), vol. 5, https://adb.anu.edu.au/biography/mackay-john-4106.
8 Edward Wybergh Docker, *The Blackbirders* (Sydney: Angus and Robertson, 1970), pp. 170–74.
9 Business Leaders Hall of Fame, 2009 Burns Philp, http://leaders.slq.qld.gov.au/inductees/burns-philp-and-company-limited.
10 Chad Cooper, "The Immigration debate in Australia: from Federation to World War One" (Canberra: Commonwealth of Australia Parliamentary Library, 2012), *Background Note*, 2012, p. 1, https://parlinfo.aph.gov.au/parlInfo/download/library/prspub/1782447/upload_binary/1782447.pdf;fileType=application/pdf.
11 McKinnon, 'Blackbirds'.
12 Tracy Flanagan, Meredith Wilkie & Susanna Iuliano, 'Australian South Sea Islanders: A century of race discrimination under Australian law', Australian Human Rights Commission, *e-Race Archives*, 1 January 2003, https://humanrights.gov.au/our-work/race-discrimination/publications/australian-south-sea-islanders-century-race.
13 McKinnon, 'Blackbirds'.
14 Hermann Joseph Hiery, *The Neglected War: The German South Pacific and the Influence of World War 1* (Honolulu: University of Hawai'i Press, 1995), p. 13.
15 Hiery, *The Neglected War*, pp. 42–44.
16 Hiery, *The Neglected War*, p. 23.
17 Hiery, *The Neglected War*, p. 25.
18 Holmes was subsequently deployed to Gallipoli, and later promoted to the rank of major general as a divisional commander in France. He was killed by a chance shell burst in July 1917 while accompanying the premier of New South Wales, W.A. Holman, who was inspecting the battlefield at Messines.
19 Hon. W.M. Hughes, 'Rabaul: Alleged Misuse of Red Cross Gifts, and Looting by Military Officers and Privates – Report', Parliament of Australia, 22 July 1915, https://parlinfo.aph.gov.au/parlInfo/download/publications/tabledpapers/HPP052016004595/upload_pdf/HPP052016004595.pdf.
20 Hiery, *The Neglected War*, p. 88.
21 Hiery, *The Neglected War*, p. 68.

22 Hiery, *The Neglected War*, p. 72.
23 Hiery, *The Neglected War*, p. 73.
24 Seumas Spark, 'White Man's War: New Guineans' experience of war 1942–45', AUS-PNG Network, Lowy Institute, 27 February 2019, https://auspng.lowyinstitute.org/article/png-experiences-of-world-war-two.
25 Matt Wade, 'Guns vs giving: The trend that says everything about our priorities', *The Sydney Morning Herald*, 8 August 2020.
26 Wade, 'Guns vs giving'.
27 Wade, 'Guns vs giving'.
28 Angela Clare, 'Official development assistance (ODA): a quick guide', (Canberra: Commonwealth of Australia Parliamentary Library,2019).
29 Saber Salem, 'Climate change and the sinking island states in the Pacific', *E-International Relations*, 9 January 2020, www.e-ir.info/2020/01/09/climate-change-and-the-sinking-island-states-in-the-pacific.
30 'Five Pacific islands lost to rising seas as climate change hits', *The Guardian*, 10 May 2016.
31 Mélanie Becker et al., 'Water level changes, subsidence, and sea level rise in the Ganges-Brahmaputra-Meghna delta', *Proceedings of the National Academy of Sciences of the United States of America*, 28 January 2020.
32 World Population Review: Papua New Guinea, https://worldpopulationreview.com/countries/papua-new-guinea-population.
33 'About Papua New Guinea', UNDP, www.pg.undp.org/content/papua_new_guinea/en/home/countryinfo.html.
34 Department of Foreign Affairs and Trade, Papua New Guinea country brief, www.dfat.gov.au/geo/papua-new-guinea/Pages/papua-new-guinea-country-brief.
35 Transparency International ranks PNG at 137th of 180 countries in its 2019 report (see www.transparency.org/en/countries/papua-new-guinea.
36 Australian Government, *2017 Foreign Policy White Paper* (Canberra: Department of Foreign Affairs and Trade, 2017), pp. 87–105, www.dfat.gov.au/publications/minisite/2017-foreign-policy-white-paper/fpwhitepaper/pdf/2017-foreign-policy-white-paper.pdf.
37 James Batley, 'Keep calm and step up: The White Paper's message on the Pacific', *The Interpreter*, 27 November 2017, www.lowyinstitute.org/the-interpreter/keep-calm-and-step-white-paper-message-pacific.
38 Australian Infrastructure Financing Facility for the Pacific, 'Enabling Prosperity across the Pacific', Department of Foreign Affairs and Trade, www.aiffp.gov.au.
39 Clare, 'Official Development Assistance (ODA): A quick guide'.
40 Oxfam, 'Budget blind to dual crises of inequality and climate change', media release, 2 April 2019, https://media.oxfam.org.au/2019/04/budget-blind-to-dual-crises-of-inequality-and-climate-change.

41 Australian Council for International Development, 'Aid cuts signal strategic blackhole', media release, 2 April 2019, https://acfid.asn.au/media-releases/aid-cuts-signal-strategic-blackhole.
42 Jonathan Pearlman, 'The budget's pitiful response', *AFA Weekly*, 3 April 2019 www.australianforeignaffairs.com/afaweekly/the-budgets-pitiful-response.
43 Department of Foreign Affairs and Trade, 'Pacific Step-up: Stepping up Australia's engagement with our Pacific family', www.dfat.gov.au/geo/pacific/Pages/the-pacific.
44 Malcolm Turnbull, 'Remarks at Pacific Island Forum', 9 September 2016, https://pmtranscripts.pmc.gov.au/release/transcript-40440.
45 Scott Morrison, 'Australia and the Pacific: A new chapter', 8 November 2018, www.pm.gov.au/media/address-australia-and-pacific-new-chapter.
46 See James Bell et al., 'International cooperation welcomed across 14 advanced economies', Pew Research Center, 21 September 2020, www.pewresearch.org/global/2020/09/21/views-on-international-cooperation.
47 Bell et al., 'International cooperation welcomed across 14 advanced economies'.
48 Scott Morrison, 'Tomorrow in the Indo-Pacific', 5 August 2020, www.pm.gov.au/media/address-aspen-security-forum-tomorrow-indo-pacific.
49 Graeme Dobell, 'Happy fourth birthday, Pacific step-up', *The Strategist*, 7 September 2020, www.aspistrategist.org.au/happy-fourth-birthday-pacific-step-up.
50 A.J. Behm, 'The Fix: Solving Australia's foreign affairs challenges', *Australian Foreign Affairs*, no. 10, October 2020, p. 96.
51 Stan Grant, 'Kiribati president says AUKUS nuclear submarine deal puts Pacific at risk', *ABC News*, 28 September 2021.
52 Stephen Howes & Holly Lawton, 'The Pacific labour scheme: Is it a flop?', *Devpolicyblog*, 29 July 2019, https://devpolicy.org/the-pacific-labour-scheme-is-it-a-flop-20190729.
53 Allan Behm, 'Re-thinking national security in the age of pandemics and climate change catastrophe', The Australia Institute, 20 April 2020, www.tai.org.au/sites/default/files/Rethinking%20National%20Security%20%5BWEB%5D.pdf.

Chapter 6. Asia Incognita

1 This is an archaic and rare term for storm clouds and thunderbolts.
2 As a schoolboy attending an inner-city school in Melbourne in the 1950s, I travelled each day on the eastern line train to the city, passing under the Stanhope Grove overhead railway bridge which continued to display some graffiti artist's 'PIG IRON BOB' in large white letters as a contribution to posterity.

3 For an extended discussion of the nature of geopolitics, see Ronald J. Granieri, 'What Is Geopolitics and Why Does It Matter?', *Orbis*, vol. 59, no. 4, 2015.

4 For an example of how a respected journal like *The Economist* can offer commentary that essentially talks past the Asian approach to relationship management, see comment 'ASEAN in 2017: A 50th anniversary to forget', *Economist Intelligence*, 28 December 2016, http://country.eiu.com/article.aspx?articleid=974957681&Country=Brunei&topic=Politics_2.

5 Francois Bernier's *Nouvelle Division de la terre par les différentes espèces ou races qui l'habitent* was published anonymously in Paris in 1684.

6 See Elizabeth Kolbert, 'There's no scientific basis for race – it's a made-up label', *National Geographic*, 12 March 2018, www.nationalgeographic.com/magazine/2018/04/race-genetics-science-africa.

7 I am indebted to Professor Richard Rigby, founding executive director of the ANU China Institute, for this brief summary of Mandarin nomenclature.

8 See the commentary by Kua Kia Soong, 'Time to end racial discrimination in Malaysia', *Malaysiakini*, 20 March 2015, www.malaysiakini.com/letters/292624.

9 Marc Rerceretnam, 'Intermarriage in Colonial Malaya and Singapore: A case study of nineteenth- and early twentieth-century Roman Catholic and Methodist Asian communities', *Journal of Southeast Asian Studies*, vol. 43, no. 2, 2012, p. 323.

10 The cultural, economic, political and social consequences of Chinese migration into South-East Asia are a fascinating study in themselves. A good starting point is C.P. Fitzgerald, *The Southern Expansion of the Chinese People* (Canberra: ANU Press, 1972).

11 For an early and comprehensive rebuttal of the 'fifth column' idea, see Stephen FitzGerald, 'China and the Overseas Chinese: Perceptions and policies', *The China Quarterly*, no. 44, 1970, pp. 1–37.

12 Lindsay Falvey, *Understanding Southeast Asia: Syncretism in commonalities* (Songkhla: Thaksin University Press, 2015), p. 113.

13 For a magisterial account of the forms of religious belief and practice, especially Islamic belief and practice, in Indonesia, see Clifford Geertz, *The Religions of Java* (Chicago: University of Chicago Press, 1976).

14 As Raymond H. Schmandt demonstrated in his 'The Medieval Just War Theory in Some Recent Literature' (*Peace Research*, vol. 13, no. 2, 1981, pp. 45–52), the offensive campaigns known as the Crusades were deemed theologically justifiable.

15 The Jesuit theologian Francisco Suárez was one of the foremost defenders of the defensive just war doctrine. See Theodor Meron, 'Common rights of Mankind in Gentili, Grotius and Suarez', *The American Journal of International Law*, vol. 85, no. 1, 1991, p. 131.

16 Falvey, *Understanding Southeast Asia*, p. 149.

17 For an interesting account of community consultation in modern Thailand, see Gertrud Buchenrieder et al., 'Participatory Local Governance and Cultural Practices in Thailand', *Cogent Social Sciences*, vol. 3, n. 1, 2017.

18 Citra Anggita & Tsuyoshi Hatori, 'Customary Practices of Musyawarah Mufakat: An Indonesian style of consensus building', *IOP Conference Series: Earth and Environmental Science*, 589, 2020, 012027.

19 For an interesting if somewhat opaque treatment of this issue, see Meghawati, 'Musyawarah and Meaning of Sovereign People in People's Democracy Perspective – Pancasila values', *Proceedings of the First International Conference on Progressive Civil Society* (ICONPROCS 2019), www.atlantis-press.com/proceedings/iconprocs-19/125908578.

20 His Royal Highness Sultan Nazrin Muizzidin Shah, 'Keynote address', ASEAN-Australia Dialogue 2018, 13 March 2018, https://asialink.unimelb.edu.au/stories/archive/keynote-address-by-his-royal-highness-sultan-nazrin-muizzuddin-shah.

21 His Royal Highness Sultan Nazrin Muizzidin Shah, 'Keynote address'.

22 Cheong Suk-Wai, 'Mysterious yet effective ASEAN', *The Straits Times*, 5 October 2017.

23 Anthony Milner & Ron Huisken, 'ASEAN Regional Forum: less might be more", *The Interpreter*, 29 March 2019, www.lowyinstitute.org/the-interpreter/asean-regional-forum-less-might-be-more.

24 Elena Holodny, 'The rise, fall and comeback of the Chinese economy over the last 800 years', *Business Insider Australia*, 9 January 2017, www.businessinsider.com.au/history-of-chinese-economy-1200-2017-2017-1?r=US&IR=T.

25 Professor Richard Rigby, Australian National University, private communication with the author.

26 PricewaterhouseCoopers (UK), *The World in 2050: Will the shift in global economic power continue?*, February 2015, p. 3, www.pwc.com.au/pdf/the-world-in-2050.pdf.

27 Mark Beeson, 'Australia and Asia: The years of living aimlessly', *Southeast Asian Affairs*, 2001, p. 55.

28 Naaman Zhou, 'Cutting Asian language courses at Australian universities hurting students' job prospects, experts say', *The Guardian*, 16 April 2021.

Chapter 7. The Four Horsemen of the New Apocalypse

1 Hugh White, 'Hugh White on China: "It would probably be the biggest war since 1945 … and it would very likely become a nuclear war"', *The Saturday Paper*, 8–14 May 2021.

2 John Culver, 'The unfinished Chinese civil war', *The Interpreter*, 20 September 2020, www.lowyinstitute.org/the-interpreter/unfinished-chinese-civil-war.

3 For a comprehensive (though somewhat dated) overview of the China–Taiwan issue, see Gary Klintworth, *China and Taiwan: From flashpoint to redefining One China*, Research Paper 15 2000-01 (Canberra: Parliamentary Library, 7 November 2000).

4 See 'Joint Communiqué of the Australian Government and the Government of the People's Republic of China concerning the Establishment of Diplomatic Relations between Australia and China', 21 December 1972, https://pmtranscripts.pmc.gov.au/release/transcript-3119.

5 See, for example, the comments attributed to Kurt Campbell, President Biden's so-called Asia tsar, at the Financial Times Global Boardroom conference on 4 May 2021 (Demeteri Sevastopulo & Kathrin Hille, 'Washington shies away from open declaration to defend Taiwan', *Financial Times*, 5 May 2021).

6 Tony Blair, 'Doctrine of the International Community', speech to the Chicago Economics Club, 22 April 1999, https://archive.globalpolicy.org/empire/humanint/1999/0422blair.htm.

7 *Taiwan Relations Act* (Public Law 96-8, 22 U.S.C. 3301 et seq.), www.ait.org.tw/our-relationship/policy-history/key-u-s-foreign-policy-documents-region/taiwan-relations-act.

8 Thomas Newdick, 'Taiwan issues rare confirmation that U.S. special operators are training on the island (updated)', *The Drive*, 10 November 2020, www.thedrive.com/the-war-zone/37549/taiwan-issues-rare-confirmation-that-u-s-special-operators-are-training-on-the-island.

9 'As Biden's emissaries go to Taiwan, China terms exercises "combat drills"', *Reuters*, 15 April 2021 www.reuters.com/world/china/china-says-its-taiwan-strait-military-drills-necessary-address-security-2021-04-14.

10 For a comprehensive analysis of the Taiwan–China issue, see Richard C. Bush, 'Taiwan's democracy and the China challenge', Brookings, 22 January 2021, www.brookings.edu/articles/taiwans-democracy-and-the-china-challenge.

11 Gareth Evans, 'Talking up war over Taiwan flouts reason, fact, judgment and Australia's national interest', *The East Asia Forum*, 9 May 2021 (reprinted on *Pearls and Irritations*, 12 May 2021, https://johnmenadue.com/talking-up-war-over-taiwan-flouts-reason-fact-judgment-and-australias-national-interest).

12 *Q&A*, ABC TV, 12 December 2019.

13 Intergovernmental Panel on Climate Change, *Climate Change and Land: An IPCC special report on climate change, desertification, land degradation, sustainable land management, food security, and greenhouse gas fluxes in*

terrestrial ecosystems, IPCC, 2019, www.ipcc.ch/site/assets/uploads/sites/4/2021/02/210202-IPCCJ7230-SRCCL-Complete-BOOK-HRES.pdf.
14 Intergovernmental Panel on Climate Change, *Climate Change and Land*, p. 446.
15 Intergovernmental Panel on Climate Change, *Climate Change and Land*, p. 89.
16 Autumn G. Hullings, 'Hunger and climate change', *Hunger Notes*, 2020, www.worldhunger.org/climate-change.
17 Intergovernmental Panel on Climate Change, *Climate Change and Land*, p. 15.
18 Intergovernmental Panel on Climate Change, *Climate Change and Land*, p. 15.
19 Intergovernmental Panel on Climate Change, *Climate Change and Land*, p. 15.
20 Intergovernmental Panel on Climate Change, *Climate Change and Land*, p. 16.
21 Intergovernmental Panel on Climate change, Climate Change 2021: The Physical Science Basis, IPCC, 2021, https://www.ipcc.ch/report/ar6/wg1/downloads/report/IPCC_AR6_WGI_Full_Report.pdf
22 Polly Hayes, 'Here's how scientists know the coronavirus came from bats and wasn't made in a lab', *The Conversation*, 13 July 2020, https://theconversation.com/heres-how-scientists-know-the-coronavirus-came-from-bats-and-wasnt-made-in-a-lab-141850.
23 This author was the Exercise Monitor for that national epidemic exercise.
24 See the remarkable article published by Albert Einstein: 'Atomic war or peace', *The Atlantic*, November 1947.
25 Office of the Historian, 'The Acheson-Lilienthal & Baruch Plans, 1946', *Milestones Series: 1945–1952*, US State Department, https://history.state.gov/milestones/1945-1952/baruch-plans.
26 Office of the Historian, 'The Acheson-Lilienthal & Baruch Plans, 1946'.
27 The French *force de frappe* doctrine is a policy based on dissuasion and retaliation in the event of a conventional war threat, as well as the threat of a nuclear war.
28 Paul Dibb, 'Should Australia develop its own nuclear deterrent?', *The Strategist*, 4 October 2018, www.aspistrategist.org.au/should-australia-develop-its-own-nuclear-deterrent.
29 White, *How to Defend Australia*, p. 231.
30 Ramesh Thakur, 'The bomb for Australia? (Part 1)', *The Strategist*, 17 January 2018, www.aspistrategist.org.au/bomb-australia-part-1; Ramesh Thakur, 'The bomb for Australia? (Part 2)', *The Strategist*, 19 January 2018, www.aspistrategist.org.au/bomb-australia-part-2; Ramesh Thakur, 'The bomb for Australia? (Part 3)', *The Strategist*, 22 January 2018, www.aspistrategist.org.au/bomb-australia-part-3.

31 John Mecklin (ed.), 'This is your COVID wake-up call: It is 100 seconds to midnight', *The Bulletin of the Atomic Scientists*, 27 January 2021, https://thebulletin.org/doomsday-clock/current-time.

32 See, for example, John Carlson, 'Is the NPT Still Relevant? How to progress the NPT's disarmament provisions', *Journal for Peace and Nuclear Disarmament*, vol. 2, no. 1, 2019.

Chapter 8. Identity, Interests and Values

1 Ernest Satow, *A Guide to Diplomatic Practice* (London: Longmans, Green & Co, 4th edition, 1957 [1917]), p. 1.

2 John Enfield (1934–1992) was a deputy secretary in the Department of the Prime Minister and Cabinet, and later secretary of the Department of Territories and Local Government, which subsequently became the Department of Territories. He later became chief executive officer of the Institution of Engineers, Australia.

3 Australian Senate, Legal and Constitutional Affairs References Committee, *Nationhood, National Identity and Democracy* (Canberra: Department of the Senate, 2021).

4 Paul Kelly, *The March of Patriots: The struggle for modern Australia* (Melbourne: Melbourne University Press, 2009), p. 328.

5 Stan Grant, *Talking to My Country* (Sydney: Harper Collins, 2016), p. 3. He deals with the same subject matter in his subsequent book *On Identity* (Sydney: Hachette, 2019).

6 Grant, *Talking to My Country*, p. 4.

7 The Uluru Statement from the Heart can be read in full at https://ulurustatement.org/the-statement.

8 See Professor Warwick Anderson's insightful treatment of this issue in 'Whatever happened to "Australian Civilisation"', ABC Religion and Ethics, 24 September 2019, www.abc.net.au/religion/whatever-happened-to-australian-civilisation/11543430.

9 Ian Cunliffe, 'Australian values for new citizens', *Pearls and Irritations*, 15 October 2020, https://johnmenadue.com/australian-values-for-new-citizens.

10 Isabel Wilkerson, *Caste: The origins of our discontents* (New York: Random House, 2020), p. 76.

11 Francis Fukuyama, *Identity* (London: Profile Books, 2019), pp. 9–10.

12 Migration Regulations 1994, *Australian Values Statement for Public Criterion 4019-2016/113* (Schedule 4, Part 3, Clause 3.1), Schedule 1, 'Australian Values Statement'.

13 Scott Morrison, Transcript of virtual 'summit' meeting with Prime Minister Narendra Modi, 4 June 2020, www.pm.gov.au/media/virtual-summit-prime-minister-india.

14 Jocelyn Chey, 'The value pack relationship with China', *Pearls and Irritations*, 11 June 2021, https://johnmenadue.com/the-value-pack-relationship-with-china.

15 Senator Penny Wong, 'Australian Values in a Time of Disruption', Griffith University, Brisbane, 3 August 2017, www.pennywong.com.au/media-hub/speeches/australian-values-in-a-time-of-disruption-griffith-asia-institute-s-perspectives-asia-lecture-griffith-university-brisbane-03-08-2017.

16 Wong, 'Australian Values in a Time of Disruption'.

17 Anthony Galloway, 'Marise Payne says Australia won't trade away values to restart China dialogue', *The Sydney Morning Herald*, 20 March 2021.

18 Carbis Bay G7 Summit Communiqué, 'Our Shared Agenda for Global Action to Build Back Better', p. 3, para. 3 www.consilium.europa.eu/media/50361/carbis-bay-g7-summit-communique.pdf.

19 Senator Penny Wong, 'Australia's National Interests in a Time of Disruption', The Lowy Institute, Sydney, 6 July 2017, www.pennywong.com.au/media-hub/speeches/australia-s-national-interests-in-a-time-of-disruption-lowy-institute-sydney-06-07-2017.

20 Jeremy Bentham, *Introduction to the Principles of Morals and Legislation* (Oxford: The Clarendon Press, 1907), p. 3.

21 Bentham, *Introduction to the Principles of Morals and Legislation*, p. 3, n. 1.

22 Bentham, *Introduction to the Principles of Morals and Legislation*, p. 2.

23 Hans J. Morgenthau, 'Six Principles of Political Realism', in *Politics Among Nations: The struggle for power and peace* (New York: Alfred A. Knopf,5th edition, 1978 [1948]), pp. 4–15.

24 Hans J. Morgenthau, *Politics Among Nations: The Struggle for Power and Peace* (New York: Alfred A. Knopf, 1st edition, 1948), p. 105.

25 Austrade, *Why Australia: Benchmark report 2021*, p. 6, www.austrade.gov.au/ArticleDocuments/10653/Why_Australia%20_Benchmark%20_Report_2021.pdf

26 Chloe Lane, 'Top universities in Australia 2021', *QS Top Universities*, www.topuniversities.com/university-rankings-articles/world-university-rankings/top-universities-australia-2021.

27 The Economist Intelligence Unit, *The Global Liveability Index 2021: How the Covid-19 pandemic affected liveability worldwide*, 2021, p. 2, https://pages.eiu.com/rs/753-RIQ-438/images/global-liveability-index-2021-free-report.pdf.

28 Michael Fullilove, *A Larger Australia*, Boyer Lectures, ABC, 2015, www.abc.net.au/radionational/programs/boyerlectures/2015-boyer-lectures/6668786.

29 Lowy Institute Blue Ribbon Panel, *Australia's Diplomatic Deficit: Reinvesting in our instruments of international policy* (Sydney: The Lowy Institute, 2009), p. viii. Public diplomacy (information diplomacy) and development assistance will be addressed in subsequent papers.

30 Lowy Institute Blue Ribbon Panel, *Australia's Diplomatic Deficit*, p. 20.

31 Alex Oliver, 'Australia's flatlining foreign affairs budget', *The Interpreter*, 10 May 2017, www.lowyinstitute.org/the-interpreter/australia-s-flatlining-foreign-affairs-budget.

32 Melissa Conley Tyler & Mitchell Vandewerdt-Holman, 'Australia's incredible shrinking Department of Foreign Affairs and Trade', *Pursuit*, 18 October 2019, https://pursuit.unimelb.edu.au/articles/australia-s-incredible-shrinking-department-of-foreign-affairs-and-trade.

33 See the National Film and Sound Archive of Australia resource 'Les Patterson' at www.nfsa.gov.au/collection/curated/les-patterson.

34 B.J. Costar, 'Gair, Vincent Clare (Vince) (1901–1980', *Australian Dictionary of Biography*, National Centre of Biography, http://adb.anu.edu.au/biography/gair-vincent-clare-vince-10267. Gair was withdrawn from Dublin for inappropriate behaviour.

35 Edmund Campion, 'Armstrong, John Ignatius (1908–1977)', *Australian Dictionary of Biography*, National Centre of Biography, http://adb.anu.edu.au/biography/armstrong-john-ignatius-9384. Armstrong was known as 'the Golden Barman'.

36 Peter Edwards, 'Kerr, Sir John Robert (1914–1991)', *Australian Dictionary of Biography*, National Centre of Biography, http://adb.anu.edu.au/biography/kerr-sir-john-robert-23431. In London, Kerr was often found in gentlemen's clubs, inebriated.

37 Daniel Flitton, 'Australia, it's time to put our political diplomats to the test', *The Interpreter*, 4 March 2019, www.lowyinstitute.org/the-interpreter/australia-s-flatlining-foreign-affairs-budget.

38 In the winter of 2000, I was privileged to attend a dinner in Sir John Gorton's honour hosted by the former Labor treasurer John Kerin. Gorton told an amusing anecdote. Sometime during his relatively short prime ministership (1968–71), Gorton said to the deputy secretary of the Department of External Affairs, K.C.O. 'Mick' Shann, that he had been rejected when he applied for a position as a diplomatic cadet immediately after World War II. 'External Affairs rejected me,' he said, 'but here I am, Prime Minister, and you all work for me.' Shann, who was renowned for his sangfroid, allegedly replied, 'Then you'll be happy to know, Prime Minister, that our standards have not slipped: you would still not cut the mustard.'

39 Wong, 'Australia's National Interests in a Time of Disruption'.

40 Wong, 'Australia's National Interests in a Time of Disruption'.

41 OECD, 'Gross domestic product (GDP)', https://data.oecd.org/gdp/gross-domestic-product-gdp.htm.

42 International Monetary Fund, 'World Economic Outlook database: April 2021', www.imf.org/en/Publications/WEO/Issues/2021/03/23/world-economic-outlook-april-2021.

43 William McInnes, 'Australia's economy overtakes Brazil, nears Russia's', *The Australian Financial Review*, 4 June 2021.

44 ACOSS and UNSWA Sydney, *Inequality in Australia 2020 Part 1: Overview*, p. 11, http://povertyandinequality.acoss.org.au/wp-content/uploads/2020/09/Inequality-in-Australia-2020-Part-1_FINAL.pdf, and *Inequality in Australia 2020 Part 2: Who is affected and why*, http://povertyandinequality.acoss.org.au/wp-content/uploads/2020/12/Inequality-in-Australia-2020-Part-2-Who-is-affected-and-why_FINAL.pdf.

Chapter 9. Imagining a New International Game Plan

1 National Commission on Terrorist Attacks Upon the United States, *The 9/11 Commission Report* (Washington: US Congress, 2004), p. 344.

2 Joint Standing Committee on Foreign Affairs, Defence and Trade, *Bougainville: The peace process and beyond* (Canberra: Parliament of Australia, 1999), chapter 2, paras 2.77–114, pp. 29–29, www.aph.gov.au/Parliamentary_Business/Committees/Joint/Completed_Inquiries/jfadt/bougainville/BVrepindx.

3 National Commission on Terrorist Attacks Upon the United States, *The 9/11 Commission Report*, pp. 339–48.

4 The branding accorded by the Department of Defence to the biennial Australia–United States joint military exercise – 'Exercise Talisman Sabre' – is a rare example of military irony.

5 Emma Shortis, *Our Exceptional Friend* (Melbourne: Hardie Grant Books, 2021), p. 232.

6 Paul Kennedy, 'Fin-de-Siècle America', *The New York Review of Books*, 28 June 1990; Joseph S. Nye Jr. (and reply by Paul Kennedy), 'Is the US declining?', *The New York Review of Books*, 11 October 1990.

7 Patrick Porter, 'Was Paul Kennedy right? American decline 30 years on', *War on the Rocks*, 17 June 2015, https://warontherocks.com/2015/06/was-paul-kennedy-right-american-decline-30-years-on.

8 Paul Kennedy, *The Rise and Fall of the Great Powers* (New York: Random House, 1987), p. 539.

9 Gore Vidal, *The Decline and Fall of the American Empire* (Berkeley: Odonian Press, 1992), p. 7. Vidal's essay 'The day the American empire ran out of gas' was published as 'Requiem for the American empire' in *The Nation* on 11 January 1986.

10 William Clinton, transcript of 'Global Challenges', Yale University, 31 October 2003, https://archive-yaleglobal.yale.edu/content/transcript-global-challenges.

11 Bruce Ackerman, 'The Decline and Fall of the American Republic', Tanner Lectures on Human Values, Princeton University, 7–8 April 2010, https://tannerlectures.utah.edu/_resources/documents/a-to-z/a/Ackerman_10.pdf, and subsequently expanded into *The Decline and Fall of the American Republic* (Harvard: Harvard University Press, 2010).

12 Eric A. Posner, 'POTUS-phobia', *The New Republic*, 23 December 2010.

13 Ackerman, 'The Decline and Fall of the American Republic', p. 18.

14 Joseph R. Biden, 'Why America must lead again', *Foreign Affairs*, March/April 2020.

15 Is the 'Biden Doctrine' Lazarus thrice-risen? *Foreign Policy* found one in 2012 (James Traub, 'The Biden Doctrine: How the vice president is shaping President Obama's foreign policy', *Foreign Policy*, 10 October 2012) and *The Atlantic* found one in 2016 (Steve Clemons, 'The Biden Doctrine: Has the vice president made a lasting contribution in foreign policy?', *The Atlantic*, 23 August 2016).

16 Hal Brands, 'The emerging Biden Doctrine: Democracy, autocracy and the defining clash of our time', *Foreign Affairs*, 28 June 2021.

17 John Keane, 'Enter the dragon: Decoding the new Chinese empire', *Australian Foreign Affairs*, no. 11, February 2021, pp. 8–9.

18 Keane, 'Enter the dragon', pp. 10–12.

19 James Traub, 'The World's oldest democracy is one of its worst', *Foreign Policy*, 6 July 2021.

20 Howard W. French, 'Can America remain preeminent?', *The New York Review*, 29 April 2021.

21 Yan Xuetong, 'Becoming strong: The new Chinese foreign policy', *Foreign Affairs*, July/August 2021.

22 Franklin D. Roosevelt, 'First Inaugural Address', 4 March 1933, https://avalon.law.yale.edu/20th_century/froos1.asp.

23 David Brophy, *China Panic: Australia's alternative to paranoia and pandering* (Melbourne: La Trobe University Press, 2021).

24 See Chapter 8, n. 40.

25 Isaiah Berlin, 'The Originality of Machiavelli', in *Against the Current* (New York: Viking Press, 1980), pp. 75–76.

26 Wang Jisi, 'The plot against China? How Beijing sees the new Washington consensus', *Foreign Affairs*, July/August 2021.

27 Jisi, 'The plot against China?.

28 Tess McClure, 'Kiwi wars: The golden fruit fuelling a feud between New Zealand and China', *Guardian Australia*, 19 June 2021.

29 See, for instance, Daniel Hurst, 'Australia joins allies in accusing China of "malicious cyber activities"', *Guardian Australia*, 19 July 2021.

30 See, for example, Charles R. Morris, 'We were pirates, too', *Foreign Policy*, 6 December 2012.

31 Kurt Tong, 'Hong Kong and the limits of decoupling: Why America struggles to punish China for its repression', *Foreign Affairs*, 14 July 2021.

32 Scott Morrison, 'Speech before the Address by the President of Indonesia', House of Representatives, 10 February 2020, www.pm.gov.au/media/speech-address-president-indonesia.

33 President Joko Widodo, 'Address to the Australian Parliament (translation)', 10 February 2020, www.aph.gov.au/Parliamentary_Business/Hansard/Hansard_Display?bid=chamber/hansardr/be8a2537-4a84-4dc2-b27b-28f392b06329/&sid=0000. President Widodo's full Indonesian text is available at https://setkab.go.id/pidato-di-hadapan-anggota-parlemen-australia-10-februari-2020-di-gedung-parlemen-canberra-australia.

34 See commentary by Gerard Henderson: 'Howard should end confusion on foreign policy', *The Age*, 3 June 2003.

35 There has been extensive international commentary on the implications of Howard's reported remarks. See, for example, David Watts, '"Deputy sheriff" policy change stuns Asians', *The Independent* (Ireland), 27 September 1999, and David Fickling, 'Australia seen as "America's deputy sheriff"', *Guardian Australia*, 10 September 2004.

36 Sharon Seah et al., *The State of Southeast Asia: 2021* (Singapore: ASEAN Studies Centre at the Institute of Southeast Asian Studies (ISEAS)-Yusof Ishak Institute, 2021).

37 See the Lowy Institute Poll 2021, available at https://poll.lowyinstitute.org/themes/indonesia.

38 *The Ugly American* was an excoriating political novel depicting US diplomatic failure in South-East Asia. Although it was somewhat overwritten and hence unfair to the efforts of many outstanding US diplomats working in South-East Asia, the novel continues to resonate wherever there is a systemic failure in US foreign policy.

39 Naaman Zhou, 'Cutting Asian language courses at Australian universities hurting students' job prospects, experts say', *Guardian Australia*, 16 April 2021.

40 Rod Neilsen, Michiko Weinmann & Sophia Slavich, '"Too foreign, difficult and suspicious": Discourses of Chinese language learning in Australia', *Asian Currents*, 19 March 2021, https://asaa.asn.au/too-foreign-difficult-and-suspicious-discourses-of-chinese-language-learning-in-australia.

41 James Massola & Peter Hartcher, 'Indonesian President Widodo says Australia should be in ASEAN', *The Sydney Morning Herald*, 15 March 2018.

42 Graeme Dobell, 'Fifty years of Foreign Affairs: The anaemia problem', *The Strategist*, 7 December 2020, www.aspistrategist.org.au/fifty-years-of-foreign-affairs-the-anaemia-problem.

43 Jonathan Pryke, 'DFAT cuts show our foreign policy's khaki tinge', The Lowy Institute, 20 July 2020, www.lowyinstitute.org/publications/dfat-cuts-show-our-foreign-policy-khaki-tinge.

44 Melissa Conley Tyler, 'Australia is spending less on diplomacy than ever before – and its influence is suffering as a result', *The Conversation*, 6 November 2019, https://theconversation.com/australia-is-spending-less-on-diplomacy-than-ever-before-and-its-influence-is-suffering-as-a-result-125722.

45 Wang Gungwu, *Community and Nation: China, Southeast Asia and Australasia* (Sydney: Asian Studies Association of Australia with Allen & Unwin, 1992), p. 334.

46 Gabrielle Chan & Gay Alcorn, 'Tony Abbott says he will "shirtfront" Vladimir Putin over downing of MH17', *Guardian Australia*, 13 October 2014.

47 For a helpful short review of 'fa'a Samoa' (Samoan culture), see 'Samoan culture: Core concepts', *SBS Cultural Atlas*, https://culturalatlas.sbs.com.au/samoan-culture/samoan-culture-core-concepts.

Chapter 10. Engagement: The Antidote to Isolation

1 Clare Wright captures the dynamism of the age in *You Daughters of Freedom: The Australians who won the vote and inspired the world* (Melbourne: Text Publishing, 2018), pp. 220–22 and pp. 296–311.

2 For an outstanding analysis of the quality of public administration in early post–World War II Australia, see Samuel Furphy (ed.), *The Seven Dwarfs and the Age of the Mandarins: Australian government administration in the post-war reconstruction era* (Canberra: ANU Press, 2015).

3 See *Australia's Strategic Planning in the 1990s* (Canberra: Department of Defence, 1992). While the classified version was agreed by cabinet on 27 November 1989, an unclassified version was not released until September 1992 by the then defence minister, Robert Ray. Available at www.defence.gov.au/SPI/publications/Australias-Strategic-Planning-1990s.pdf.

4 Gareth Evans, 'Ministerial statement', *House of Representatives Hansard*, 6 December 1989, www.gevans.org/speeches/old/1989/061289_fm_regionalsecurity.pdf.

5 'Rudd full of stunts and slogans: Downer', *ABC News*, 30 March 2008, www.abc.net.au/news/2008-03-30/rudd-full-of-stunts-and-slogans-downer/2386856.

6 For commentary on the impact of political sectarianism on parliamentary practice, see Allan Behm, *No, Minister* (Melbourne: Melbourne University Press, 2015), p. 102.

7 Behm, *No, Minister*, pp. 149–50.

8 Geoffrey Barker, 'Losing their Mooreings', *The Australian Financial Review*, 2 August 1999.

9 Scott Morrison, Speech, Institute of Public Administration, 19 August 2019, www.pm.gov.au/media/speech-institute-public-administration.

10 Allan Behm, Lynne Bennington & James Cummane, 'A Value-creating Model for Effective Policy Services', *Journal of Management Development*, vol. 19, no. 3, 1 April 2000, pp. 162–78.

11 See, for example, Anne Davies, 'Berejiklian concedes $140m grant scheme was pork-barrelling, but says "it's not unique to our government"', *Guardian Australia*, 26 November 2020.

12 'Finance minister's bankrupt defence', *The Australian Financial Review*, 5 July 2021.

13 Simon Longstaff, 'Car park rorts rot the body politic', *The Australian Financial Review*, 8 July 2021.

14 Jonathan Daley, *Gridlock: Removing barriers to policy reform* (Melbourne: The Grattan Institute, 2021), p. 48, https://grattan.edu.au/wp-content/uploads/2021/07/Gridlock-Grattan-Report.pdf.

15 'Public Trust in Government: 1958–2021', Pew Research Center, 17 May 2021, www.pewresearch.org/politics/2021/05/17/public-trust-in-government-1958-2021.

16 Jennifer Rankin, 'Bitter EU summit exposes trust deficit among leaders with no end in sight', *The Guardian*, 21 July 2020.

17 Mark Evans, 'Trust in politicians and government is at an all-time low. The next government must work to fix that', *The Conversation*, 25 February 2019, https://theconversation.com/trust-in-politicians-and-government-is-at-an-all-time-low-the-next-government-must-work-to-fix-that-110886.

18 Richard Denniss & Allan Behm, 'Double game: How Australian diplomacy protects fossil fuels', *Australian Foreign Affairs*, no. 12, July 2021, pp. 49–68.

19 Nick Perry, 'Jacinda Ardern apologises for New Zealand's "dawn raids" on Pacific people', *The Sydney Morning Herald*, 1 August 2021.

20 The Uluru Statement from the Heart, https://ulurustatement.org/the-statement.

21 Australian Government, *Closing the Gap in Partnership*, www.closingthegap.gov.au.

22 Australian Institute of Aboriginal and Torres Strait Islander Studies, *The Stolen Generations*, https://aiatsis.gov.au/explore/stolen-generations.

Acknowledgements

No Enemies No Friends was largely written between January and August 2021, surrounded by COVID-19 lockdowns, the closure of libraries and the newest technique for extending the length of the day – working from home. In all of this, I have enjoyed the unstinting support of my colleagues at The Australia Institute, particularly of the Institute's Director, Ben Oquist, the Chief Economist, Richard Denniss and Rod Campbell, the Director of Research. For one who has hit the half-way point in his eighth decade, it is a privilege to work with such bright, capable, dedicated and enthusiastic young people who make up the team at The Australia Institute. They are a critical part of Australia's public policy future.

The emergence of *No Enemies No Friends* is a consequence of over five decades of conversation, conference attendance, essay writing, studying the works of serious international scholars, and reading the books and articles written by friends and colleagues. Many of them are referenced in this book. It is also a product of six years or so working in Parliament House, first with Greg Combet and subsequently with Penny Wong. Both are brilliant in argument and, like good leaders everywhere, attract team members who are also articulate, clever and unafraid, especially when it comes to tilting at windmills to find new answers to old questions and imaginative answers to new questions. I owe much to my Ministerial and Parliamentary Staff colleagues.

In a career spanning over fifty years, I have been privileged to work with outstanding people in Australia, China, India, Indonesia, Japan, Malaysia, New Zealand, Singapore, Thailand and the United States – academics, diplomats, journalists, military officers, politicians and public servants. I owe a particular debt to the late Sir James Plimsoll and the late John Enfield, both of whom shared with me their profound understanding of national security and what drives it. The late General John Baker, with whom I worked closely in a vain attempt to transform *Plan Nocturne* into a campaign plan of some utility in the direct defence of Australia (the Defence juggernaut was too big for both of us), had an enormous impact on my appreciation of Clausewitz's dictum 'war is the continuation of policy by other means'. And the late Paul Barratt, a friend and mentor for many years and to whom this book is dedicated, was in constant conversation as this book was in its development stage. He would have enjoyed the result.

A couple of the chapters in this book draw upon papers published over the past two years on The Australia Institute's website in preparation for *Rethinking Diplomacy: A Conversation*, a colloquium hosted by the Australia Institute in early December 2020. Some thirty people covering a broad spectrum of Australia's foreign policy thinkers and commentariat attended the colloquium. Many of the thoughts and themes raised at the colloquium have found their way into this book. I cannot over-express my gratitude to the participants.

Because of its currency and topicality, the strategic implications of Taiwan's role in north Asia, addressed in chapter 7, was the subject of a co-authored paper issued by The Australia Institute. I am very grateful to my co-author, Melissa Conley Tyler, for her advice and guidance.

There are many others whose ideas reverberate throughout this book. In particular, professors Michael Leigh (a friend for most of my working life) and Tony Milner, together with Ian Buchanan (formerly of Booz Allen Hamilton) and Andrew Parker (Price Waterhouse Cooper), have fabulous insights into the inner workings of Southeast Asia. Dr Shiro Armstrong, along with Professors Peter Drysdale, Stephen Fitzgerald, Jane Golley, James Laurenceson, James Curran and Richard Rigby have provided countless tutorials on China, Japan and South Korea.

The Department of Foreign Affairs and Trade has counted among its diplomats some of the most gifted people in Australia. I am particularly grateful to Howard Bamsey (without peer on climate policy), Allan Gyngell, Louise Hand, Roger Holdich, John McCarthy (like James Plimsoll, Ambassador to almost everywhere that matters), Geoff Miller (whose contributions to John Menadue's *Pearls and Irritations* continue to enlighten), Greg Moriarty (currently Secretary to the Department of Defence) and Harinder Sidhu.

In the Defence world, Hugh White, Paul Dibb, Richard Brabin-Smith, Bill Schofield, Ross Thomas, Ross Babbage and Michael Scrafton have been long-time friends and colleagues, and formidable proponents of the art of contestability. The Australian Defence Force boasts some wonderful minds, and I am indebted to many now retired former colleagues. Admiral Chris Barrie, former Chief of the Defence Force, and I have worked closely together on a variety of projects over the past decade, with much contemplation and discussion of 'what was that all about?' Vice Admirals Rob Walls and Tim Barrett, Rear Admirals Peter Briggs and Rowan Moffitt, Lieutenant General Des Mueller, Major Generals Peter Abigail, Peter Dunn, Michael Smith and the late Michael Clifford, and Air Vice Marshal Peter Nicholson have all influenced my thinking, sometimes provoking and sometimes moderating my tendency to explore the heights and plumb the depths of strategic policy possibilities.

The fourth estate makes an enormous contribution to Australia's public discourse and the public policy issues that must be ventilated and debated if we are to maintain a robust and vibrant democracy. Paul Bongiorno, Graeme Dobell, Michelle Grattan, Virginia Hausegger, Mark Kenny, Katharine Murphy, Deborah Snow, Laura Tingle, Tony Walker, Jack Waterford and Marian Wilkinson – to name just some of the journalists whose work has influenced my thinking – share the remarkable ability to ask questions that demand answers. Some of them have managed to straddle the academia/media divide, while others, particularly Stephen Spencer and Patrick Walters, have negotiated the journalist/policy adviser interface with dexterity and impact. In the relentless and unforgiving world of the media, each of these wonderful people are heroic.

For me, writing is intensely personal. But writing is totally pointless unless it is socialised. To paraphrase somebody or other, writing is human but publishing is divine. This book is a tribute to those who think that books, reading and story-telling are among the cornerstones of civilisation. I am deeply indebted to Jeanne Ryckmans, my fellow member on the Canberra Writers Festival board, for her inspiration in identifying Upswell as the most apposite imprint for *No Enemies No Friends*. A new publishing house, it is agile, bold and deeply invested in bringing fresh ideas and voices to our national conversation. I could not have imagined a better or more supportive publisher than Terri-ann White. The experience has been exhilarating, and the magic effected by Julian Welch as copy editor improved the original manuscript immensely. It is a matter of great pride for me to be listed among Upswell's authors.

All authors will tell you that book-writing induces a kind of obsession, where one's waking and sleeping moments are consumed by the relentless pressure to create meaningful sentences, paragraphs and chapters. I do not know how people deal with that obsession without the constant care, love, support and toleration of their families. I cannot express adequately my love and thanks to my wife Rhyan, who has endured both me and the COVID-19 lockdown for the entire time this book was underway. And both of us have endured the prolonged absence of our daughter Phyllida, whose constant pastoral care via FaceTime has cheered us mightily.

All of these, and many others, have made this book possible. But in acknowledging them and expressing my boundless thanks, I also acknowledge that any errors and misperceptions contained in this book are mine.

About Upswell

Upswell Publishing was established in 2021 by Terri-ann White as a not-for-profit press. A perceived gap in the market for distinctive literary works in fiction, poetry and narrative non-fiction was the motivation. In her years as a bookseller, writer and then publisher, Terri-ann has maintained a watch on literary books and the way they insinuate themselves into a cultural space and are then located within our literary and cultural inheritance. She is interested in making books to last: books with the potential to still be noticed, and noted, after decades and thus be ripe to influence new literary histories.

About this typeface

Book designer Becky Chilcott chose Foundry Origin not only as a strong, carefully considered, and dependable typeface, but also to honour her late friend and mentor, type designer Freda Sack, who oversaw the project. Designed by Freda's long-standing colleague, Stuart de Rozario, much like Upswell Publishing, Foundry Origin was created out of the desire to say something new.